D0336816

The LOST PILOTS

ALSO BY COREY MEAD

WAR PLAY: VIDEO GAMES AND THE FUTURE OF ARMED CONFLICT

ANGELIC MUSIC: THE STORY OF BENJAMIN FRANKLIN'S GLASS ARMONICA

The LOST PILOTS

COREY MEAD

THE SPECTACULAR RISE AND SCANDALOUS FALL OF AVIATION'S GOLDEN COUPLE

MACMILLAN

First published 2018 by Flatiron Books, New York

First published in the UK 2018 by Macmillan
an imprint of Pan Macmillan
20 New Wharf Road, London N1 9RR
Associated companies throughout the world
www.panmacmillan.com

ISBN 978-1-5098-2849-4

Photographic section credits:
p. 1 (top): Lost Aviator Gallery
p. 2 (top): Lost Aviator Gallery; (bottom): AP Photo
p. 3 (top): Lost Aviator Gallery; (bottom): St. Louis University Libraries
p. 4 (bottom): City of Toronto Archives, Fonds 1266, Item 18331
p. 6 (top): Lost Aviator Gallery; (bottom): Davis-Monthan Aviation Field Register
p. 7 (top): *The Courier Mail*, Brisbane, Australia
p. 8 (bottom): Lost Aviator Gallery

1 3 5 7 9 8 6 4 2

A CIP catalogue record for this book is available from the British Library.

Designed by Anna Gorovoy
Maps by Rhys Davies
Printed and bound by CPI Group (UK) Ltd, Croydon, CR0 4YY

For my family

CONTENTS

I have just escaped a most unpleasant death . . .

—CAPTAIN WILLIAM LANCASTER'S SAHARA DIARY

Life at its best is short anyway . . .

—JESSIE KEITH-MILLER

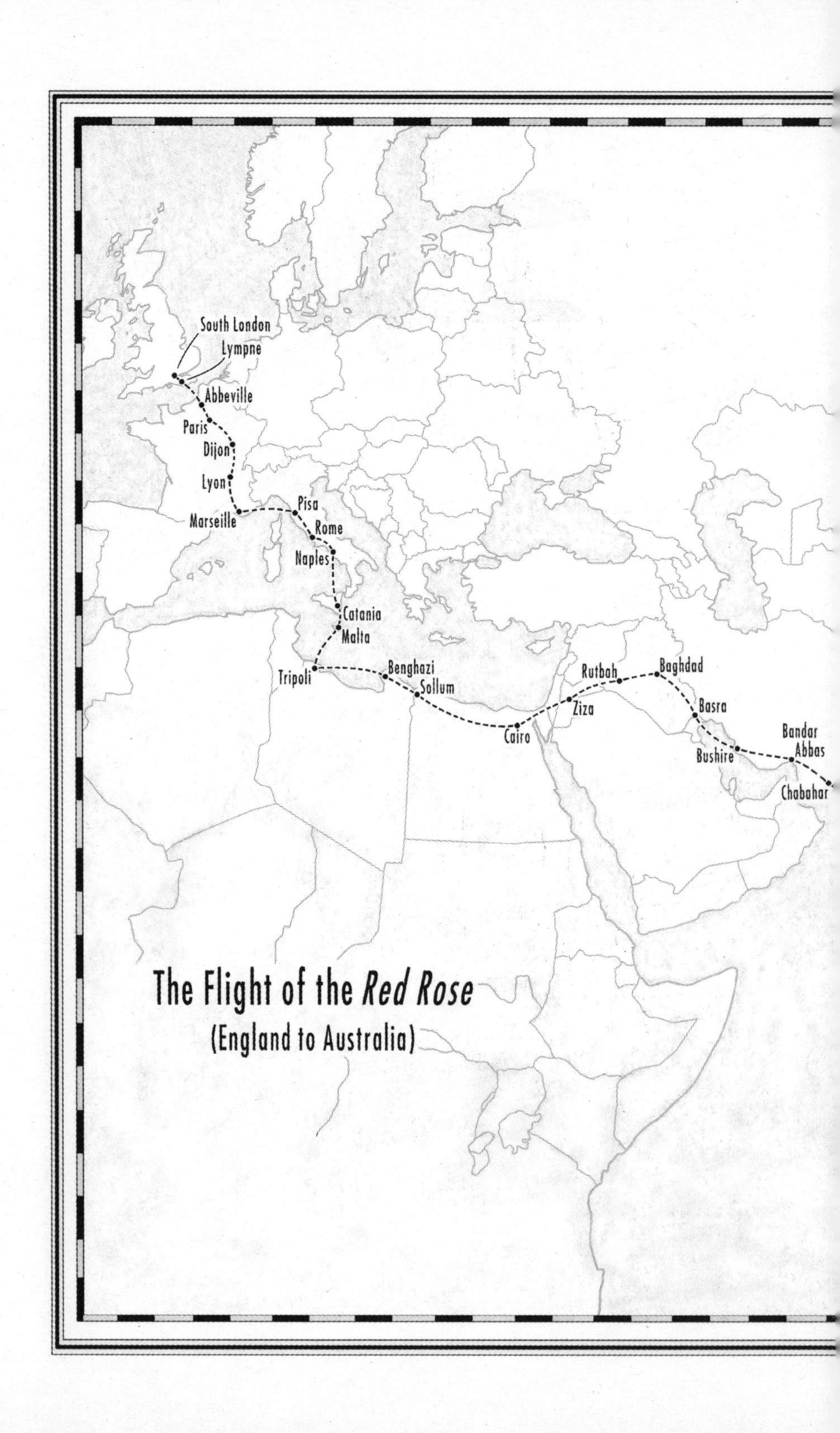
South London
Lympne
Abbeville
Paris
Dijon
Lyon
Marseille
Pisa
Rome
Naples
Catania
Malta
Tripoli
Benghazi
Sollum
Cairo
Ziza
Rutbah
Baghdad
Basra
Bushire
Bandar
Abbas
Chabahar
The Flight of the *Red Rose*
(England to Australia)

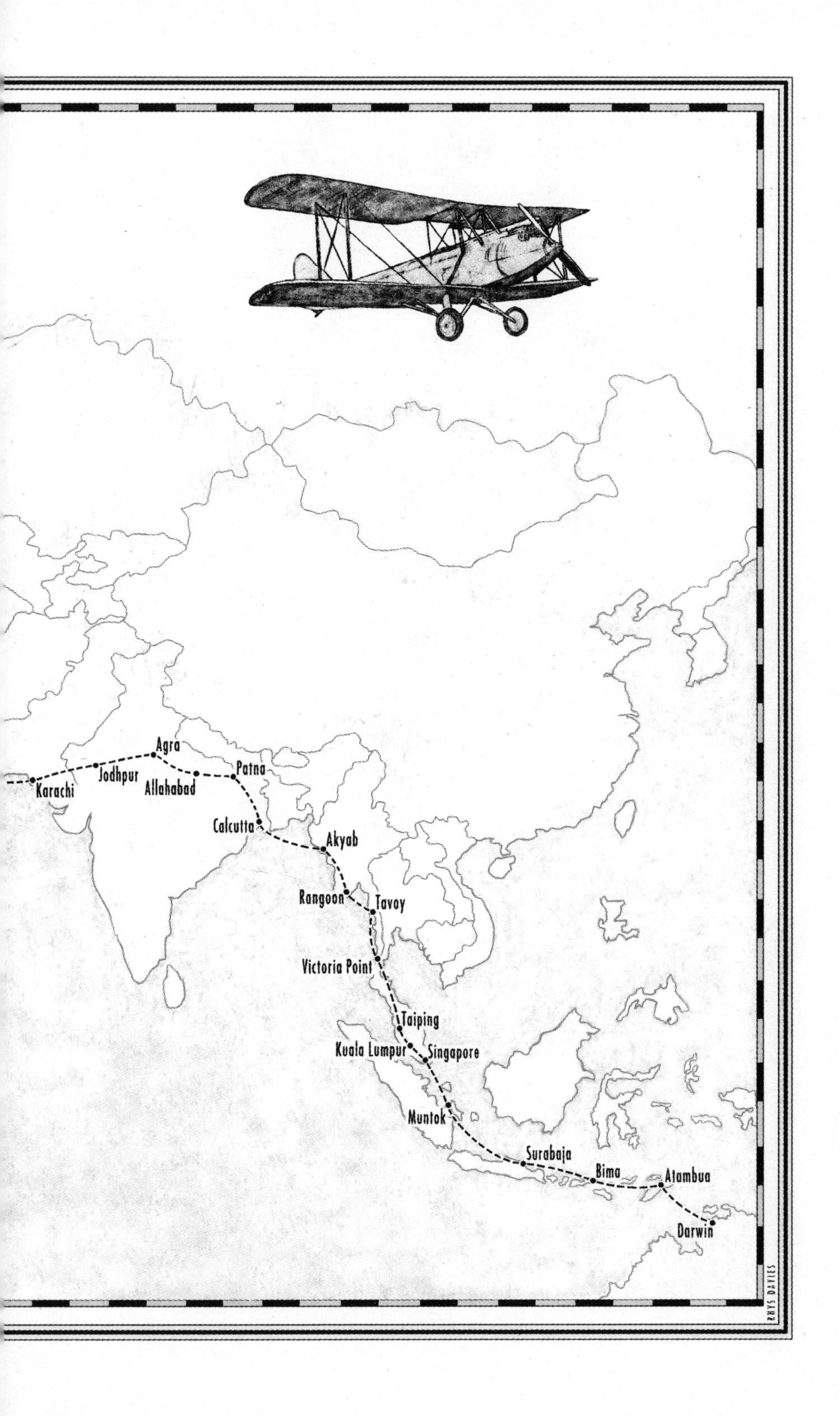
Agra
Jodhpur
Karachi
Allahabad
Patna
Calcutta
Akyab
Rangoon
Tavoy
Victoria Point
Taiping
Kuala Lumpur
Singapore
Muntok
Surabaja
Bima
Atambua
Darwin
RHYS DAVIES

PROLOGUE A TIME LIKE THIS

The Dade County Courthouse on bustling Flagler Street in downtown Miami was the tallest building in the state of Florida. By some accounts, it was the tallest building south of Baltimore, and the tallest municipal building in the United States. Completed four years earlier, at a cost of more than four million dollars, the twenty-eight-story neoclassical structure, with its gleaming white terra-cotta exterior and distinctive ziggurat roofline, was dazzlingly lighted at night and could be seen, the rumor went, for fifty miles by land and a hundred miles by sea. The courthouse included the requisite courtrooms, judicial chambers, law library, and administrative offices, in addition to serving as Miami's City Hall. It also housed, on its top nine floors, the Miami City Jail.

The date was August 2, 1932. At a quarter past nine in the morning, the celebrated British aviator Captain William Lancaster received a guarded escort from his twenty-second-floor jail cell down to a sixth-floor courtroom to begin his long-awaited trial. Lancaster had spent the summer in captivity, charged with the murder of a Miami writer named Haden Clarke. For months the story had transfixed newspaper readers around the globe. The trial had been moved from the regular circuit courtroom to the larger criminal courtroom to accommodate the crush of expected spectators.

Hours before the court opened, hundreds of people milled about the courtroom, some jammed tightly against the door. Bailiffs could hardly move the throng to allow the forty-three witnesses and one hundred prospective jurors to enter the room. Outside the courthouse, mobs of would-be spectators fought to gain entry to the building. Women of all ages, including many with children, predominated in the crowd. Because of the international interest the case had generated, three "noiseless" telegraph instruments belonging to the International Press Services had been allowed in the courtroom for the first time in Dade County's history.

Shortly before 9:30 a.m., Lancaster—wearing a light brown suit, gray shirt, and tan tie—entered the room in the company of his attorneys, James Carson and James "Happy" Lathero, both of whom were attired, like true Southern gentlemen, in white suits. Lancaster appeared relaxed, even good-humored. Behind him, a large American flag rippled in the breeze from the open courtroom windows. As he posed for photographs, the flag's folds fell across his shoulders. Lancaster laughed. He dropped his lighthearted facade just long enough to ask the news correspondents to send a message to his father in England: "Don't worry, everything is all right—Bill." When a photographer asked him to smile, he demurred, saying, "It's hard to smile at a time like this."

Garnering just as much attention from reporters that day was Mrs. Jessie Keith-Miller, Captain Lancaster's longtime flying partner and lover, and one of the pioneering female aviators of the period. At the time of Haden Clarke's death by gunshot, Jessie and the young writer had been romantically involved. Now, at the courthouse, Jessie looked visibly nervous as she stood for the photographers. Her face tense, she stared straight ahead, not even the hint of a smile breaking her tightly compressed lips. The newspapers noted her slim figure, stylish white silk dress, white hat, white shoes with yellow insteps, and flesh-colored stockings.

When Bill Lancaster and Jessie Keith-Miller had first met, five years earlier, they were both trapped in unhappy marriages. Over the course of a record-setting six-month flight from England to Australia, they had fallen in love. Fame and adulation had followed, leading them to America, where aviators were the newly crowned heroes of the so-called Golden Age of

Aviation. But the Great Depression had dried up their fortunes, and Jessie had found comfort in the arms of another man—until the tragedy that had led her and Lancaster to a packed Miami courthouse on a sweltering August day. Now "one of the most sensational hearings in the history of Florida," as the *Miami Herald* dubbed it, was about to begin.

PART I RED ROSE

1

BRIGHT YOUNG THINGS

On a muggy June night in 1927, a whirl of music, laughter, and conversation spilled from the open windows of an artist's Baker Street studio in London. Paintings crowded the studio's walls, but actual furniture was sparse, with only a low sofa, a few scattered cushions, and a single chair in which to sit. The party guests that night didn't care; as they weaved throughout the crowded, cigarette-smoke-filled room, they felt an immutable kinship with the chaos and promise of the blossoming Jazz Age. They were young women in pearls and fashionable dresses, and young men in suits, their jackets abandoned in the heat, eagerly clutching sweating tumblers of gin and tonic. They were the Bright Young Things of London, a pleasure-seeking assortment of wealthy socialites, bohemian artists, and middle-class rule-breakers, who gloried in their own irresponsibility and blissfully debauched fun. But beneath the bright, shiny facade, though they were not eager to admit it, the traumatic shadow of World War I lingered always over their frivolity, adding to it an air of desperation, a last-ditch alcohol-soaked escape from the black dog that trailed in their paths, no matter how privileged their social status and connections.

One of the party guests, a dark-haired, full-lipped twenty-five-year-old

Australian woman with sparkling eyes who shared a one-room apartment downstairs, stood entranced at the scene before her, thrilled by the vitality of her newly adopted city. Jessie Keith-Miller—jokingly called "Chubbie" by her friends, a childhood nickname that had evolved into a winking reference to her slender five-foot-one frame—had arrived in London only weeks before, leaving behind Australia and a husband to whom she was unhappily married. This was her first London party, and it was filled with the kinds of glamorous, intriguing artists and bohemians who she had dreamed would fill her new life.

With the party in full swing, Jessie followed the party's host, George, around the room. He introduced her to a smattering of acquaintances, before stopping in front of a tall, lean, well-dressed man with a high forehead, thinning brown hair, and a crinkly smile. "This is Flying Captain Bill Lancaster," George told Jessie. "He's flying to Australia. That should give you something in common—you ought to get together."

Lancaster radiated geniality and good cheer, and he was in a chatty mood. In no time at all the handsome pilot was telling Jessie about his plans for an upcoming solo flight to Australia, a feat that had never been attempted with the type of "light" airplane he intended to fly, one that would weigh significantly less than the heavier variety of plane that previous fliers had employed. (In aviation, the terms "heavy" and "light" refer simply to an aircraft's takeoff weight.) Though the idea had been germinating for some time, Lancaster's imagination had been newly fired by an event that had electrified the world just one month earlier.

On May 20, 1927, at Roosevelt Field on Long Island, Charles Lindbergh, an unknown U.S. Air Mail pilot, had climbed into his self-designed lightweight aircraft, the *Spirit of St. Louis*, to begin the first solo nonstop flight across the Atlantic. Thirty-three hours later, an exhausted Lindbergh touched down at Le Bourget Airport in Paris before an ecstatic crowd of more than a hundred thousand spectators. In that instant, Lindbergh's life, and the world of aviation, were forever changed.

Lindbergh became the most famous man of his day, while aviators themselves became the age's new idols. In the words of aviatrix Elinor Smith Sullivan, at that time the youngest U.S.-government-licensed pilot on record, "[Before Lindbergh's flight] people seemed to think we [aviators] were from outer space or something. But after Charles Lindbergh's flight, we could do no wrong. It's hard to describe the impact Lindbergh had on people. Even the first walk on the moon doesn't come close. The twenties was such an innocent time, and people were still so religious—I think they felt like this man was sent by God to do this." Speaking the month after Lindbergh's flight, former secretary of state Charles Evans Hughes captured the common mood: "Colonel Lindbergh has displaced everything. . . . He fills all our thought. He has displaced politics. . . . [H]e has lifted us into the upper air that is his home."

As Lindbergh biographer Thomas Kessner writes, "It is impossible today to comprehend the scale of his popularity, the void he filled in a bloody era searching for fresh heroes and new departures. War on a scale no one had ever imagined had drained the world of optimism. And in an age desperately searching for a moral equivalent of war, he demonstrated transcendence without menace." The groundbreaking employment of aircraft in World War I—the first major conflict to feature such large-scale use of flying machines—had proven aviation's effectiveness as a tool of death and destruction, but Lindbergh recovered its essential thrill. After his record-setting flight, applications in the United States for pilot's licenses soared, the numbers tripling in the remaining months of 1927 alone. The number of licensed aircraft almost immediately quadrupled, as a long-skeptical public embraced air travel with the fervor of the newly converted.

Though he didn't mention it to Jessie Keith-Miller at the Baker Street party, Bill Lancaster had witnessed World War I's atrocities firsthand, from the gory battlefield trenches, and his natural recklessness, combined with his inborn optimism, made him a perfect example of the 1920s breed of flier. With Lindbergh as his model, Lancaster seemed to take it as a given that the flight from England to Australia he envisioned would bring him worldwide fame.

Lancaster's knowledge of Australia was limited, however, and so, as he chatted with Jessie, he peppered her with questions about her country's airfields, local routes, and weather. Twelve months earlier Lancaster had left his job as a Royal Air Force (RAF) pilot, and now, at age twenty-nine, with flying jobs growing scarce and a wife and two children to support, he was anxious to make a name for himself. Though Jessie could answer few of his questions, and though she could barely hear him above the noise of the party, Lancaster was positive she could help him simply by virtue of her being Australian. No doubt her impish buoyancy and wide, winning smile added to her considerable appeal. "Come and have tea with me tomorrow at the Authors' Club at Whitehall," he urged her. "I'll show you the plans I've made so far."

The party's freely flowing alcohol may have enhanced the moment, but Lancaster's invitation was a perfect match for Jessie's own impulsiveness. It was a far cry from the circumscribed nature of her upbringing in a family marked by religious conservatism and Victorian sternness. Her father, Charles Beveridge, was a clergyman's son; her mother, Ethelwyn, a clergyman's daughter; her uncle ran a parish in Melbourne.

She was born Jessie Maude Beveridge on September 13, 1901, in the tiny western Australia settlement of Southern Cross, little more than a decade after the town's founding by gold prospectors. Her father had arrived in town four years earlier to manage the local branch of the Commercial Bank, setting up residence in a small apartment above the bank. The year after Jessie another daughter, Eleanor, was born, but, tragically, she died an infant.

In 1905 the Beveridge family moved to Perth, where Jessie's mother gave birth to a son named Thomas. Here, in the capital city, Jessie and Thomas formed an indissoluble bond, one that grew only more robust with each passing year. When Jessie was seven, the Commercial Bank relocated her father to a branch in the mining town of Broken Hill, halfway across the country, where the family finally bought their own house. Jessie and Thomas attended Convent High School, where Jessie excelled in singing, piano, and music theory. By all accounts she could have had a fine career as a professional musician if she had so chosen.

In 1916 the bank transferred Charles to a new branch in the agricultural town of Timaru, New Zealand. Jessie attended the elite Craighead School, a newly founded private institution dedicated to producing "refined" and "cultured" young women. At Craighead, Jessie was a socially popular star athlete, but just three years later the family moved once again, this time to Melbourne, where Charles worked in the bank's main office. By this point Jessie was fed up with relocating—each time the family moved, she had to go through the lengthy and painful process of reestablishing herself and gaining new friends. She also felt oppressed by her family's staunchly religious lifestyle, which entailed endless visits to church and nonstop Bible reading. For an energetic, audacious spirit like hers, the atmosphere was insufferably claustrophobic. Jessie was keen for an escape.

At the age of seventeen Jessie met a *Weekly Times* journalist named Keith Miller, who was five years older. Though Miller's personality was far more sober than hers, Jessie, desperate to leave her family, unhesitatingly said yes when Miller proposed to her the following year. The two were married in a Melbourne suburb on December 3, 1919. It soon became apparent, however, that the young couple had little in common. "We were quite maladjusted," Jessie recalled later in life. "It was like two babies getting married. Our characters were poles apart." Jessie was headstrong and temperamental, whereas Keith was calm and steady. The quickly apparent gulf between their personalities was exacerbated by an inability to have children: the couple lost one baby born twelve weeks early, and two subsequent miscarriages convinced doctors that Jessie wasn't fit to bear a child.

Eventually the couple settled into a rhythm as friends, but they both accepted that they were no longer in love. Keith wanted a traditional wife who would stay at home, whereas Jessie wanted to travel the world and have "the right to live my own life." She was still itching to break the bonds of her sheltered existence.

Not long after, Jessie's father passed away from throat cancer at the relatively young age of fifty-seven. Two years later, her beloved brother, Thomas, who had become a midshipman in the navy, died suddenly of cerebral meningitis at age twenty-one. Jessie, caught utterly off guard, was devastated. As children, she and Tommy had spent hours lying on the rug in front of the fireplace, concocting plans to travel the world in search of adventure. He had been her closest confidant, her most intimate sounding board, the person who had kept her sane in the midst of her family's upheavals and cloyingly pious beliefs. Now her world seemed permanently scarred by misfortune: Tommy and her father were dead, her sister, Eleanor, had died an infant, and Jessie was stuck in a passionless marriage. Emotionally, she was hollowed-out—if not suicidal, then certainly deeply depressed. She felt trapped at the bottom of the world, doomed to wither, barren and alone, beneath the unforgiving Australian sun.

In the throes of her depression, Jessie decided her only option was to find something worth living for—even if she had no idea what that might be. For months she cast around fruitlessly for ideas, until finally a workable plan presented itself. Her father's family lived in England; at the urging of her aunt, she would go and visit them in an attempt to escape her gloom. Pleading with Keith that the trip was essential to her mental health, Jessie found employment as a door-to-door carpet sweeper saleswoman in order to save up funds for her trip. She even invited Keith to accompany her to England, but he demurred, possibly because his journalism career was well established in Australia. The two may have made a poor married couple, but they were on friendly-enough terms, and Keith agreed to Jessie's plan: she would live in England for six months while he provided her with a three-pound weekly allowance. He asked only that she earn enough money to pay for her return voyage home.

The driven, headstrong Jessie made a powerful saleswoman. As one of her customers later recalled, Jessie had knocked on the door of his Melbourne apartment sporting an ear-to-ear grin. When he opened up, Jessie had "thrust a neat, suede-shoed foot between the door and the sash, and refused to remove it until I had agreed to buy a newfangled carpet sweeper that I did not want." When the customer later spotted Jessie at a club, he asked a female friend who she was. With a knowing smile, the woman replied that Jessie was "a hurricane saleswoman."

As soon as she had saved up enough money, Jessie, with her devoted friend Margaret Starr in tow, purchased a third-class ticket for the voyage to England. She and Margaret planned to stay in London for six months. When they arrived in the city, in the spring of 1927, they rented a flat and began insinuating themselves into the local community of Australian expats. The freedom and stimulation Jessie had craved for so long were finally hers for the taking.

Now, at the Baker Street party, chatting with Bill Lancaster about his plans to fly to Australia, Jessie had a sudden vision of how she might further change her life.

2

A NIMBLE LIFTOFF

History surrounded Bill Lancaster and Jessie Keith-Miller as they sat within the elegant stone walls of the Authors' Club at Whitehall Place, a stone's throw from both the Thames River and Trafalgar Square. This was where Oscar Wilde had furiously condemned the censorship of his controversial play *Salome*; where Sir Arthur Conan Doyle had for years reigned undefeated as billiards champion; where guest speakers like Mark Twain, Rudyard Kipling, and Emile Zola had been honored; where Ford Madox Ford had gotten rip-roaring drunk on the night he returned from combat in France. In later years the building would serve as MI6's secret headquarters, but for now its glittering chandeliers and elaborately tiled floors bespoke a snobbish yet accessible gentility.

Jessie had hardly taken her seat before Lancaster launched into an animated spiel about his upcoming flight. The England-to-Australia route had been conquered twice before, but by so-called heavy airplanes. Lancaster intended to make his mark by flying the route in a *light* airplane—specifically, the eighty-five-horsepower ADC Cirrus engine-powered Avro Avian, designed and built only a few months earlier. The Avro Avian was set to transform modern light flying, Lancaster claimed, with its eighty-mile-an-hour cruising speed and nine-hundred-mile range.

Jessie may have been an amateur when it came to aviation, but she exhibited a no-nonsense approach that cut through any bravado in Lancaster's presentation. She pressed him for details: Could Lancaster actually *get* an Avro Avian?

Here Lancaster's confident manner began to falter. His father might help him, Lancaster said, but under Jessie's continued questioning he admitted that his father had thus far refused to finance the trip. From what Jessie could garner, the only concrete elements of Lancaster's plan were that he knew which airplane he preferred and which route he planned to take. But these meant nothing without the financial means to make them happen. Jessie pressed him further. Aside from the plane, how would fuel be paid for? What about food and equipment, not to mention visas, licenses, landing fees, service charges, and maps?

Jessie may have been sensible and strong-minded, but she was also fun-loving and lively. Despite Lancaster's lack of preparation, Jessie found him an appealing character, and not just because of his charm and looks. He was clearly an experienced pilot, and his eagerness for the journey was addictive in its way. Like her, he seemed ready for any adventure, keen to immerse himself in new worlds, yearning for escape from the constraining dailiness of his life. Most importantly, Lancaster's money problems aligned perfectly with the idea that had spontaneously flowered in Jessie's mind at the party the night before. After a few more questions, she came to the point.

"You said the plane was a two-seater?" she asked.

"Yes," he replied.

"If I can raise the money, say fifty percent of the total outlay, can I come with you?"

A look of astonishment crossed Lancaster's face, and he briefly scrambled for words. Whatever assistance he may have wanted from Jessie, this was clearly not it. Once Lancaster gathered his thoughts, he told Jessie that it would be impossible for her to join him on his journey. "In the first place there's the extra weight," he protested. "And you can't imagine what the flight would be like—you'd have to rough it everywhere. Besides, it's dangerous. I'm confident for myself but I couldn't take on the responsibility of a woman passenger."

Jessie barely registered Lancaster's words. As she sat in the Authors' Club, the flight suddenly represented for Jessie everything she'd yearned for: thrills, exploration, a headlong voyage into unfamiliar landscapes. The planned route would be the longest flight ever made by a woman. It seemed that together, they could achieve something legendary. And Jessie's argument was irrefutable: without her input, Lancaster was incapable of gathering the necessary money.

A still-hesitant Lancaster offered another reason why Jessie couldn't come on the flight—he confessed that, although he was currently living with his parents, he was married and had two daughters. He also claimed, truthfully or not, that he and his wife, Kiki, weren't living together because of a scandal involving Kiki, but that he wasn't seeking a divorce because of the sordid details that would be revealed in court, thereby damaging his children. Given the conservative moral tenor of the times, the fact of a married man and a married woman traveling together in such close circumstances for such a long period of time would complicate immensely the task of lining up sponsorship and support from businesses and the press, Lancaster argued. The hint of impropriety would be too great.

While Lancaster had a point, Jessie also felt he was employing this reason, and the story about Kiki, as an excuse to put off making a decision. As she would eventually come to learn, Lancaster had a habit of telling what Jessie called "little white lies," lies that usually had their basis in truth but which he spun to portray himself in the most flattering light. "I don't know whether he was capable of any big deceit," Jessie once said, but "I could never quite make out which was absolutely the truth and what was said on the spur of the moment."

When they reconvened a few days after their Authors' Club meeting, Jessie pressed her advantage. "Look, Bill, you've been talking about this flight for months, or so everyone tells me, and what have you got?" Her manner was unyielding. "The truth is that you haven't a hope of getting started without money. I've got Australian contacts who'll help with money, and I'm a woman, which will help with publicity. It seems to me it's a case of either you take me or you don't go at all."

After thinking things over, Lancaster had come to the reluctant conclusion that Jessie was right: without her help, the journey would not happen. Thus decided, he agreed to form a business partnership with Jessie. The two later insisted that the decision was purely professional—because they each had spouses, they joined together for aviation purposes only. But they were kindred free-flying spirits, young and in bloom, dismissive of convention, with large, immensely appealing personalities. The attraction, even unstated, must have been immediate.

To kick off their affiliation, the two met the next day at Stanfords, the world's finest map store, in Covent Garden. Situated in a charmingly refurbished Victorian home, Stanfords' multiple floors were filled to bursting with travel guides, gorgeously crafted handmade globes, intricately detailed atlases, and stirring narratives of heroic expeditions. In the shop, an RAF officer helped Lancaster and Jessie plan the route of their flight, which would proceed in stages, with RAF airfields making up the bulk of their landing fields. Stanfords would convert these plans into strip maps that folded up into a book.

Seeing an opportunity to shore up her deal with Lancaster, Jessie forked over the money for the maps on the spot. Barely a week before, Jessie had been an innocent adrift in a thrillingly intimidating new city. Now her life possessed an exhilarating purpose, a concrete goal on which to focus her energies. She, along with Lancaster, had a sudden future to plan for.

Bill Lancaster's path to his partnership with Jessie had been winding, but his flying skills were well established. Born William Newton Lancaster on February 14, 1898, in the industrial city of Birmingham, he had been raised in South London by his father, Edward, and his mother, Maud, a first cousin of Edward's. The family was upper middle-class. Edward was one of England's top civil engineers, with several leading technical books on engineering to his name, while Maud was the author of a best-selling guidebook for housewives, and an active follower of the Spiritualist movement. Maud devoted most of her time to volunteering with a local Christian charity organization called Mission of Flowers, where she was known as "Sister Red Rose." The neighbors considered her an unconventional but loving mother.

When he was a teenager, Lancaster headed off for Australia with his brother, Jack, as junior members of a royal commission. The year was 1914; by the time Lancaster and Jack reached Australia, the commission had been canceled due to the outbreak of World War I. After working a series of odd jobs, Lancaster joined the Australian military's Light Horse infantry, after which he was transferred back to England as a mechanical specialist.

The trenches in which Lancaster soon found himself were fetid, blood-soaked pits, and he gazed with longing at the fighter pilots zipping overhead, who appeared exempted from the human misery below. Never before had aviation been used so heavily in war—indeed, the extraordinary advances made by aviation in World War I still form the core of today's military and civilian flight—and Lancaster, like countless numbers of his fellow soldiers, was awed and inspired by the tough new breed of flying jockeys. Within a matter of weeks, he put in for a transfer to the Flying Corps. He gained his wish in July 1917, and spent the rest of that summer receiving pilot training. But soon after beginning his new position that fall, he crashed in a snowstorm. Shortly before the war ended in 1918, Lancaster's military contract was canceled for medical reasons.

Returning to London, Lancaster briefly flirted with dental school, but he abandoned these plans after the Royal Air Force (RAF) granted him a new appointment as second lieutenant. The RAF, the world's first independent air force, had come into existence only a few months earlier, on April 1, 1918, but it now provided the lifeline that Lancaster had been seeking. Lancaster had a ground's-eye view as the RAF rapidly transformed itself into the largest air force in the world.

That same year, Lancaster met a woman named Annie Maud Mervyn-Colomb, whose husband had died in battle three years earlier. Lancaster was two years younger than the woman he nicknamed "Kiki," and he was, in many ways, profoundly immature. But he nonetheless recognized Kiki's polished bearing, her innate morality, and her thoughtful, generous nature. Lancaster was a twenty-one-year-old bundle of unfocused energy, and Kiki's composed manner helped settle him, however temporarily. The two were married in April 1919.

With Kiki in tow, Lancaster headed to India two years later for a posting with the highly regarded 31 Squadron. The pilots of the 31 were as dedicated and professional as any fliers in the world, and they were fiercely proud of their good name. Next to them, Lancaster seemed out of his depth, even if he himself failed to recognize this. He possessed a youthful foolhardiness, a sort of innocent arrogance, which was coupled with a fun-loving, easygoing manner. To the reserved, self-consciously modest squadron officers, these qualities represented a marked breach of social conduct.

Lancaster was an outcast in another way, as well: he was married and living off base, which meant his social interaction with his fellow fliers was minimal. This, again, was considered a breach of conduct. When Kiki gave birth to a daughter, Patricia, in early 1922, the family's already thin finances were stretched to the point that Lancaster frequently went into arrears on monthly bills. To the squadron, this was yet another mark against him.

The following summer Lancaster was assigned to RAF Halton in England, which proved a more welcoming environment than India. While Lancaster was still regarded as an oddity, his behavior elicited bemused acceptance rather than social rebuke. He remained boastful, and his hijinks were frequently juvenile, but Halton lacked the buttoned-up atmosphere that had made these qualities so damning in India.

Lancaster's most memorable incident during this period occurred when International Rodeo rolled into Wembley Stadium in London. As part of the event, cowboys from America, Canada, and Australia competed in displays of riding, roping, and steer wrestling, while select audience members participated in a bucking bronco challenge. In practice, few spectators actually embraced this latter challenge, and none of them, no matter how seasoned, lasted long on the bronco. But when Lancaster was informed of the challenge, he announced, in his typically cocksure way, that he could win it. His fellow officers at Halton thought he was deluded, but they were eager to encourage his attempt. His failure, they thought, might curb his braggadocio.

Thus Lancaster had a full car of passengers as he drove to the rodeo, with several more RAF associates making the journey to Wembley by rail. Later that night, as his compatriots looked on, secretly rooting for his failure, Lancaster stunned the crowd by winning the challenge—and the ten-pound reward. That he had performed the feat wearing a pin-striped suit and bowler hat only added to his triumph. Lancaster's victory did little to temper his conceit, but it caused the men at Halton to treat him with a newfound respect.

In the fall of 1924, Lancaster's duties were shifted to RAF Manston, where the crew soon discovered that Lancaster was an intrepid and capricious risk-taker. When their boxing team faced Uxbridge in a championship series that winter, the team's lack of a welterweight threatened to doom their chances at victory. Though Lancaster had little experience—and though he was ill equipped against his powerful opponent—he agreed to step into the ring. The Uxbridge challenger's large, strong frame dwarfed his own; in less than a round the knockout blow had been delivered. But Lancaster received a point just for joining the match, which ultimately propelled Manston into the championship seat.

The beating Lancaster received in the ring didn't affect his penchant for athletic stunts. When Manston held a swimming competition soon after the boxing match, Lancaster engaged in a Houdini-like performance. He was sewn into a large sack and lifted onto the high diving board. Stepping from the board, Lancaster plunged under the water for a full thirty seconds before bobbing up to raucous applause from the crowd. In fact, he had secretly placed a knife in the sack, which he used to cut himself out. But to his Manston comrades, the incident was emblematic of Lancaster's freewheeling persona.

As a pilot, Lancaster was adroit, if reckless. What set him apart was not his skills, but his radical self-assurance. This partially stemmed from his mastery of engineering: he knew he could fix any mechanical problems his aircraft encountered. Lancaster's fellow pilots viewed this ability with envy, but he was too well liked, despite his irresponsibility, for them to resent him. He may not have been career officer material, but no one at Manston doubted that high adventure lay in Lancaster's future.

As the humid London summer labored its stifling way to fall, and Lancaster and Jessie worked tirelessly to plan their record-attempting flight, Jessie fretted that Lancaster's wife, Kiki, would be disturbed by the idea of her husband traveling with another woman. In a change of story, Lancaster had told Jessie that he and Kiki were living apart due to financial constraints—Kiki was living on the south coast, the only place that she could find a job. Meanwhile, his parents were taking care of his daughter Pat and a second daughter, Nina Ann, who had been born earlier that year. Whatever attraction Lancaster and Jessie felt for each other was submerged and private, with no intention to act, and Jessie's concern for Kiki's feelings was genuine. So, at her insistence, she and Lancaster headed south to meet with Kiki in person. Happily, Jessie's apprehensions proved unfounded.

"My dear, I couldn't care less who he flies with or what he does, as long as he sends me some money," Kiki promised Jessie.

Lancaster's parents, however, were scandalized at the thought of him joining forces with a woman to whom he wasn't married. But when they met Jessie, they found themselves pleasingly surprised by her frankness and sincerity. Her willingness to pay for the journey's maps further indicated that she was serious about the endeavor.

Following the meeting at their house, Maud Lancaster made Jessie accompany her on a visit to her favorite spirit medium to determine whether the spirits thought Jessie was the right person for the flight. The medium went into a deep trance, after which he confirmed that the spirits believed Jessie would make an excellent flying partner for Lancaster. When Maud looked away, the medium caught Jessie's eye and gave her a big wink. Reassured, and always eager to help out their son, Edward and Maud Lancaster agreed to help finance a plane, on the condition that the aviators distribute pamphlets for Maud's beloved Mission of Flowers charity at every stop along their route.

There were other expenses, as well. Lancaster and Jessie needed to provide a deposit for the cables they would send during their trip, while passports and flying kits were an additional expenditure. The luxury fashion house Burberry made up their flight kits and, in a show of support for their journey, gave them a 50 percent discount in the process. Putting her saleswoman skills to work, Jessie proved a natural at seeking out potential funders for their journey. She wrote letters to the London offices of Australian firms asking for their sponsorship, and she gained the support of the Australian high commissioner to the UK, Sir Granville Ryrie. She also secured pledges from Shell and British Petroleum to provide the necessary gasoline, which would be stored at regular stops along the flight path, and from Wakefield & Co. to provide the oil. These services were provided free of charge; the promoters knew that a triumphant journey would generate positive exposure for their companies.

Help also came from several London-based Australians. The cattle baron Sir Sidney Kidman, one of Jessie's contacts, donated money for the trip. The rugged Kidman owned the largest cattle operation on the planet, his empire covering an astonishing 3 percent of the Australian landmass. Jessie obtained additional financial help from Baron Clive Baillieu, an Australian-British businessman and former champion rower, and James Nevin Tait, an Australian film producer and concert promoter. When Jessie visited the Pickfords moving company to arrange for her trunks to be delivered to Australia—she would pick them up at journey's end—the firm agreed to pay for the service at the urging of trailblazing Australian masseuse Lizzie Armstrong.

Not everyone was so enthusiastic. When Lancaster described his and Jessie's plans to Sir Keith Smith, a former military pilot who in 1919 had flown from England to Australia in a record-setting twenty-seven days, Smith replied, "Oh, well it is a very good way in which to commit suicide." But apparently not wishing Lancaster and Jessie to suffer such a fate, Smith provided them with all the assistance he could.

For the airplane itself, Lancaster turned to the Lancashire-based company Avro, one of the world's first and finest aircraft manufacturers. Avro was eager to be associated with a potentially record-setting journey, especially after Lancaster assured them that he intended to promote how dependable their plane was, not to be a daredevil. In September 1927 the company gave Lancaster a significant discount on their brand-new Avian III biplane, whose streamlined body resembled that of a silver wasp with wide, rounded-off wings that could fold up vertically. Lancaster and Jessie, in a tribute to Lancaster's mother, named their plane the *Red Rose*, and those words, framing the image of a rose, were tidily painted in black on the aircraft's front sides. The plane featured fresh overload tanks, modified center-section struts, and a narrower tubular-steel interframe, which meant reduced room for suitcases and spare tires. The plane's small luggage compartment only had room for the bare essentials: emergency rations, maps, a few spare parts and tools, some oil, a gun and ammunition, and their clothes and toiletries.

As it happened, only late in her preparations for the journey did Jessie consider what to bring. She faced the dual considerations of trying to minimize the plane's weight while also making sure she had the necessary amenities. In the end, her gear for the trip fit into a small leather bag. She packed a comb and mirror, one change of underwear, one pair of socks, one pair of silk stockings, one clean shirt, one pair of shorts, one box of face powder, one pair of satin evening shoes, and one black sheer fabric evening gown.

Her toiletries consisted simply of a toothbrush, a tube of toothpaste, and a small cake of soap. She wore low-heeled leather shoes and breeches, short trousers fastened just below the knee. With sexist condescension, the *Manchester Guardian* newspaper noted that this was "probably the smallest amount of luggage ever taken by a woman on a journey of this length."

A final issue remained: Who would insure the plane, and what would they charge? Lancaster's lack of fame was a liability for insurers, and for the aviation world as a whole. Unlike Charles Lindbergh, Lancaster was an unproven entity. Professional aviators thought that bringing a female passenger represented pure gimmickry, which was enhanced by the news that Lancaster would be distributing pamphlets for his mother's Christian charity. But for Lancaster and Jessie the flight was serious business indeed.

On the chilly, wet morning of October 10, Lancaster drove to Woodford Aerodrome in Manchester to inspect his new aircraft. He made a short test flight in which the plane performed flawlessly. "London to Australia in Light Plane," read the *Manchester Guardian* headline announcing Lancaster's visit, describing him as "not only an adventurous airman but a well-known athlete," the latter a reference to his RAF boxing match. Declaring full confidence in the Avian's capabilities, Lancaster flew to Croydon Airport in South London later that afternoon. This would be the starting point for his and Jessie's journey.

On the flight to Australia, Lancaster, sitting in the rear cockpit, would be the lead pilot, but Jessie was eager to master the art of aviation as well. (The *Red Rose*'s front cockpit would feature a dual control panel so that Jessie could fly the plane herself.) To provide her with lessons, Lancaster brought in an old World War I pilot friend of his named T. Neville Stack, who had recently flown from England to India. Jessie was transfixed as soon as Stack took her up in the air. "I thought it was marvelous," Jessie later said. "I simply adored it. I took to it absolutely. Never a qualm, never a moment of airsickness, nothing. Bill always said I was a natural pilot."

Lancaster planned to give her additional instruction, but when he showed up two hours late for her first lesson with him, he found Jessie already in the air, flying solo. For ten minutes she soared nimbly over his head. After making a smooth landing, she took off again before Lancaster had time to join her in the cockpit. She repeated this action several more times in order to make her point: she was born to be a pilot.

Aviation was an intensely male-dominated field at the time, and for women who wanted to participate, the confidence and audacity that Jessie exhibited were essential. From the beginning, female aviators had faced an onslaught of taunts and criticisms that women were mentally and physically unfit for flying. Claude Grahame-White, one of England's first star aviators, expressed the dominant prejudice, proclaiming, "Women lack qualities which make for safety in aviation. They are temperamentally unfitted for the sport." Grahame-White believed, among other things, that a woman's sense of balance was inferior to that of a man. Arnold Kruckman, the aviation editor for the *New York American*, opined that women were far too sensitive emotionally to handle the stress of flying, and that they lacked discipline, "the natural heritage of many men." Orville and Wilbur Wright at first thought women shouldn't fly, a belief they held in common with celebrated American aviator Glenn Curtiss. Prominent German pilot Hellmuth Hirth agreed; he also shared the anxiety of other male aviators that their public regard would drop considerably if women joined the field. If women could perform the same spectacular and daring aviation feats as men, Hirth and others fretted, then perhaps those feats were not so special.

Another reason for the bias against female pilots was that flying was *dangerous*: early aviators were killed at an astonishing rate. While it was fine and well for a young man to risk his life in an airplane, for a young woman to do so was thought unnatural. As the *New York Times* sniffed, "It would be well to exclude women from a field of activity in which their presence is unnecessary from any point of view."

One way international aero clubs enacted this bigotry in aviation's early years was by banning women from flying competitively against men. Women were restricted instead to their own contests at their own airfields. And yet these exhibitions attracted rapturous fans of both sexes, who thrilled at the sight of these talented and daring women in the air.

For the pilots themselves, the risk was beside the point. "Most of us spread the perils of a lifetime over a number of years," said the intrepid French baroness Raymonde de Laroche, the first woman to fly a heavier-than-air machine into the air alone, and the first woman in the world to receive an airplane pilot's license. "Others may pack them into a matter of only a few hours. In any case, whatever is to happen will happen—it may well be that I shall tempt Fate once too often. Who knows? But it is in the air that I have dedicated myself, and I fly always without the slightest fear." De Laroche herself was a case study in flying's dangers: ten years after her revolutionary flight of 1909, she died in a plane crash at Le Crotoy airfield in France.

On August 1, 1911, screenwriter Harriet Quimby became the first American woman to receive a pilot's license. She was also the first woman to fly across the English Channel, though her achievement was little noted due to massive media coverage of the RMS *Titanic*'s sinking the day before. "I'm going in for everything in aviation that men have done," Quimby declared, "altitude, speed, endurance, and the rest. . . . Flying is a fine, dignified sport for women, healthful and stimulating to the mind, and there is no reason to be afraid so long as one is careful." On that last point, Quimby was unfortunately mistaken. In 1912, she fell victim to tragedy when her two-seat monoplane crashed over Boston Harbor, killing her and her male passenger.

Quimby was followed in America by such daredevil pilots as Ruth Law and Katherine Stinson in 1912, women who became known as much for their death-defying stunts, like wingwalking, as for their flying skills. In those early years of aviation the field possessed, especially in America, an unabashedly circus-like atmosphere, and the hair-raising stunts performed by people like Blanche Stuart Scott and Jessie Woods only contributed to aviators' superhuman reputation among spectators on the ground. The telescopic focus on aerial acrobatics in America, and the concomitant risks that fliers increasingly had to endure to stand out in the crowd, eventually drove many women out of the field. Their European counterparts, by contrast, had greater freedom to concentrate on pursuing extended cross-border and international flights.

The most famous female aviator of all, Amelia Earhart, began her flying lessons on January 3, 1921, in Long Beach, California. By October of the following year, Earhart had flown her own biplane fourteen thousand feet into the air, setting a new women's record. In May 1923 she became only the sixteenth woman in the world to earn an international pilot's license. As her reputation grew, Earhart wrote newspaper columns that advocated vigorously for female aviators, and she became vice president of the American Aeronautical Society's Boston chapter. With her close-cropped hair, aviator helmet, and leather jacket, Earhart's now-iconic look mirrored that of the era's other female pilots—all of those intrepid fliers whom, for the general public, she would eventually come to represent.

As Lancaster and Jessie prepared for their journey, Amelia Earhart was still months away from the seminal flight across the Atlantic that would turn her into an international celebrity. But as their scheduled day of departure drew near, Lancaster and Jessie's momentum was briefly halted by superstition. They had intended to leave on October 13, but to fly without insurance on such a day felt overly risky. They decided to postpone their departure for twenty-four hours. If insurance for the plane hadn't materialized in that time, they would begin their journey regardless. Otherwise the press would dismiss them as amateurs, and Lancaster and Jessie would continue depleting their already-shaky finances. What's more, Kiki, who had traveled to London with the children to see Lancaster off, had to get back to her job. The Australian high commissioner to the UK and his family were also due at their departure, and Lancaster and Jessie felt determined to impress them. No matter the consequences, they had to leave Croydon Airport behind.

On October 14, 1927, a group of journalists and supporters clustered around the *Red Rose* to witness the grand event. Lancaster and Jessie had twenty-five pounds sterling in their pockets. "Woman Flying to Australia" read the understated headline in the *Manchester Guardian*. The *Sydney Times* called Jessie a "heroic woman" who was "credited with being the driving force of the enterprise [who] has handled all the business details."

When the Australian high commissioner arrived, he handed them an official letter of support. "I am an Australian," Jessie announced to the reporters, "and have always wanted to be the first woman to fly from London to Australia." (The "always" was a significant exaggeration.) "The flight is not intended in any way to be a stunt," she added reassuringly; "it is purely a utility flight to demonstrate the practicability of the light airplane as a means of covering long distances."

Lancaster also delivered a short speech, emphasizing yet again that his and Jessie's purpose was to test the Avian III model, not to engage in attention-grabbing exploits. Kiki looked on proudly, bestowing goodbye kisses to both fliers. A bowl of scarlet petals was scattered over the plane, with each softly curling petal representing the *Red Rose*. Once Lancaster was settled in the rear cockpit and Jessie in the front, five-year-old Pat climbed into Kiki's arms to scrawl a goodbye note on the plane's lower right side. The time was 2:35 p.m., and the heavy fog that had covered the airport all morning had finally lifted enough to allow their departure. Raising his hand in farewell, Lancaster guided the plane down the unpaved runway. Achieving a nimble liftoff, the *Red Rose* angled up into the autumn afternoon.

3

SINGLE-MINDED ABANDON

Even as they began their journey, Lancaster and Jessie knew relatively little about each other as people. During the months of hectic preparation for their flight, their interactions had, of necessity, centered on the myriad details that such an ambitious undertaking required. Though they enjoyed a friendly, effortless bond, and though their pulses quickened at the thought of their impending shared adventure, they had divulged relatively little of their personal lives. Not that that was an issue of concern for them: they were interested in action, not reflection; in experience, not rumination. They both lived in the moment, and the fact that they delighted in each other's company was appreciated but unremarked upon. Nor did either acknowledge the undeniable fact that, even as friends, they appeared far more suited to each other than to their respective spouses.

Their journey had been plotted to follow a dotted path of RAF airfields stretching from London to Australia. These stations were where most of their landings would occur, and where the two aviators would lodge. Lancaster and Jessie had been advised that, due to weather conditions, they should spend the first night of their journey in the quaint French town of Abbeville instead of flying on to Paris. And indeed, the fog remained so thick as the *Red Rose* flew over the English Channel that it obscured the water below.

Lancaster and Jessie arrived at Abbeville at nightfall, but there were no lights on at the airfield to guide them, and so they landed instead in a small field outside of town. A group of French farmers approached the plane and gave Lancaster directions for the short hop to the airport. Because there was so little room to taxi the plane, he was forced to lighten the load: Jessie, her luggage in tow, would have to walk the two miles to the airport. Two of the farmers accompanied her, while Lancaster flew on ahead. As she carried her luggage from the field into the town, Jessie was struck by how unreal her new circumstances felt. In a matter of hours, it seemed, her life had become something wholly new. "My mind," she wrote in the first of a series of dispatches for an Australian newspaper, "was a confusion of hopes, inhibitions, and great desires."

The next morning she and Lancaster headed for Paris. Shortly after flying over Beauvais's massive (and still unfinished) thirteenth-century Gothic cathedral, they spotted a large French airliner, with passengers milling about it, stranded in a field below. Concerned, they circled the *Red Rose* back around, but the passengers waved that everything was safe: it had been a forced landing, not an accident. When they reached Le Bourget Airport in Paris, they were met by pilots from Imperial Airways, a British commercial air transport company, who provided lively conversation and humor as Lancaster and Jessie spent the afternoon tinkering with the plane's engine and refueling its gas tanks. The weather conditions, however, remained dismal. Jessie felt, she wrote, as if "all the fogs in the world were dogging" them. Despite the gloom, the group later went out on the town for a mouth-watering dinner with wine. Joyously tipsy, Lancaster and Jessie took off their shoes and splashed laughingly in the fountains outside the Folies Bergère cabaret. To be young and free in one of the world's great cities, surrounded by pilots who accepted her instantly, without comment, as one of their own—Jessie felt a warm sense of belonging that night that she would hold close in her memory over the months to come.

Not until Lancaster and Jessie were flying toward the port city of Marseille one day later did the sky finally brighten and sunlight break through the clouds. But stiff crosswinds continued to batter the plane as they flew over the Rhône Valley, marveling from their cockpits at the quaint castles and churches nestled on the hillsides below. At one point the *Red Rose* ripped into an air pocket and plunged precipitously. Jessie, who wasn't buckled in, launched straight up from her seat and cracked her head on the center wing section; dazed, she slammed back down with a jarring thwack. It was a painful and early reminder to always wear her seat belt. When the drained aviators finally reached Marseille, the gleaming Mediterranean abutting the city provided them with their first glimpse of blue water on the trip, a positive omen after the soggy weather of the previous days.

After stabling the *Red Rose* at the airport, where they met up with another group of aviators, Lancaster and Jessie took the train into the city, taking notice of its bustling, boat-lined quays. Famished after their long day flying, they ate at a cheap, cramped restaurant; chickens strode brazenly beneath the tables as Lancaster, Jessie, and their companions feasted on thick hunks of bread and cheese, sardines and onions, and cheap vinegar-like wine. As in Paris, Jessie felt an immediate bond with these pilots, who bade no notice of her gender and treated her instead with the respect due a fellow flier. This was a pattern that would continue throughout the journey; the people who obsessed over her status as one of the world's few female aviators were journalists and civilians, not other pilots. Aviators were still a rare enough breed that they felt bound by a comradeship that superseded any markers of personal identity.

Lancaster spent these early days of the journey studying which flight patterns and which on-the-ground servicing the *Red Rose* best responded to. He shared his mechanical knowledge with Jessie, who was anxious to learn. Soon she was checking clearances, cleaning spark plugs, re-oiling engine parts, and straining fuel, which required standing on the plane's fuselage and pouring gasoline through chamois leather into the tanks. This latter task was risky: frequently wind would blow the gasoline back over her, burning her skin. Jessie would often pilot the plane herself while Lancaster rested, although he still insisted on performing all takeoffs and landings. The plane had no radio, so the two communicated via a small hatch between the cockpits. Lancaster would tap Jessie's head to gain her attention, then pass her a handwritten message through the hatch.

As they headed toward Italy, continued foggy weather added to the strain of their journey. Lancaster had to fly uncomfortably low to the sea just to make out the water; even the plane's nose was invisible in the murky haze.

Mountains rose straight up from the water's edge, further boxing them in. The skies had cleared just enough by the time they reached Pisa that Lancaster and Jessie were able to marvel from the air at the famed Leaning Tower, which they circled twice. Rain continued to pour on and off during Lancaster and Jessie's flight to Rome, but the view turned dramatic as the city appeared in the distance. The numerous bridges spanning the Tiber "seemed like so many clips cutting a silver ribbon into sections," Jessie breathlessly noted, "and not even the Caesars dreamed of such an approach as ours to the city of Seven Hills."

A day later Lancaster and Jessie flew close enough to Mount Vesuvius to witness smoke curling from its crater "as if from an evil pot." Touching down at Catania, a port city on Sicily's eastern coast, they were greeted by General Italo Balbo, one of the principal architects of the Italian Fascists' rise to power, who with gracious formality presented them with a personal note from Mussolini extolling his best wishes for a successful journey. Zealous Italian Air Force pilots, clothed in immaculately tailored dark gray uniforms, scurried around the *Red Rose*, scrawling "Viva Mussolini" all over its fuselage. Lancaster and Jessie couldn't help but grin at the energetic scene.

Their jovial mood soon came to an abrupt halt: as Jessie gripped a hand pump to refuel the gas tanks, she crushed her knuckles on the side of the plane. The pain was immediate; blood flowed over her torn skin, staining the side of the *Red Rose*. Alarmed Italian officers hustled to locate some iodine for her wounds. They had just finished dousing the cuts when, to Jessie's horror, an oblivious General Balbo strode over to kiss her hand in farewell. As the general raised his head, Jessie saw with dismay that his mouth was smeared with blood and iodine. For a tense moment there was only silence, and then the pointy-bearded Balbo burst out laughing at the mess. Jessie relievedly joined in.

Their next stop was the island of Malta, where Lancaster and Jessie spent the weekend among the ancient fortresses and megalithic temples. At night they were feted by the local RAF command, as they had been at almost every previous stop. Only eight days into their journey, Jessie was already finding her lone evening gown essential. Yet at every gathering she sensed a certain coolness among the air force officers' wives, who she felt disapproved of her nontraditional pursuits. This only served to make her value even more the companionship of her fellow pilots, not to mention Lancaster himself. A shared glance, an appreciative smile, a reassuring hand on the back—the friendly gestures of affection that she and Lancaster increasingly shared in the midst of their social whirl grew more meaningful with each passing day.

After Malta they departed for Tripoli, but rough winds and poor visibility turned their 225-mile trek across the Mediterranean into a slog. For diversion during the dreary haul, Lancaster and Jessie swooped down low over the decks of a large steamer ship and gave the passengers onboard what Jessie felt sure was "the shock of their lives." The weather was so poor that Lancaster and Jessie didn't spot the Libyan coast until they were almost on top of it, but they managed nonetheless to land within two miles of their intended destination. The Italian Air Force officers at Tripoli greeted them enthusiastically, bestowing on Jessie a gigantic bouquet of flowers that nearly dwarfed her tiny frame. Then they whisked them off to an afternoon dance, where, in between breaks for tea and cake, Lancaster and Jessie gamely waltzed, tangoed, and did the Charleston to the tune of a live orchestra. The celebration continued that night with an elaborate dinner at the British Consulate.

Climbing into the *Red Rose* the next morning, Jessie felt obliged to squeeze the enormous flower bouquet into her cockpit so that the officers who presented it to her wouldn't feel insulted. Only when Tripoli was behind her did she toss the bouquet overboard.

After a short flight the *Red Rose* touched down at Homs in western Syria to take on gas and oil. The night before, the air force had warned Lancaster and Jessie that Italy was skirmishing with North Africa's Arab population, which was resisting Italian efforts to build a road from Benghazi to Tripoli. "If you have to make a forced landing anywhere along the coast," the Italians had cautioned them, "you are in for a bad time." They had suggested that Lancaster and Jessie tie the Union Jack onto their plane as a safety measure. At Homs, however, the aviators found the locals who greeted them to be nothing but hospitable. Perhaps the Italian officers had been overstating the region's threat. But later that afternoon they were flying toward Benghazi when Jessie, craning her neck, noticed four puffs of smoke in the air beneath the plane. The Italians hadn't been exaggerating after all: Bedouin tribesmen on the ground were firing at the *Red Rose*.

Before Jessie could fully process this information, she heard an alarmed shout from Lancaster. Raising her head, she was stunned to see a colossal wall of sand heading straight for them, kicked up by forty-five-mile-an-hour winds. Only moments before, the sky had been pure blue; now she barely had time to jam her goggles down over her eyes before the sandstorm surrounded the plane, stinging her and Lancaster's faces unmercifully. Lancaster dropped the plane as low to the ground as possible, but in the massive storm visibility was practically nil. Reaching Benghazi, their intended destination, would be impossible. Their only option was to follow the coastline to Sirte, a town two hundred miles closer. "The sand was terrible, and was getting worse every minute," Jessie later recounted. "It gritted in our teeth, got into our hair and ears, and dribbled down our necks. The carburetor was choked with this loosened desert, and the machine was in a filthy condition."

After what felt like an eternity the *Red Rose* finally limped into the Italian military airport at Sirte. Lancaster and Jessie had brought with them the Italian newspapers from Rome, which featured their story splashed across the front pages. Because neither aviator spoke Italian, the newspapers afforded them an introduction they could not have made themselves. The air force commander, a bachelor, appeared pleased to see them, but he seemed at a loss as to where to house Jessie. No other women were visible in the town. At last Jessie was given quarters in the barracks, while Lancaster shared the relative luxury of the commandant's lodgings. Jessie's room had hard stone floors and an iron bed frame, not to mention cockroaches scampering madly all over the ground. When she walked, the cockroaches, much to her revulsion, scurried over her feet. But she put on her best brave face, and the air force officers responded by preparing her and Lancaster a wonderful meal.

The language barrier was difficult enough to overcome that communication at dinner consisted mostly of gestures, smiles, and generic flattery. Jessie was made to understand that she was the first white woman to ever visit the town, while the commanding officer, having quite warmed up to her, gifted her with an aerial photograph of the base. After dinner the satiated group sat on the dining hall's verandah and smoked Italian cigarettes. The wind was still blowing at high speed, and the gulf heat felt unbearable. Jessie was far from eager to return to her cockroach-infested room, but she desperately needed rest, so she turned in early. The punishing wind turned the walk back to her barracks into a feat of endurance. She stretched uncomfortably under the mosquito netting over her bed as she struggled to fall asleep in her dismal quarters.

The Italian officers woke Lancaster and Jessie at 5 a.m., plying them with strong, sweet black coffee for the morning's flight to Benghazi, a straight shot across the bay from Sirte. Once in the air, the aviators flew for two hours before spotting the bazaars and colored roofs of the first town on the bay's far side. Hungry after skipping breakfast, they landed in the hopes of searching out food, but ended up settling for more coffee instead. Camels roamed freely on the town's dusty outskirts, provoking in Jessie a sudden urge to ride one. She was always searching out new experiences, and being carried on a camel would be a first for her. But when she and Lancaster asked a local if Jessie could borrow his camel, the language barrier proved insurmountable. The man merely shrugged his shoulders at the impertinent request and led his camel away. So Lancaster and Jessie hopped back in the *Red Rose* and pushed onward through a strong headwind until they reached Benghazi, marveling from the air at the sparkling sea and the city's pure white buildings of Moorish design.

Next they flew east for the Egyptian village of Sallum, a Bedouin community and former ancient Roman port, but a hard wind fought them the whole way, and once at Sallum they couldn't locate the airport, which was unmarked. Lancaster spiraled up above the steep cliffs on which the village was perched, barely clearing them, but he found no place to land. Even in the midst of such hair-raising circumstances, as Lancaster circled frantically while vicious winds thrashed the plane, Jessie couldn't help but feel awed by the blue beauty of the Mediterranean below. At last a desperate Lancaster, in an imprudent attempt to mark a landing zone, tossed several smoke bombs overboard. When the bombs exploded, sending out plumes of smoke, the previously deserted landscape came alive, with panicked soldiers and villagers running from all directions in the mistaken belief they were being attacked from the air.

When the *Red Rose* finally touched down, Lancaster and Jessie were greeted by Egyptian soldiers from a nearby base aiming rifles at their faces, along with an infuriated commanding officer asking them in flawless English to state their business. Lancaster, attempting to defuse the tension, quickly adopted a posh British accent as he explained their situation and inquired politely whether the soldiers might be willing to spare any food.

Jessie knew by now that this performance was vintage Lancaster: reckless, friendly, and intrepid all at once. At times she didn't know whether to be livid with him or to embrace him. She only knew that the two of them were inseparable, and not just because of their physical circumstances. Thoughts of their respective spouses, in far-off England and Australia, were receding with each shared escapade, with each exhilarating or terrifying moment spent speeding above the earth in their cramped but close-set cockpits.

Lancaster and Jessie arrived in Cairo, their next major destination, on October 29. Landing at RAF Heliopolis, on the city's outskirts, they were given a fulsome welcome by a group of Lancaster's former RAF mates. Equally uplifting was their visit to the great pyramid at Giza; Jessie's heart raced as she climbed the small, worn steps of the ancient tomb. As they spent the weekend in the city carousing with Lancaster's old friends, the story of their journey also began to attract greater media interest. A two-week flight from England to Cairo was not remarkable in itself, but the route had never before been attempted with a passenger, nor had a light airplane been utilized in this particular manner. The aviation world, too, was waking up to the fact that Lancaster and Jessie were serious, and that their journey was far more than a gimmick. Boosted by this new attention and forty-eight hours of carefree socializing, they prepared for their next flight. The route would be their toughest yet, taking them over nearly landmark-free desert as they made their way to Baghdad. Because the *Red Rose* was too small to carry any emergency water or food, the RAF commander at Heliopolis insisted they be guided by a British biplane troop carrier.

Just after dawn, Lancaster and Jessie again took to the air, the troop carrier in front of them. As they flew over densely cultivated lands, the delta of the Nile resembled a collection of tiny silver lakes to the north. "The sails of the strange craft on the river looked like little bits of paper blown by the breeze," Jessie wrote, "and spread beneath us was a living picture of the maps we carried in the cockpit." They soared over the Suez Canal—in Jessie's words, a "tinsel ribbon shining in the sunlight"—and the Dead Sea, which, though it looked small from the air, took them a significant time to cross. They kept slamming into air pockets, low-pressure regions that forced the *Red Rose* abruptly downward. At one point the plane plunged a heart-stopping five hundred feet.

Finally they landed, along with the troop carrier, at the small Wahhabi village of Ziza, east of the Dead Sea, to refuel. Because of strong headwinds, the RAF decided the group should spend the night in Ziza. Jessie found the setting dismal, but she gamely shared the rations of the men stationed at the bare-bones air depot. Rusted tin lids served as plates, and an old tin mug served as a community cup, but the dinner, a stew of tinned corned beef and onions, proved surprisingly tasty. The RAF squadron leader, a cheery sort, lightened the mood by playing songs on his ukulele, which he pulled from under a box of salted fish in the troop carrier's fuselage. There was little water for washing up later, however—everyone had to rinse from the same small dishful. The meager beds Lancaster and Jessie slept in were practically open to the desert.

They departed early, and for the first time on their trip Lancaster and Jessie grasped the true vastness of the desert. "There is no glitter about the unending spread of sand early in the morning," Jessie wrote, "and instead of the gilded beauty which comes with the sun it seems to reflect the blue of the sky, measuring distance with it." They flew for hours without spotting any villages or palm-ringed oases or desert nomads in long robes. "The sun became a scorcher, and whatever breeze there was came from some blast furnace," Jessie reported. "We opened our shirts at the throats in order to gain a little respite." Black hills flanked the flat surfaces below; massive basalt boulders rose from the mountainous valleys.

As they flew over the Iraqi province of Al Anbar, Lancaster passed Jessie a note: "What are you doing with your feet? Are you thumping them on the floor?" Jessie responded that she was doing no such thing. "Well, something is happening!" Lancaster replied. Then Jessie smelled fire, and she began to imagine the worst. For a pulse-quickening twenty minutes the burning smell continued as Lancaster and Jessie waited for the *Red Rose* to burst into flames. They decided, in their petrified state, to make an emergency landing at Rutbah Wells, which for the past three years had served as a rest stop for Imperial Airways. As they descended, they could see nomadic tribes' black goatskin tents dotting the town; in the distance, a group of rugged hills floated above the otherwise flat expanse. The town's immense old fort, an ungainly gray building, had been transformed into a rest house for the airline.

Upon landing, Lancaster and Jessie discovered that one of the generators in the *Red Rose*'s ignition system had sheared, and was smoldering away. They spent the afternoon devising a temporary fix, before joining the RAF's

Armoured Car Company for an open-air dinner. The group ate in the desert beside a roaring campfire, with kerosene cans serving as chairs, saucepan lids substituting for plates, and two mugs of tea shared communally. As wild animals stalked outside the fire's perimeter, Lancaster and Jessie feasted on stewed gazelle.

Later that night, as Jessie tried vainly to sleep, a fierce windstorm blew in. Worried that the *Red Rose* might flip over, she stumbled through the dark, the sand whipping against her face, to check how well it was secured. At one point she heard a man's voice calling out to her in Arabic, but because she didn't speak the language, she pressed on. Suddenly she came up short—the man, a guard, was standing directly before her, pointing a rifle at her nose. Jessie realized with a start that he must have been yelling "Halt!" Despite the heavy wind, she eventually managed to light a match, and in the dim glow of the flame identified herself as one of the fliers. The apologetic guard escorted her to the plane and helped her tie it down. But hardly had it been secured when a torrential rain began pelting the desert, accompanied by even more lashing winds, forcing Jessie, with Lancaster's help, to fold the *Red Rose*'s wings vertically and wheel the airplane into the fort, where they were spending the night. The moment was historic: never before had an airplane been small enough to fit into the premises. Photographs were excitedly snapped in the morning to mark the occasion.

Despite a rainstorm so intense that no other planes were flying, Lancaster and Jessie, freezing and exhausted, made it to Baghdad one day later. The Tigris River, Jessie wrote, "squirmed over the countryside like an angry snake." As the main British base in Iraq, RAF Hinaidi, just outside the city, featured all the necessary amenities: wide barracks, a modern hospital, recreational areas, maintenance and communication units, and massive hangars. But in the fearsome storm, Baghdad itself resembled a faded tapestry, its ancient glories seemingly past.

The rainstorm flooded the airport, forcing Lancaster and Jessie to remain at the base for the next four days. Though frustrated by the wait, Lancaster used the opportunity to add an extra fuel tank to the *Red Rose*, boosting its flying time to approximately ten hours. Jessie purchased a pair of shorts from the base's Iraqi tailor, as her flying outfit was proving intolerable in the suffocating heat. When the aviators visited Baghdad, exploring narrow streets that wound haphazardly through miles of flat roofs, the city's poverty shocked them. With their blinkered mentality, they had naively expected to find a gleaming gold city straight out of *One Thousand and One Nights*. For the disillusioned Jessie, the high point of her five days in Baghdad came when an RAF officer gifted her with a gold-lined ring made of elephant hair for good luck. It was a ring she would wear for the rest of her life.

At last the *Red Rose* escaped Baghdad for the port city of Basra, one of the rumored locations of the historic Garden of Eden. Lancaster and Jessie flew over vast expanses of marshland and swamp stippled by small villages and intersected by the muddy wanderings of the Tigris and Euphrates rivers. After such desolate landscape, they found Basra to be a hive of activity, its teeming canals populated by thousands of small boats. The Shatt al-Arab river was lined with thick groupings of date palm trees that provided the city's main export of sweet fruit. Tight streets wove through rows of tumble-down mud huts, their passageways navigated by camel caravans bearing sellable goods. Brutal tragedy marked the scene as well: an outbreak of cholera had recently killed over a thousand people, and Jessie witnessed the dead stacked like cordwood on barges in the river, waiting for inspection by the local British medical officer.

Because they were waiting for a replacement engine part to be delivered from England, Lancaster and Jessie's journey ground to a halt. Their frustration over the delay was compounded by a cholera outbreak at the base, which forced them into seven days of quarantine. Jessie was given a room at the British Consulate, while Lancaster stayed at the RAF officers' mess. After weeks of frenetic movement, enduring such stasis proved wholly unwelcome, and once their quarantine was complete, they happily became nightly dinner guests on the HMS *Enterprise*, a Royal Navy light cruiser that had arrived in the city to quell a pro-German revolt. The ritual, by this point in their journey, was familiar: formal meals in evening wear, heavy drinking, boisterous dancing, and ceaseless socializing with local British dignitaries. In Basra, the two aviators were enlivened by the routine.

They were also thrilled, after a week of separation, to be back in each other's company. As much as Lancaster and Jessie had initially centered their relationship on business, and on the immense effort required to propel a journey like theirs, the days had drawn them, perhaps inevitably, ever closer emotionally. The space they shared was in essence a world within a world: on the outside was the protective womb of the British Empire, which allowed them to traverse the globe despite knowing almost nothing of the local peoples and cultures, not to mention any languages besides English. Nor did they find this fact unusual. As biographer Chrystopher Spicer writes, "They were totally confident that because of their white skin and British passports they would be protected and looked after wherever they went." Such was the reach and power of the flag under which they flew.

Inside that sheltered space existed the two of them as a unit, navigating a daily onslaught of occurrences that practically no man and woman in the history of the world had experienced together. It would have been almost impossible for the kinship they felt not to deepen with each new exhilarating takeoff, or narrowly avoided danger, or festive greeting by RAF compatriots and political elites. The attachment was fostered both between themselves and in how others perceived and treated them. As the celebrated guests at each new stop, they were treated, gender differences aside, as a single entity. This joining together was cultivated whether they were sleeping in barren tents on a windblown expanse or carousing with other revelers in the dining hall of an RAF airfield. As people, Lancaster and Jessie were up for anything, and their vastly compatible spirits took unalloyed pleasure in their sheer like-mindedness. It was a far cry from what each viewed as the mismatch of their respective marriages.

All told, Lancaster and Jessie spent more than two weeks at Basra before the *Red Rose*'s ignition was at last repaired, and they were able to depart for RAF Bushire in Iran. The RAF warned them to follow the Iranian coast instead of crossing the Arabian Gulf—"The water is shark-infested and you'd have no chance if you came down," they were told—but Lancaster was determined to save time, and crossing the Gulf would halve their distance. As the *Red Rose* flew over the Gulf's glistening waters, over its mangrove trees and coral reefs, the new ignition began to sputter. The clear sea below highlighted the truth of the RAF's warning: sharks thronged the water. Jessie was consumed by terror, and by the time the plane reached the Iranian coast, she felt utterly wrung out.

As her pulse began to regain its normal rhythm, Jessie gazed from the plane at the land flanking the Gulf, struck by its lack of vegetation. "The whole expanse resembled nothing so much as a boundless field which had been turned over by the harrow," she wrote, "and before crops could be planted storms had washed it mercilessly, and the sun had baked it again into a myriad of fantastic patterns." A lovely colored mist swirled over the landscape, enhancing the tone of the yellow clay. Jessie thought of the Grand Canyon in America, which she had never visited, and imagined it looked the same.

The city of Bushire on the Gulf, Lancaster and Jessie's destination, was a white city on a spit of land; from the air, Jessie thought it looked like "a huge chunk of coral." Her impression was correct: many of the city's residences were built from coral and shells.

Rather than friendly RAF cohorts, Lancaster and Jessie were confronted at Bushire by a squad of scowling Persian soldiers wielding bayonet-tipped rifles. In an effort to win them over, the two aviators handed the soldiers their cigarettes, but further exchanges were stymied by the language barrier. Lancaster asked repeatedly for food and lodging, along with fuel and oil for their airplane, but to no avail. The stress of the flight, the soaring temperature, her growling stomach: all of these drove Jessie nearly to tears. Their uncomfortable limbo was finally broken when a Persian officer appeared on the scene and guided them to an unused barracks.

Lancaster and Jessie were six weeks into their flight, during which the potent mixture of thrills and peril, along with their forced stay at Basra, had changed them. The blur of exotic locales, the near-death escapes, the navigation of encounters that ranged from the absurd to the profound—these dynamic experiences forged between them a connection whose intensity was not dissimilar from that of soldiers in war. Sharks in the Gulf and rifle-bearing soldiers were only their latest adventures, and now they were alone in an abandoned room, exhausted from their trials, and unleashed from their normal tethers. Their homes and their families seemed a world away; only the current moment seemed tangible. The electricity that had crackled between them since the first night they met burst into sparks.

With single-minded abandon, Lancaster and Jessie removed their clothes and made weary, intense love.

4

ARRIVAL

There were no regrets the next morning; there was only the exhilaration of newly revealed love. And while Lancaster and Jessie's situation was made immeasurably more complicated because both were married, that reality seemed, for now, a world away—not just physically, but emotionally. Jessie's marriage was over in all but name anyway, a fact of which Lancaster was aware. But Jessie was less certain about Lancaster's relationship with Kiki. She knew the two of them were living apart for financial reasons, but Lancaster had implied that their separation was more serious than that.

Whatever the truth of Lancaster's marriage, the morality of the time dictated that he and Jessie had to keep their new relationship intensely private. To the press, and even to their friends, they would continue to play the role of dutiful spouses to their respective partners. Anything else would lead to outraged condemnation of Lancaster and Jessie from all quarters: their corporate sponsors; the general reading and viewing public; the RAF; the British and Australian governments. Jessie, as a woman, would be the recipient of particularly vicious slandering.

———

Following Bushire and brief stopovers on Iran's southern coast, Lancaster and Jessie headed for the port city of Karachi, Pakistan, a sprawling metropolis of grand European edifices, wide gravel-paved streets, organized marketplaces, and a state-of-the-art British airfield. As they flew, the *Red Rose* was subsumed by a series of sandstorms and clouds so thick that Lancaster had to repeatedly shut off the engine and dive close to the water—perilously so—to gain his bearings. At higher altitudes the swirling sand was so thick that Lancaster and Jessie couldn't even see the plane's nose. As the hours trudged by, the two aviators grew famished. They never carried food in the *Red Rose*; any added weight would have upset the plane's delicate balance.

After nine and a half hours of white-knuckle flying, during which the blowing sand clotted their eyes, mouths, and noses, Lancaster and Jessie at last reached Karachi, where the local RAF officers plied them with whiskey and soda. Lancaster took a rejuvenating shower at the officers' mess and borrowed an officer's clean shirt. Jessie felt grimy and drained from the long flight, too, but when she asked to use the bathroom, the commanding officer politely refused. RAF dictates stipulated that women were forbidden in the mess hall.

Lancaster and Jessie had now flown more than six thousand miles and accumulated a total of ninety-two hours in the air. The press reported that the aviators were nearly halfway to their destination, while Avro and Wakefield Oil extolled Lancaster and Jessie's achievements in their advertisements. They also cabled much-needed funds. Given this new approbation, Lancaster didn't mind that the journey was progressing slower than he'd initially hoped, and he was amenable when the RAF asked him and Jessie to remain in Karachi a little longer. The air force was preparing a grand performance in honor of Afghanistan's King Amanullah Khan, who was attempting to modernize his country based on Western precepts.

The *Red Rose* was housed in an enormous one-story building next to the airport, and it was here that Lancaster and Jessie waited for King Amanullah and his fifty-man retinue. The occasion was significant: Jessie would be the first white woman to greet Amanullah outside of his home country. Because she had never met a king before, she was uncharacteristically nervous when Amanullah first approached, but the king, dressed in Western garb, quickly broke the ice. "How do you do?" he inquired in French, sticking out his hand. He asked Jessie if she was a pilot, and if she liked flying, and he took a keen interest as she and Lancaster showed him the *Red Rose*. For twenty minutes the king chatted with the pair, even signing their logbook. Then, with another handshake, he bid them farewell.

Lancaster and Jessie subsequently followed the path of the Ganges River as they headed for Calcutta. The land hugging the sacred river was a patchwork of small fields in every shade of green, but the journey was a desolate one: hundreds of dead bodies, many of them children, floated on the Ganges's filthy surface. Crocodiles sunning on the river's banks plopped into the water as the *Red Rose*'s engine buzzed overhead. "The combination of corpse and crocodile," Jessie wrote grimly, "is not a happy one." The searing heat and bumpy air further exhausted the weary aviators. As they approached their destination, smoke belching from modern factories surrounded the towers and mosques of the centuries-old city.

Lancaster and Jessie's arrival at Dum Dum Airport in Calcutta on December 19 heralded a new world record—8,500 miles—for distance flown in a light plane. For Jessie, the accomplishment was even more remarkable: it heralded the longest distance ever flown by a woman in an airplane, and the longest distance ever flown by a woman with a copilot. The RAF officers who greeted them proffered two cold bottles of beer to toast their accomplishment. Lancaster and Jessie spent a day savoring their achievement before pushing onward toward Singapore, but after a painfully early 4:30 a.m. takeoff, they were forced to return to Calcutta one hour later. Lancaster had absentmindedly left under his pillow the considerable sum of money they had received from Avro and Wakefield, sparking Jessie's fury. By the time they got back to the hotel, the money was gone. Lancaster frantically cabled the police commissioner, but no assistance was forthcoming. Just the day before, they had been comparatively rich, but now Lancaster and Jessie were utterly broke, lacking even the funds to pay for that morning's fuel. They signed on credit instead. The buoyancy of the previous day was replaced with dismay. With no other options, Jessie sent a plea to her family to cable some funds.

After leaving Calcutta for the second time, Lancaster and Jessie headed to Burma, then hugged the heavily wooded coast southward before hopping the Irrawaddy River and aiming for Rangoon. The landscape was stunning. "The sea was a magnificent blue, dotted here and there with lovely little green islands," Jessie wrote. "Stretches of white curving beaches were an invitation to come and sun-bake on the sand. Towards the seashore [was] a jungle of mangrove swamps, but in the valleys between the mountains were paddy-fields irrigated with astonishing precision." Coming into Rangoon they flew over flat, heavily cultivated country in which innumerable workers toiled the arable land.

Their intended landing field was a racetrack in the city, but three miles from their destination, the *Red Rose*'s engine gave two stomach-churning belches and then died. Lancaster shouted to Jessie: "Hold your legs up! I think we're going to crash!" Jessie was too paralyzed with fear to follow his advice. Forced to rely purely on wind currents, Lancaster steered the plane just over the tip of an expanse of thickly forested mountains. A river appeared below, and beyond it muddy fields of rice that stretched into the distance. With an expert hand, Lancaster guided the plane into a flawless landing on one of the fields.

The two aviators stepped out of the *Red Rose* into the dripping, swampy heat; startled Burmese field-workers soon ran over to check on them. Removing his sweat-soaked shirt, Lancaster poked around the engine until he found the culprit: a broken piston. The only option was to contact Calcutta for a replacement, which would take up to ten days to arrive. One of the Burmese spoke some English, and he led Lancaster on a two-mile walk to the nearest train station for a telephone. Jessie, meanwhile, spent two and a half hours in the scorching midday sun. Steam rose from the marshy ground as she tried in vain to keep the locals from swarming over the *Red Rose* to explore its every nook and cranny.

Finally Lancaster returned with a local British couple named the Taits, who carried baskets filled with iced soda water. The Taits advised Lancaster and Jessie to move the plane immediately so that venomous krait snakes couldn't hide inside it. But the advice proved moot: without a working piston, the plane was stuck. "Close everything up before we go, then, so that the snakes can't get in," the Taits cautioned.

Lancaster and Jessie passed the Christmas holiday in Rangoon, killing time until, just after the New Year, the piston arrived, and the *Red Rose* was fixed. Right before takeoff, the Taits offered a final warning about poisonous snakes, but Lancaster and Jessie laughingly dismissed it, believing the couple was just trying to frighten them. Once aloft, they steered out to the coast, then angled south for the port city of Tavoy, on the Dawei River's northern tip.

About thirty minutes into the flight, Lancaster felt something brushing along his back. A moment later he looked down, only to see a three-foot-long snake slithering out from between his feet. Petrified, he took his foot off the rudder and tried to stomp on it, but the snake squirmed away. Before Lancaster could regain control, the plane began a steep dive.

In the front cockpit, Jessie turned around and shouted, "What's the matter?" Lancaster let out a bellow: "Snake!" Jessie glanced down, and saw the snake's twisting body pushing out from the little trapdoor through which she and Lancaster passed their notes. The snake, blunt-tailed and brown-colored, was a venomous krait; a single bite, Jessie knew, could kill her. Acting quickly, she jerked her feet up into a cross-legged position on the seat, while yanking her control stick from its socket. Taut with fear, she began bashing her control stick down on the snake's triangular head. Her pace grew frantic, but no matter how hard she clobbered it, and how much blood jetted from its body, the snake continued to struggle. Eventually, after several more furious whacks, the snake's movement stopped. It was dead, its blood splattered all over the cockpit. A revolted Jessie picked it up and threw it over the cockpit's side.

Over the next few days they traveled up the Malay Peninsula, stopping over at Taiping, after which they left the paddy fields behind them and entered a region where rubber and tin were the prime commodities. At times they flew through clouds so thick that they could not tell whether their plane would clear the mountains ahead of them. Then they would climb above the dense cloudbanks to find, in Jessie's words, "a heavenly blue sky and brilliant sunshine. The clouds looked so solid one could almost have landed, and the shadow of [the *Red Rose*] looked like a sinister bird in our wake. As the sun caught the propeller a halo seemed to form" around the plane, and was mirrored against the clouds. At other times they maneuvered through gushing tropical storms.

Touching down at Kuala Lumpur, Lancaster and Jessie found, to their great embarrassment, that the airport at which they landed was crowded with beautifully dressed government officials and wives who had come to greet them, while the aviators themselves were filthy and covered in grease. They borrowed clothes for a formal luncheon that was held in their honor, and in the afternoon had a grand time playing tennis and swimming in borrowed bathing suits. "I patched up my one black frock for dinner," Jessie reported, "and powdered my nose with the last of my powder. It almost seemed like civilization again to play bridge before turning in." 1928 was not yet a week old.

Lancaster and Jessie next aimed for Singapore, but hard rain throughout their flight soaked their freshly borrowed clothes and made the journey a dismal one. The pounding storm transformed the ground into a ghastly swamp, and the *Red Rose*'s engine stalled as the plane slid to a halt in several feet of water. Despite the poor conditions, a swarm of local residents swished through the lake around the plane to greet the drenched aviators.

Singapore was Lancaster and Jessie's major destination thus far, and they received a hearty welcome, with the acting governor officially greeting their arrival. The Singapore Aero Club, an assemblage of aviation enthusiasts from various countries, provided them with lodging and threw a luncheon in their honor. The menu featured such items as "consommé a la *Red Rose*" and "Lancaster croquettes." Back in England, the London *Aeroplane* declared its admiration for the two pilots. "Their effort thoroughly deserves to succeed," the editor trumpeted. "They have already done far more than has ever been done by any light airplane. . . . The flying people at Croydon, where they made their meager preparations, treated their scheme as a joke and refused to believe that they would get much farther than France. But in spite of it all they have made good."

Less than three thousand miles now remained between Lancaster and Jessie and their ultimate goal of Darwin, Australia. They would have to navigate the nearly eighteen thousand islands of the Dutch East Indies before they reached their destination. Their pace would remain measured, with the heaviest flying before noon, and mechanical checkups every afternoon. They spent a day in Singapore overhauling the *Red Rose*'s engine and performing repairs.

When they departed the next morning, seemingly the entire town gathered at the harbor to see them off. Acknowledging the crowd, Lancaster and Jessie circled the *Red Rose* low over the harbor, the surface of which was covered with all manner of boats, then headed for the coast of Sumatra. "Somewhere around here we'll be crossing the Equator," Jessie realized as they flew—and indeed, later that day she became the first woman to cross the equator in an airplane. From the air, the jungle covering Sumatra resembled a flattened green rug, the trees merged thickly into each other.

"The landscape seemed to have compressed breadth but no depth," Jessie reported, as "[p]alm-fringed bays alternated with mangrove swamps, and tiny emerald islands with a lacy edge of white dotted the coastline." They spotted a herd of elephants through a slight break in the trees.

Lancaster and Jessie flew across the sea to the northern tip of Bangka Island, east of Sumatra, where they had a bumpy landing on a makeshift runway angled down a modest hill. When Jessie hopped down from the plane, the grass rose up to her waist. But the island's Dutch residents had turned out in full force to greet them, and the aviators were cheered by the hospitality they were shown. The Dutch, Jessie wrote, "had fixed up a reception at the club for us that night, [where] a long speech was read in near perfect English. They had the whole story of the flight itemized, and did not miss one detail of importance." About a hundred people attended the gathering, and Jessie and Lancaster gleefully clinked champagne-filled glasses with all of them.

Early the next morning the two aviators climbed back into the *Red Rose*. The entire Dutch community, in a grand show of support, was there to see them off. Despite the runway's downward slope, Lancaster achieved an easy liftoff into the humid tropical air. Jessie was just peering down from her cockpit to wave goodbye to the crowd when the plane, having climbed to 150 feet, abruptly lost power. With no engine noise, the air went eerily silent. A puzzled Jessie thought Lancaster was planning to land again, until she realized he was madly attempting to restart the engine. As he struggled, the plane gave a sickening lurch.

Lancaster's options were nonexistent: he didn't have enough altitude to turn back to the runway, but all he saw in front was a hillside covered in trees and houses. Trying to avoid certain death, he tipped the plane on its side so the right wing would hit the ground first, absorbing the shock and preventing Jessie, who was seated up front, from being killed by the engine. The moments began to crawl; to Jessie, hours seemed to pass before the earth came rushing up and the *Red Rose* collided violently with the ground. The force of the crash flipped the plane head over heels, ripping the landing gear from its bottom. As the *Red Rose* somersaulted, Jessie's consciousness went blank.

When she recovered from her shock, Jessie was hanging upside down; the plane was flopped on its back, and only the seat straps kept her from plunging headfirst to the ground. Hot fuel from the broken tank was raining down on her face, popping and sizzling as it went, pouring into her nose, and searing her blurry eyes. Jessie tried to move but she was ensnared within a jumble of wires. Again and again she called out Lancaster's name; receiving no response, she pictured him crushed in his cockpit. She was sure that at any moment the plane would burst into flames.

Then she spied a possible exit. Jessie took off her helmet and began to squirm feet-first through a small opening. As she later described it, a "screw being taken out its socket was nothing [compared] to me wriggling round and round to negotiate that opening to freedom. I took all the skin off myself in the process. But you cannot imagine how glad I was to be standing outside the broken machine instead of being imprisoned under the debris."

When she got clear of the wreckage Jessie spotted Lancaster sprawled on his face in the dirt several yards away. Though she could barely walk, Jessie forced her lurching body to where he lay. She turned him over and saw blood pouring from his mouth. Worried about internal injuries, she held him up so that he wouldn't choke. Lancaster's body remained unmoving, as if he were dead, and his teeth protruded straight through his bottom lip. Still, Jessie could see his shallow breathing. She pulled his lip free from his teeth and tried to stop the bleeding, but it was no use.

A group of Dutch soldiers who had witnessed the crash came sprinting up. As Lancaster regained consciousness, they helped Jessie pull him to his feet. Despite his injuries Lancaster was desperate to go examine the plane's damage, and the Dutchmen had to struggle to get him into a car instead. They drove the battered pilots to the nearest hospital, where a doctor slathered Jessie with iodine and informed her that she'd sustained a broken nose. She had a massive bump on her forehead and two black eyes. Lancaster, meanwhile, had suffered a concussion and needed stitches in his lip. But he had it fixed in his mind that, for insurance purposes, he needed to take photographs of the damaged *Red Rose* immediately; medical attention could wait. The doctors had to physically restrain Lancaster to prevent him from leaving the hospital.

When Lancaster and Jessie returned to the crash site the following day, they were aghast at what they saw. The plane looked practically demolished. As Lancaster inspected the wreckage, he realized that the crash had been due to human error—his own. In keeping with his characteristic absentmindedness, he had accidentally left his fuel switches in the "off" position when the plane took off; with no fuel, the engine had simply stopped.

Though their journey now appeared over, Lancaster and Jessie were praised for their gumption. *Flight* magazine affirmed that the *Red Rose* "had put up a splendid flight of greater distance than any hitherto made with a machine of such low power. . . . [T]o have got as far as it did is a very fine performance." The London *Aeroplane* seconded that opinion, though the editor didn't sound the final trumpet just yet.

The *Aeroplane* noted that the potential record was now threatened, however, by the emergence of Herbert John Louis "Bert" Hinkler, the so-called "Australian Lone Eagle," another pioneering aviator who had logged time with the Royal Air Force during the war, and then become a test pilot for Avro in subsequent years. Hinkler had already set a number of flying records, including a nonstop flight from England to Latvia, but his earlier attempt to fly from England to Australia had ended in a disastrous crash over Europe. Now that Lancaster and Jessie had apparently failed, too, Hinkler announced his renewed intention to fly a light airplane from England to Darwin in a brisk two weeks.

Despite their injuries, Lancaster and Jessie were not quite ready to call it a day. They decided their best option was to return to Singapore, where the remains of the *Red Rose* could be sent for repairs. The sympathetic Dutch on Bangka Island arranged passage for the two aviators on a Chinese boat. When they climbed on board, the Chinese captain looked shocked: he didn't know about their plane crash, and he was taken aback by their decrepit appearance.

After arriving in Singapore, Lancaster and Jessie were taken to the British colonial secretary's cozy bungalow. There they languished for a week without money, until, to their supreme relief, a wealthy local British rubber broker named Sam Hayes, who admired the pluck they'd shown in traveling so far, offered his financial support to fix their plane. Like many in Singapore, Hayes believed that Lancaster and Jessie deserved to claim their world record. Yet despite Lancaster's mechanical expertise, the *Red Rose*'s potential repairs proved to be beyond his capabilities.

Here, at their lowest point, Lancaster and Jessie were buoyed by some remarkable news: a contingent of RAF engineers was just at that moment docking in Singapore's harbor. The lead officer had followed the *Red Rose*'s progress with admiration, and so he was taken aback when he finally met the daring aviators: Lancaster's stitched face was still raw with scars, while Jessie presented a bandit-like appearance, with deep black rings around her eyes. He quickly realized that appearances were deceiving, and that the pair still burned with the ambition to reach Australia. So with Sam Hayes providing the money, the RAF engineers agreed to perform the repairs.

For the next two months, until the replacement parts arrived, Lancaster and Jessie lingered in Singapore in a hazy state of suspension. Lancaster lived at the British Government House at Seletar, fourteen miles outside the city, while Jessie stayed with a member of the Singapore Flying Club. With so many eyes upon them, the two aviators were forced to keep up the illusion that they were business partners only and were yearning to reunite with their spouses once the journey finally ended. Much of their socializing during this period occurred separately; Lancaster, in Seletar, dutifully made the rounds of the governing British colonial set, while Jessie had greater involvement with the RAF engineers in the city.

As the days stretched by, the aviator Bert Hinkler's proposed record-setting flight to Australia turned into a reality: on February 7, Hinkler departed from Croydon Airport in London—in an Avro Avian, no less. He was scheduled to arrive in Singapore twelve days later, much to the outrage of local members of the Singapore Flying Club. To them, Hinkler was committing the criminally unsportsmanlike offense of exploiting Lancaster and Jessie's misfortune for his own selfish glory. In retribution, Lancaster and Jessie's supporters threatened to sabotage Hinkler's plane during his stopover. Jessie was furious, as well—she felt that Hinkler was exploiting their misfortune.

Lancaster, however, was wholly gracious, at least in public. (The fact that Hinkler's wife and Kiki Lancaster were close friends may have played a role.) He announced that Hinkler was perfectly justified in attempting his flight, and on the night of Hinkler's arrival, he bedded down in Hinkler's cockpit to protect the plane from saboteurs, while Hinkler slept in more comfortable quarters.

Perhaps Lancaster's generous actions were another example of his inherently genial nature. Or maybe he was simply distracted by the most prominent—if secret—facet of his new life: his profound love for Jessie. Theirs was a love that couldn't be acted upon at the moment, as conventional society, in Singapore and elsewhere, would have reacted in shock to their illicit union, but their social separation didn't diminish the extent of their feelings for one another. If anything, the clandestine nature of their relationship, and their inability, due to their public profile, to express their love physically after their lone night in Iran, only heightened its effect.

The *Red Rose*'s replacement parts finally arrived from England, but the complicated repairs took weeks to complete. Finally, on March 12, Lancaster and Jessie returned to the sky. Jessie packed only a tennis dress, a change of shirts and shorts, and a toothbrush; the rest of their luggage was left behind in Singapore. After flying to Batavia (the present-day city of Jakarta), they skirted eastward over the Dutch East Indies islands of Java and Sumatra. At some identified spot along the way a hungry mosquito infected Jessie with malaria; for months afterward she battled its deleterious effects. Five days later, the aviators landed in a scrubby clearing in Atambua, Timor. Darwin, their final destination, on the other side of the Timor Sea, was a mere five hundred miles away. Their life-altering journey was almost complete.

Torrential monsoon rains delayed Lancaster and Jessie's plans for takeoff. A Royal Dutch Shell official cabled them that the landing ground at Darwin had become a swamp. Lancaster and Jessie didn't know, however, that a portion of the runway had been cleared for them. The news of the *Red Rose*'s arrival had electrified the town; seemingly every man, woman, and child in Darwin had gathered at the airfield to welcome it. The officials there were unaware of the Shell representative's message, and so, as the hours ticked by with no sign of Lancaster and Jessie, the crowd began to worry that the aviators had plunged to their deaths among the reefs and uninhabited islands of the Timor Sea.

Killing time in Atambua, Lancaster and Jessie were oblivious to the drama unfolding at their hoped-for destination. As night fell, Lancaster cabled Darwin with the latest update: he and Jessie planned to depart at 7 a.m. the next morning. He received nothing back, which he took as silent confirmation. The next morning, after takeoff, the Dutch officials at Atambua cabled Darwin with the news.

Hardly had Lancaster and Jessie leveled off, though, when they were assaulted with the slashing rain and battering wind of the worst storm they had yet encountered. The sheer mass of water cascading down from the sky seemed almost incomprehensible, and yet its volume kept increasing. Just as things seemed at their worst, the *Red Rose*'s engine began to malfunction. At moments it would settle down and the plane would gain height, but then it would sputter and the plane would drop precipitously. For ten minutes, Lancaster worked furiously to keep the plane horizontal. Then the engine gave an explosive cough, and the *Red Rose* started to sink.

Jessie immediately comprehended the dire nature of their situation. As she struggled to reconcile herself to her onrushing death, she felt a tap on her head, and glimpsed down to see that Lancaster was handing her a message through the cockpit's trapdoor. Unfolding the note, Jessie read Lancaster's parting words: "I'm afraid she won't stay the course. I don't think we're going to make it, but we've done our best."

Jessie may have been in love with Lancaster, but in some respects they were still coming to know each other as people, and Lancaster's note had the effect of deepening Jessie's appreciation of him even further. The note wasn't sentimental or melodramatic or filled with woe—it was as straightforward as Jessie prided herself on being. What's more, it bespoke respect for Jessie as a *pilot*, not just a woman. Despite her terror, she removed her seat belt, turned around in her seat, and gravely shook Lancaster's hand.

Hours passed with no relief from the torrential rain, or from the *Red Rose*'s continual gut-wrenching plunges downward. At one point the plane plummeted to within seven hundred feet of the ocean's roiling waves, and Lancaster kissed his hand to the sea and sky. But even as the hours ticked brutally by, Jessie sensed that Lancaster remained fully focused on his flying; he evinced not the slightest hint of worry. With catastrophe looming at every moment, his strength was a balm.

After nearly eight pummeling hours in the air, Lancaster and Jessie spotted Darwin in the distance. They looked at each other and turned their thumbs up at the exact same moment. As they circled above the airfield, they could see, even through the lashing rain, that it looked abandoned; the ground had turned into a lake. Lancaster buzzed the plane in a circle, looking for the least waterlogged place. Spotting his most promising option, he brought the *Red Rose* sliding down into a muddy, soppy mess.

The plane's wheels skidded though two inches of water before finally slowing to a halt. "My God, what an awful landing-ground," Lancaster moaned. Completely spent, he and Jessie could at first do nothing but sprawl limply in their cockpits. They didn't even have matches to light their desperately yearned-for cigarettes.

PART II A NEW WORLD

5

GRAND WELCOMES

The next day saw Lancaster and Jessie in finer spirits. Having awoken to the news that the two aviators had arrived, Australian officials hurried to provide them with the grand welcome they deserved. The Darwin Town Hall hosted a stirring reception in their honor, while the prime minister's office soon invited them down to Canberra, the nation's capital, to celebrate their achievement within the regal confines of the magnificent white brick, three-story Parliament House. And that achievement was substantial indeed: the first two-person flight from England to Australia in a light airplane, and, of even greater significance, the longest flight ever made by a woman. Lancaster and Jessie's feat had "fired the imagination of the people," the *Brisbane Courier* crowed, while the London *Aeroplane* declared, "The arrival of the Avian Red Rose at Port Darwin marks the success, though not the end, of one of the pluckiest flights in the history of flying."

Aviators were the world's thrilling new heroes: just one day later, in America, Charles Lindbergh was presented with the Congressional Medal of Honor for his first transatlantic flight. Three weeks later, the first ever east-west transatlantic flight by airplane took place from Ireland to Canada. With the world trapped in an uneasy peace post–World War I, and acts of political violence marring the landscape from Chicago to China, aviators remained a shining example of the upside of the technological upheavals that had placed destruction on a global scale within humankind's reach.

Jessie, weak with malaria, had been hoping to gather some much-needed rest after their journey, but Lancaster had scheduled a pre–6 a.m. appointment at the Darwin airfield on the morning after their arrival in Australia, squashing Jessie's dreams of relaxation. Lancaster's unwillingness to rest stemmed in part from financial reality. While the positive press from England, Australia, and elsewhere was heartening, it didn't come with a paycheck. The aircraft, oil, and fuel companies that had sponsored the journey would provide necessary short-term cash, but Lancaster and Jessie knew that significant earnings would only result from them selling their story to newspapers and making lecture appearances in as many cities as possible. Already these fees would be less than desired because of Bert Hinkler's earlier flight.

As it turned out, the real star in Australia was Jessie, not Lancaster. The manager of Shell Australia, which had provided the flight's fuel, sent a telegram expressing the common sentiment: "[Jessie's] success in being the first woman to fly to Australia is a fitting culmination to splendid achievements [of] her countrymen." Hinkler's flight had robbed Lancaster of the opportunity to set the record as a male, and so it was Jessie whose accomplishment truly stood out. The "women of Australia should give Mrs. Miller a tremendous welcome," declared one influential socialite, for putting "women on the map." Women in the future, the head of the Country Women's Association predicted, "may follow where she has not feared to lead." By the end of the month, Jessie had signed a lucrative £250-a-week contract with Union Theaters for a lecture tour of her homeland. Jessie herself never failed to give full credit to Lancaster, but her story—an Australian citizen becoming the first female to fly to Australia—was simply irresistible. As Ralph Barker points out, three months later Amelia Earhart became famous "simply by flying the Atlantic as a passenger, an achievement not to be compared with Jessie's."

Lancaster and Jessie remained firmly in love, and once the hectic initial onslaught of media attention had passed, they were able to sneak occasional time to be physical, which they hadn't done since that ragged night in Iran. Their business affiliation, while still in place, was deeply emotional now.

Jessie paid her husband a brief visit in Sydney, and she and Lancaster attended a horse race with him in Williamstown, but these were little more than photo ops; the marriage, as far as Jessie was concerned, was over. But Jessie insisted that she and Lancaster continue to send Kiki one-third of their earnings, as they had promised, while Kiki reciprocated with a warm telegram for Jessie: "Three cheers for your success; hearty congratulations. Love, Kiki." Despite this interaction, Jessie remained unsure of the exact status of Lancaster and Kiki's marriage. Perhaps, she thought, Lancaster was too careless an individual to give it much thought himself.

During the two months of Jessie's lecture tour, as they zigzagged across the Australian continent's vast reaches, hitting big cities and midsize towns, they were welcomed by adoring crowds—nowhere more so than in Sydney, where a staggering hundred thousand people greeted them at the airfield with another fifty thousand waiting outside the fence. Throughout the tour Lancaster played the role of personal escort, introducing Jessie at events and sharing with audiences color lantern slides of the places and people they'd encountered on their journey. In his downtime he picked up freelance flying gigs. "I would be happy to render any assistance in civil aviation," Lancaster announced to the press by way of promotion, "if I were approached and asked to do so." He also found time to meet up with his brother, Jack, another former World War I fighter pilot who had resettled permanently in Australia. Though travel and lodging were expensive, Jessie still earned enough money from her lectures that she and Lancaster enjoyed a healthy profit. The pace, however, was exhausting, all the more so for Jessie because of her malaria. "Sometimes I wish I had never done it," Jessie confessed wearily at one formal dinner reception. "I really feel scared stiff and want to creep away to bed. . . . I thought we would just arrive quietly, you know."

One of Lancaster's freelance flying jobs during this time period turned out to be pivotal, and led to the next phase in his and Jessie's post-journey lives. On June 8, legendary Australian aviators Charles Kingsford Smith and Charles Ulm, along with the Americans Harry Lyon and James Warner, touched down at Eagle Farm Airport in Brisbane in their Fokker monoplane *Southern Cross.* This marked the completion of the first ever transpacific flight, from the United States to Australia, an eighty-three-hour and thirty-eight-minute journey across open seas, and one of the most astounding aviation achievements of the age. A rapturous crowd of forty thousand greeted the aviators in Brisbane. Lancaster flew a photographer to Eagle Farm Airport to document the historic moment.

Lancaster and Jessie were only too aware that the *Southern Cross*'s arrival meant their own time in the spotlight was now coming to an end. There would be no rest following Jessie's lecture tour; they needed to line up subsequent jobs before their achievements were forgotten. Here Harry Lyon, the *Southern Cross*'s gregarious American navigator, came cheerfully to the rescue.

Lyon was the son of a prominent rear admiral in the navy, but he himself had failed out of the U.S. Naval Academy, embarking instead on an unremarkable career in the merchant marine. It was only through a high-placed friend in the Marine Department that Lyon ended up as navigator on the *Southern Cross*—a job prospect that he at first found ludicrous, given that he had absolutely no experience with aircraft navigation. Lyon hadn't even *flown* in an airplane more than once or twice before.

During his short time in Australia, Lyon, who hailed from the tiny village of Paris Hills, Maine, had become a beloved figure for his oversized personality and relentless good humor. He sported a thicket of black hair, jug ears, a broad nose, and a beaming, big-lipped smile. Fame, for this rural boy, was a pleasure he was only too eager to embrace. Now Lyon told Lancaster and Jessie that a Hollywood studio had contacted him with a $75,000 proposal—an immense sum for the time—to work on a film about flying. Lyon's Australian crewmates, Kingsford Smith and Ulm, were forgoing the offer in order to stay in their home country. Might Lancaster and Jessie like to replace them? After the film there were plans for a transatlantic flight, to be followed by a flight from Australia to America.

Financially, Lyon's offer was enticing, and the word "Hollywood" may have held glamour, as well. Lancaster and Jessie were also eager to embark on the lecture circuit in America, hoping that it would prove as profitable as Jessie's Australian junket. But what America promised them as much as anything was a chance to avoid their respective marriages without having to face the consequences of either personal turmoil or public reprobation. Their partnership could continue untroubled—it was perfectly natural that a successful flying team would head for Hollywood to make a film, after all, and thus no undue public suspicion would arise. Lancaster and Jessie were delighted to accept Lyon's offer.

On June 23, just fifteen days after the *Southern Cross*'s arrival in Australia, Lancaster, Jessie, and Lyon, along with James Warner, boarded the SS *Sonoma* for passage to San Francisco. Jessie didn't even have time to bid her husband farewell. The group received a lively, raucous farewell as they waved to the crowd before leaving the harbor. The ear-splitting whistling and applause continued for what seemed an impossibly long time. When the *Sonoma* finally pulled out, the celebratory tooting of the other boats in the harbor only added to the cacophony.

The greeting was even more rapturous when they arrived in San Francisco three weeks later, following brief stopovers in Fiji and Hawaii. A contingent of planes accompanied the ship as it steamed through the golden opening in the bay, escorted by boats crammed with prominent local citizens. Lyon and Warner, as Americans and as newly crowned heroes, were the focus of attention, but Lancaster and Jessie received an enthusiastic welcome, as well. All four aviators were paraded in open cars through the city's famously hilly streets as ticker tape fell around them. When they arrived at City Hall, a magnificent Beaux Arts structure in the city's Civic Center, town officials inquired as to their preferred choice of alcohol. Lancaster and Jessie were perplexed. "I thought you had prohibition in America," Jessie ventured. The officials broke into loud guffaws. With wolfish grins, they threw open a cupboard; housed inside was a gleaming collection of bottles, complete with refrigerated compartments. The women in the room confided to Jessie that they had never drunk so much as they had since Prohibition.

A few days later Lancaster, Jessie, Lyon, and Warner flew to Los Angeles—Jessie did most of the piloting—where they were greeted with an official reception at the lavish Biltmore downtown. But when they drove over to Hollywood, they were distressed to find that the proposed film project had been canceled; the financing had unexpectedly dried up. In a matter of moments, their imagined futures—and imagined profits—had vanished. Anxious and fuming after this whipsaw of emotions, the aviators considered suing the studio, but they were advised not to pursue the matter, as the efforts would deplete their hard-won finances. This counsel appeared particularly sage as another project swiftly popped up to boost their fortunes. The Cunningham-Hall Aircraft Corporation, a brand-new American manufacturer, was building a powerful new monoplane, and it wanted Lancaster, Jessie, and Lyon to perform a test flight—from New York to London and back—when the venture was complete. If all went according to schedule, the plane would be ready within the next couple of months. In the meantime, the aviators could continue planning their own proposed transatlantic journey, though without Warner, who had dropped out following a spat with Lyon.

With excess time on his hands, Lyon descended in Los Angeles into a punishing routine of all-night drinking and carousing. Lancaster and Jessie enjoyed their alcohol, too, but it never hampered their productivity. Lyon was far less disciplined, and though he was always an amusing companion, the myriad pleasures of L.A. nightlife were rendering him a drunken, bumbling mess. Lancaster and Jessie pressured him to fly home to Maine to dry out in order to salvage their three-way partnership. With inebriated insistence, Lyon said he wouldn't consider it unless they came, too. To Lancaster and Jessie, this idea seemed ridiculous: How could they possibly build their careers if they were stuck in Maine? But as Lyon kept pushing, Lancaster and Jessie reconsidered. They wanted to stick together as a three-person team, and they could live rent-free with Lyon's mother while preparing for their Cunningham-Hall Aircraft flight.

In August 1928, four and a half months after landing in Darwin, the trio flew to Maine, where the village of Paris Hills welcomed Lyon like a returning hero, with a rousing parade, speeches by local dignitaries, and a fine reception at the country club. But as the August weeks crept by—and with a profound lack of action in their rustic Maine location—all three aviators grew fidgety with boredom and anxiety. Matters were made worse by frequent cables from Cunningham-Hall Aircraft postponing the completion date of their airplane.

With their restlessness at its pitch, the three headed to New York City to seek out additional work. What awaited them in the city could not have been further from the tranquility of Maine. In New York, their reputations were such that the luxury Biltmore Hotel offered them free suites, a perk reserved for celebrity guests. The city's wealthy and intellectual classes happily embraced them, throwing frequent parties and celebrations in honor of their achievements in aviation. Operating from their home base in the Biltmore, Lancaster, Jessie, and Lyon attended endless meetings with agents, managers, and lecture bureaus.

But against all expectations, and despite an effusive stream of promises, firm offers of employment never quite materialized. In the meantime, their money was rapidly draining away, despite their free lodging. Keeping up the social pretenses that staying in a high-end hotel demanded was far from cheap. In an effort to economize, the three took to sneaking out of the hotel for five-cent meals at a nearby Automat. To their embarrassment, one of the Biltmore's bellhops strolled into the Automat one evening as they sat eating their meat pies. Thinking quickly, Lancaster affected an imperious accent: "Quite an experience to eat in a place like this," he told the bellhop. "Frightfully interesting." From then on they ate at an Automat several blocks farther away.

Of the several thousand pounds Lancaster and Jessie had saved from Jessie's Australian lecture tour, they had given a chunk to Kiki, put another chunk in savings, and spent most of the rest on daily expenses. Their monetary situation already precarious, they took another blow when Cunningham-Hall Aircraft again postponed their project for financial reasons. With at least three months to go before the company's monoplane would be ready, they needed to find another contract to support themselves in the meantime, even as they continued to insist that their own transatlantic flight was still in the offing, provided funding could be located.

Their most promising New York contact so far was the famed publisher George Putnam, a fellow aviation enthusiast. In July 1927 Putnam had published Charles Lindbergh's blockbuster autobiography *We*, one of the best-selling nonfiction books of all time up to that point. (Four years later, Putnam would marry Amelia Earhart, whose book *20 Hrs., 40 Min.* he helped write and published.) Now Lancaster and Lyon pitched Putnam on the idea of financing a flight from New York to Bermuda; as of yet no plane had reached the subtropical British colony. After some consideration, Putnam agreed to put up the money—on the condition that he could join them on the flight. But the journey was not to be: problems with fueling kept delaying the flight, until Putnam, fed up, withdrew his support.

Not long after, Lancaster and Jessie decided to end their partnership with Lyon. As much as they liked him personally, and as much as they enjoyed alcohol themselves, Lyon's dissipated behavior simply made him too unreliable a partner. Nor, from a practical standpoint, had the partnership generated any financial reward. Lyon had become "a dead loss," as Jessie bluntly put it. The happy-go-lucky Lyon took no offense at the separation; he even continued to tell reporters, inaccurately, that he and Lancaster had plans for a future round-the-world flight.

Despite its financial difficulties, Cunningham-Hall Aircraft continued to provide Lancaster and Jessie with regular updates on the monoplane's progress. In November, Cunningham-Hall invited Lancaster back to California to thrash out the fine details of the aircraft's finished design. Lancaster's schedule had suddenly tightened, however. He had recently proposed to a Manhattan banking firm a licensing deal in which the Cirrus engine model that powered the *Red Rose* would be built in America. Now, at month's end, the contract was approved, and Lancaster was appointed chief test and demonstration pilot, a New York–based position. Flying to Los Angeles was out of the question.

Instead, Lancaster gave Jessie a thorough rundown on the Cunningham-Hall monoplane, and she flew out in his place. Once in California, Jessie immediately signed up for a radio operator course at the YMCA, taking cheap lodging nearby. Her independence was again on display: the class, Jessie aside, consisted exclusively of men. At night she would bring a small tapping machine back to her apartment to practice Morse code. Before long she was an expert in wireless theory and in working and repairing radios, with the impressive test scores to prove it. As Jessie saw it, her newfound radio operator skills meant that one less crew member would be required for future flights.

Twenty-five hundred miles away, in New York City, Lancaster found himself on the receiving end of increasingly plaintive letters from Kiki. During the journey itself, and in the months since, Kiki had magnanimously supported the children in England while Lancaster sought his fortune overseas. She did not resent it; on the contrary, she'd eagerly followed the media reports of Lancaster and Jessie's progress, and had kept a proud collection of all the letters she'd received.

Still, despite her generous personality, Kiki couldn't help but feel jealous of Lancaster and Jessie's adventures. Though she enjoyed her work, life in a cramped apartment in Southwest London couldn't compete with what she imagined as the glamour of her husband's new life in America. Lancaster had plans to visit her when he flew the Cunningham-Hall Corporation's plane to London, but that date remained uncertain. Kiki was eager to see him, and she didn't want to wait. Perhaps egged on by Lancaster's parents, who were eager to see their son reunite with his wife and children, Kiki told Lancaster that she would meet him in New York for the Christmas holidays.

When she arrived in Manhattan, Kiki ran headfirst into a farcical manifestation of Prohibition. She carried with her, at Lancaster's request, the *Red Rose*'s old compass, which Lancaster had invested with almost totem-like powers, and which the Avian company had just repaired. The customs inspectors in New York, however, blocked her entry. The compass contained alcohol, the inspectors declared, and was thus illegal in America. If she didn't break the compass's glass and pour the alcohol out, they would have to impound it. Kiki, astonished at this ridiculous demand, summoned Lancaster, who used his charms to convince the inspectors that the compass's pure alcohol didn't fall under the Eighteenth Amendment's purview. The *New York Times* plastered the incident on its front page.

For both Kiki and Lancaster, the Christmas holiday was unsatisfying: Kiki missed the children, while Lancaster yearned for Jessie. But with January's arrival, their reunion was enlivened by a piece of new business. The Manhattan firm with which Lancaster had negotiated a deal to manufacture Cirrus engines had shipped to America two Avro Avians—complete with said engines—for public display. Lancaster would be the firm's test pilot, tasked with exhibiting the efficiency and reliability of the Cirrus part.

The Irish aviator Mary, Lady Heath, known in America as "Britain's Lady Lindy," was also involved in the Cirrus venture. A longtime friend of Lancaster's, and one of the world's most famous women after her recent record-setting flight from South Africa to England, Lady Heath had been the first woman to hold a commercial pilot's license in England, as well as the first woman to parachute from an airplane. Now she was due at the annual Miami All-American Air Races in early January 1929, and, for publicity's sake, Cirrus's American backers wanted Lancaster to join her at the show.

He would make the flight down in one of the Avro Avians with seventeen-year-old American aviatrix Elinor Smith as his copilot. Lady Heath, with Kiki as her passenger, would travel to the air meet in her de Havilland Moth light biplane.

When the two women took off in the de Havilland from New York, Lancaster and Smith briefly followed, but their Avro Avian was no match for Lady Heath's far fleeter craft. Heath and Kiki hadn't gone far, however, before biting wintry winds forced an emergency landing in a farmer's field. Two days later, Lady Heath overshot the landing strip at Savannah, but the farmer in whose field the de Havilland touched down proved far less understanding than his compatriot to the north. Only after a great deal of appeasement did he agree to fetch some fuel. Yet Kiki and Lady Heath's travails weren't finished: they ran out of gas just short of Daytona and had to land on a narrow strip of beach.

Despite these brief setbacks, the Miami air show was a happy experience for all, with Lady Heath and Amelia Earhart the two stars of the event, and Lancaster displaying the Avro Avian for the crowd. Kiki watched the proceedings from the privacy of the Miami mayor's viewing box.

Lancaster and Elinor Smith's return flight to New York featured its own dramatic turn. During the final hop of the journey, the two aviators mysteriously failed to arrive at Curtiss Field airport on Long Island after departing from Philadelphia shortly before noon. Anxious airport authorities kept the floodlights burning at Curtiss Field all night, while a search was mounted for the wreckage of the missing airplane in the wooded areas of central New Jersey.

Unbeknownst to the authorities, Lancaster and Smith had been forced down in a small field near Belleville, New Jersey, during their flight. It wasn't until the following morning, when the pair, having abandoned their aircraft, arrived quietly in New York by train, that the mystery of their whereabouts was cleared up.

Toward the end of January, Kiki boarded a return ship for England. For her, the visit to America had been decidedly stimulating, and once back home she made a detailed scrapbook of her holiday adventure. Lancaster, however—truthfully or not—told Jessie that he had repeatedly raised the issue of divorce during Kiki's visit, but that she'd refused to consider the possibility unless he could provide enough money to secure his children's future.

Religion played a role, as well, Lancaster claimed: the devoutly Catholic Kiki simply didn't believe in divorce. Did Kiki also suspect that Lancaster and Jessie were having an affair? Perhaps. But as a supremely moral person, Kiki may simply have found it unimaginable that Lancaster would abandon his family for such an appalling act of deceit.

6

FLYING SOLO

The year 1929 was shaping up to be another remarkable one for aviation. The U.S. admiral Richard Byrd had become the first man to fly over the South Pole; closer to home, the American engineer Robert Goddard had tested the first rocket to carry scientific equipment. The U.S. Army Air Corps, employing aerial refueling, instigated a record-breaking six-day nonstop endurance flight over Southern California, while the famed Army Air Corps pilot Jimmy Doolittle achieved the first completely "blind"—that is, instrument-free—takeoff, flight, and landing. Across the ocean, the German airship *Graf Zeppelin* completed its extraordinary circumnavigation of the Northern Hemisphere. In a telling indication of the times, the aviation-themed film *Wings* even won the year's Academy Award for Outstanding Picture. Not that the news was uniformly positive: 1929 also featured the greatest number of fatal civil aircraft crashes in United States history.

There were brewing signs of economic instability, as well. On March 25, after the Federal Reserve warned of excessive speculation, the stock market experienced a mini-collapse, as worried investors began unloading their stocks and interest rates skyrocketed to 20 percent. Though the market quickly rebounded, its shaky foundation had been revealed, and steel production, construction, and automobile sales remained sluggish throughout the spring.

With Kiki back in England, Lancaster was living at Manhattan's Army and Navy Club, while Jessie, newly returned from Los Angeles, rented an apartment on West 56th Street. Though Kiki was across the Atlantic, Lancaster and Jessie were required, as always, to maintain the public facade that they were business partners only. This facade would remain the dominant factor in their relationship over the coming years; even among friends, they could not display any overt signs of physical affection, promulgating instead the continued fiction they were merely "pals." (Whether or not their friends believed them is another matter.) Their notoriety as famous fliers—economic hardships notwithstanding—ensured that watchful eyes were always upon them, especially given the social swirl with which they were forever surrounded. As such, any concrete moments for physical, or even emotional, privacy remained frustratingly fleeting. Weeks or months could pass without the two of them enjoying any truly meaningful time on their own. And yet, despite these considerable obstacles, they remained firmly in love with each other, and steadfast in their belief that one day they would marry and enjoy a relationship free of any such stifling constraints. They had survived the extraordinary rigors of their record-setting journey; next to those, any setbacks seemed relatively minor.

For now, however, it remained imperative that they establish separate careers as a sign of their independence. To that end, Jessie began studying for her pilot's license at Red Bank Flying Instructors in New Jersey, where, to no one's surprise, she made a characteristically sizeable impression. In the mornings, spectators would gather at the school's airfield to watch Jessie fly; despite her fame, the sight of a woman aviatrix was still rare enough to cause a sensation. Jessie gleefully described the scenario to a friend in Melbourne: "I have been thoroughly enjoying life lately . . . I go out to the field every morning at 8:30 and say, 'Hullo everybody, can I have my ship?' They all grin and say, 'Sure, Mrs. Miller, we'll get her out'. . . . Then I cast an eye at the wind indicator, adjust my goggles and taxi for the take-off. It's the life!" For entertainment she would race the famous *Blue Comet* train of the New Jersey Central Railroad as it sped by below on its way from Atlantic City. No matter how quickly she flew, the train always won in the home stretch. The Central Railroad's management, aware of the public relations angle, soon began paying Jessie to ensure her continued participation.

Lancaster's future was looking brighter, as well. By March 1929, American Cirrus Engines Incorporated had produced its first engine, and Lancaster was handed his first major duty as demonstration pilot: participating in a light airplane flight contest that stretched from New York through the Caribbean to Mexico, and back. Amelia Earhart and George Putnam were among the judges. But while a gold medal win would certainly please the company, it wasn't Lancaster's primary mission; his duty was to prove the engine's quality. On March 4 Lancaster and his competitors began their journey.

Lancaster retraced the path to Miami that he had navigated back in January, before heading to Havana, Haiti, and Puerto Rico. At each stop along the way he hyped the engine's capabilities. He crossed down through Martinique before arriving, in first place, in Barbados, and then flying on to Trinidad. There he spent five days displaying the Cirrus engine, before hopping back in the plane for the next leg of the journey, to Venezuela.

But disaster struck as Lancaster lifted off from the landing strip: after hitting an air pocket, his Avian nose-dived back to earth, smashing headlong into the ground and shattering its front end. Lancaster was badly injured, putting an immediate halt to any momentum in his career. Instead, for three months he lay recuperating in a Trinidad hospital bed, where his wounds proved agonizingly slow to heal. For his subsequent return to the United States, Lancaster had to be stretchered on board the SS *Vausan*, which was steaming its way to New Jersey. After arriving in Hoboken, he was taken by ambulance to a hospital in Englewood, where he spent another several weeks recuperating. Only at the beginning of August was he finally discharged.

Jessie was deeply distraught by Lancaster's injuries, but she had little time to comfort him. American Cirrus Engines Incorporated had brusquely canceled Lancaster's contract following his near-fatal crash, and Jessie had to scramble to bring in money for their partnership. Having breezed through her pilot's course in New Jersey, Jessie was now only the third woman to earn a private license in New York, and one of only thirty-four licensed female pilots in America—a number all the more astonishing when compared to the country's thousands of licensed male pilots at the time.

For Jessie, opportunity in the wake of Lancaster's crash in Trinidad arose in the form of the nation's first Women's Air Derby, jokingly but insultingly termed the "Powder-Puff Derby" by humorist Will Rogers. Founded by air-race impresario Cliff Henderson, who five years later would ban women pilots from participating in one of the world's most prestigious competitions, the Women's Air Derby was part of the 1929 National Air Races and Aeronautical Exposition. Its route would cover 2,700 miles, from Santa Monica, California, to Cleveland, Ohio. To participate, pilots were required to have a minimum of one hundred hours of solo flight; twenty-five of these hours must have been cross-country. While these same rules applied to the men competing in the national races, the Women's Air Derby involved an additional, sexist requirement: the aircraft's horsepower had to be "appropriate for a woman." Pilot Opal Kunz, for example, owned a three-hundred-horsepower plane that judges viewed as "too fast for a woman to fly." She was forced to race in a different plane.

Jessie viewed the Derby as essential to raising her profile as a pilot, and in her direct, persistent way she persuaded the head of the Bell Aircraft Corporation, Lawrence Bell, to provide her with a lightweight Fleet biplane for the occasion. Because Jessie was so much smaller than most pilots, the Bell engineers had to essentially construct a new open cockpit around her.

Jessie followed a relaxed schedule as she flew the Fleet biplane from New York to Los Angeles, focusing more on familiarizing herself with the plane than on speed. On August 18, 1929, she joined nineteen other contestants—including five other light aircraft pilots—in Santa Monica to begin the race. The lighter aircraft went first. The first major stop was Phoenix, Arizona, though only six contestants made it that night, with Jessie the only light airplane pilot among them. But their evening was soon interrupted by disastrous news: pilot Marvel Crosson had gone down in the Arizona desert, apparently after suffering carbon monoxide poisoning. Her broken body was discovered two hundred feet from her plane.

Jessie roomed in Phoenix that night with Amelia Earhart, the sentimental favorite to win the Derby, whose celebrated Atlantic flight had occurred just ten months earlier. Now, though they were deeply distressed by Crosson's death, Earhart and Jessie remained convinced that the Derby needed to continue. They spent hours that night venting about the public prejudice against women aviators, such as the double standard regarding pilot deaths:

if a man died it was considered a natural part of flying's inherent danger, whereas a woman's death was considered improper and intolerable. Earhart's natural reserve slowly wore off and she became warm and animated. By the end of the night the two women had formed a friendship that would last until Earhart's disappearance in 1937.

The next morning the other pilots voiced their agreement with Jessie and Earhart's conclusion: the Derby had to continue. Crosson's death only "made it all the more necessary that we keep flying," Earhart later explained. "We all felt terrible, but we knew now that we *had* to finish."

Accidents continued to plague the contestants throughout the race: Ruth Nichols crashed but survived; Blanche Noyes's plane caught fire in the air; Margaret Perry contracted typhoid fever; Pancho Barnes's plane smashed into a car that drove unexpectedly onto the runway as she was attempting to land. The day after Phoenix, Jessie herself faced disaster when her biplane ran out of fuel and she had to make an improvised landing in the scorching desert sands outside of Douglas. (The problem lay with a faulty fuel gauge.) But the pilots pressed onward, their movements obsessively detailed by a clamoring press corps. When they arrived at the finish line in Cleveland, the pilots were greeted by a roaring crowd of eighteen thousand spectators. Jessie placed a respectable third in her class. Soon afterward she also became, along with Earhart and the others, one of the founding members of the Ninety-Nines, an organization dedicated to advancing women's roles in aviation.

So pleased was Lawrence Bell by Jessie's performance, and by the front-page publicity she'd provided his company, that he registered her for another event in the National Air Races: the fifty-mile closed-circuit race for women, which Jessie proceeded to win. (Lady Heath took second place, although later in the meet she plowed her plane through a Cleveland factory roof and was gravely wounded.) In later events Jessie took two other medals, for second and third place. Her strong overall performance helped the female pilots vie successfully for the spotlight with such crowd favorites as Charles Lindbergh himself. For her very first outing as a solo pilot, Jessie could have hardly met with greater success. She was understandably ecstatic.

Following her Derby performance, the Long Island–based Fairchild Aviation Corporation asked Jessie to pilot one of its aircraft in the 1929 Ford Reliability Tour, a 5,100-mile series of aerial contests featuring thirty-five male fliers and three female ones. Once again Jessie proved her strength and endurance in the cockpit over the contest's rough miles, placing eighth overall. She was the only woman to complete the competition, the other two having withdrawn in the race's initial stages. Jessie's groundbreaking performance brought with it a rush of media acclaim, which Fairchild acknowledged with a thousand-dollar bonus. Oil and gas companies wanted in on the action, too. The floodgates had opened, and Jessie was momentarily drowning in money.

The same could not be said of Lancaster. After being dumped by American Cirrus Engines following his life-threatening crash, he was struggling with both his physical recovery and his need to find another source of income. He was genuinely encouraging of Jessie's success, crisscrossing the country to greet her at airports thousands of miles away, but he was also traditionally masculine, and his pride must have been wounded as Jessie's ascendant fortunes matched his own declining status. But their partnership remained rock solid, and Lancaster, wounded pride or not, took remarkably unselfish pleasure in Jessie's newfound success.

7

A CHANGE IN FORTUNE

On October 29, 1929, Black Tuesday swept Wall Street like a typhoon, as investors traded an astonishing sixteen million shares on the New York Stock Exchange in a single day. Three million shares changed hands in the first thirty minutes alone, while deafening cries of "Sell! Sell! Sell!" engulfed the trading floor and rumors spread of investors jumping from buildings in despair. By midafternoon billions of dollars were lost and thousands of investors wiped out. The market continued to plummet over the ensuing weeks, finally reaching its nadir in mid-November. These events helped plunge America, and the rest of the Western industrialized world, into the Great Depression, at the time the worst economic downturn in the history of the world.

Like everyone else, freelance pilots in America were battered by the financial collapse. The worlds of civil and sporting aviation, whose growth had seemed limitless just months before, constricted in on themselves, and even newly crowned stars like Jessie abruptly found themselves fighting for employment. The effects of the crash on her and Lancaster were swift: the Cunningham-Hall Aircraft Corporation finally canceled its long-delayed monoplane project, and Lancaster's subsequent job, as a Victor

Aircraft test pilot, was terminated after the company was forced into receivership.

Jessie's flight competition earnings were rapidly draining due to outstanding bills and day-to-day living expenses for two, and by early 1930 she and Lancaster were fretfully searching for a source of replenishment. Their situation was further complicated by the arrival in New York City of Jessie's widowed mother, Ethelwyn, who moved into Jessie's apartment on West 56th Street. Ethelwyn had never been a fan of Lancaster's, and, with a mother's intuition, she did her best to discourage his presence around Jessie. Adding to the difficulties, the cost of caring for and feeding her mother ate into Jessie's already pinched savings.

Finally, at a cocktail party in March, Lancaster and Jessie met a Dutchman named C. P. Stork who was seeking demonstration pilots who could double as salespeople for his growing Stork Corporation. He immediately offered them employment for the generous salary of six hundred dollars a month each, not including commissions. There was only one catch, Stork told them. "Have you both got commercial licenses?"

Jessie was about to answer with a regretful "no" when Lancaster jumped in. "Yes, we've got those all right," he assured Stork.

"That's good, because you must have them to fly prospective customers about and demonstrate aircraft," Stork said. "When can you start?"

"Monday," Lancaster answered.

Jessie knew this was a blatant lie, but she kept her mouth shut until they had left Stork's office and were in the elevator.

"We haven't got commercial licenses," she reprimanded Lancaster. "What are we going to do?"

"Get them," he replied, in his usual nonchalant manner. Didn't Jessie remember their friend J. R. Booth from the Ottawa Flying Club, whom they'd met during the Ford Reliability Tour? Booth had assured them he could always be counted on for assistance. Now, Lancaster said, they had three days before their next meeting with Stork, and it just so happened that Canadian licenses were binding in America.

The following morning Lancaster and Jessie stepped out on the Ottawa train platform into a cold so piercing and raw that it felt like a punch to the stomach. Luckily, Booth handed them two raccoon fur–lined jackets to offset the chill. The licensing exams had been arranged, he told them. "We'll get everything organized this morning," Booth announced, "and then I'll take you to the Silver Slipper for lunch."

Lunch with Booth proved to be more liquid-based than food-based, and Jessie's head was swimming when she went for her eye test that afternoon.

"What's the matter with you?" the doctor asked, as Jessie struggled to focus on the letters on the eye chart.

She admitted, in her typically forthright manner, that she was fairly drunk.

The doctor, unperturbed, proved accommodating. "We'll do the rest of the examination first, then," he reassured Jessie. "By the time you've finished that you'll be sober." Fortunately, his prediction was correct.

Both Jessie and Lancaster passed their flying tests with ease. True to Booth's word, they received their commercial licenses late that afternoon. Jessie, inadvertently setting another record, proved to be the first woman to receive such a license in Canada. By midnight, she and Lancaster were back home in Manhattan.

For the next six months the two aviators worked for Stork, but with the Depression in full swing, their total airplane sales numbered fewer than five. Still, hard times were everywhere, and their pathetic sales records didn't harm their reputations as pilots. When aircraft manufacturer Edward Stinson insisted they undergo training on his Stinson Juniors before displaying the planes to the public, he was, like everyone, impressed with the results. "You fly as well as any man," he wrote to Jessie, in the characteristically sexist manner that marked the times.

By the time September rolled around, the Stork Corporation's fortunes, like those of so many others in America, had drastically waned, and Lancaster and Jessie were forced to battle for contracts in an aviation landscape so barren that even the finest pilots—Lancaster and Jessie included—struggled to find freelance work. From a financial standpoint, their wisest move would have been to relocate to England, where their celebrity was such that their images were still prominently featured in advertisements for the country's foremost aircraft manufacturers. But returning to England would have meant dealing with Kiki and the children, and Lancaster, never a man for deep reflection, preferred to stay in America, pursuing the familiar if dodgy world of one-off competitions and headline-seeking feats.

Their Stork Corporation salaries had been healthy enough that Jessie and Lancaster had grown accustomed to a certain level of high living, with enough money left over to put into savings. But after an entire August without employment, and with no additional prospects in September, Lancaster had to face the increasing hopelessness of his situation. This, again, forced the onus of responsibility onto Jessie, who, as a female pilot, remained a rare breed and thus a more newsworthy figure. Her boldness and her taste for adventure may have offended mainstream sentiment, but they also ensured a continual audience for her exploits. She was as aware of this as Lancaster and, ever the dutiful partner, set about trying to line up another headline-grabbing flight.

She first approached the Wright Aeronautical Corporation, pitching them on the idea of setting a coast-to-coast record. The company readily agreed to give her a six-month loan on their powerful, 165-horsepower J-6 Whirlwind engine. The day after her meeting with Wright, Jessie caught wind of an obtainable airframe, the Alexander Bullet, out in Denver, Colorado. The Bullet was a low-wing cabin monoplane that featured a retractable landing gear, and while it wasn't anyone's ideal choice, this only worked in Jessie's favor in procuring it. The Bullet's 125-mile cruising speed was more than sufficient for her plans. With her usual capacity to inspire confidence in others, she persuaded the company's owner, J. Don Alexander, to lend her the model. The company's mechanics even mounted the Whirlwind engine and refurbished the Bullet's frame.

When Jessie returned from her time in Colorado, she was confronted once again with the strain of living with her mother, Ethelwyn. "Frankly," she admitted later, "it was getting a little wearing having mother, as she disapproved of everything." Foremost on that list, of course, was Lancaster, whom Ethelwyn continued to treat with barely concealed disdain.

As an added stress, Jessie learned, as her Alexander Bullet was being renovated, that she was not alone in planning a record-setting coast-to-coast flight. The celebrated Brooklyn-born aviatrix Laura Ingalls, who during World War II would be sent to prison as a Nazi spy, had got the jump on Jessie, flying from New York to Los Angeles in just over thirty hours—a new record. The media celebrated Ingalls's achievement, but Jessie, rather than being discouraged, decided this was a positive: her own attempt would receive all the more exposure due to Ingalls's publicity. On October 12, 1930, she departed New York in the restored Bullet, navigating a series of storm systems that stretched from Pennsylvania across the Midwestern states. And yet her pace did not slow. Five stops and four days later, she arrived in Los Angeles, having set a new record of twenty-five hours and forty-four minutes.

But such was the nature of competitive flight in that heady era that even as Jessie flew westward at an unprecedented rate, Laura Ingalls was flying eastward even faster. Ingalls immediately usurped Jessie's record with a flight time to New York of twenty-four hours and fifty-five minutes—forty-nine minutes faster than Jessie's dash to the West Coast. Not to be outdone, Jessie retaliated a few days later with a twenty-one-hour, forty-seven-minute flight from Los Angeles to New York, a decisive new record. Jessie's triumph was complete: she now held the record for both westward and eastward flights.

There wasn't a cash purse attached to Jessie's achievement, but the money flowed in anyway, with advertisers and the media paying generous fees for interviews and photographs. Lancaster, sidelined as a pilot, took on the role of Jessie's agent and manager, operating as her go-between when it came to drawing up contracts.

Jessie's track record was now such that other aircraft companies came knocking at her door. She soon accepted a $1,000 offer from the president of Aerial Enterprises Incorporated to fly round-trip, all expenses paid, from Pittsburgh to Havana. In late November her Bullet departed chilly Pittsburgh for the warmer environs of Miami and Cuba.

Jessie's flight down the eastern seaboard proved rougher than expected, with vicious headwinds battering the Bullet, severely slowing her progress. What Jessie had planned as a one-day hop to Miami doubled in length when her plane ran out of fuel. After spending the night in Charleston, she made it to Miami in time for lunch, then departed for Havana, which she reached in time for dinner. The Cuban government gave her an effusive welcome.

Aerial Enterprises Incorporated had urged a quick return to Pittsburgh, but nasty weather kept Jessie grounded in Havana for the next several days. Aerial's president proved less than sympathetic, however, pressuring Jessie on a daily basis to hustle back to Pennsylvania before the media's attention completely waned. With the president's words in her ear, Jessie decided to leave Cuba on November 28, although the weather remained poor.

Though aviation enthusiasts in Colorado Springs referred to the Bullet as a "jinx craft," Jessie placed great faith in her plane, despite the ominous warnings that had attended her initial use of it. Whatever the Bullet's spin test pilots had encountered, she had personally found the aircraft dependable, despite her joking comment in Havana that it was an "un-airworthy crate." Nor did she profess worry that her Bullet lacked a radio set and bank and turn dials. Jessie knew the Florida coast well, and she felt sure that she would be able to locate it. She would only be two hours in the air! She did take one precaution in deference to the projected thirty-mile-an-hour winds: she filled her reserve fuel tanks, despite the extra time this took. Now the Bullet would fly nine hours before it needed refueling.

Despite her brave facade, Jessie, in a moment of raw candor in Havana, confessed the truth of her emotions: "Everybody gives me credit for being brave . . . and I never let them think otherwise. But really I am afraid, desperately afraid, when I'm over water or mountains or rough country. . . . I feel many times like giving up because I know it's eventually going to get me. But I can't—people would think me a coward. I guess I've just got to keep on until it does get me. Life at its best is short anyway, so I guess I have no complaint coming."

Shortly before she took off for Miami, Jessie told the press of a disturbing premonition: "I don't why it is but something tells me I'm going down. I've had the feeling ever since I crossed on the way over from Florida and somehow or other I can't shake it off."

Where was Jessie? Her projected arrival time of 11 a.m. in Miami had come and gone, but there had been no glimpse of her since a Pan American pilot had spotted her Bullet over the Florida Straits. That afternoon the Cuban government sent two planes on a search mission, joined by Curtiss Air Station seaplanes from the marine base in Miami, but all were forced to return once night fell. From its tropical radio station, the Key West Naval Station sent hourly announcements of Jessie's disappearance to all ships in Gulf and Atlantic waters, but this proved equally fruitless; there was nothing to report. The coast guard station at Fort Lauderdale also heard nothing from local picket boats. *The New York Times* reported the common sentiment: "As nightfall obscured the waters of the Florida Straits, hope for the safety of Mrs. J. M. Keith-Miller, Australian aviatrix, faded until searchers here conceded her no more than a thousand-to-one chance of a safe landing."

In New York City, Jessie's mother gave a statement to the press. "I am very anxious about my daughter, but I shall not give up hope that she is safe," Mrs. Beveridge said. "It's the sea I am worried about, of course. I am sure that if my daughter was able to bring her plane to a point over land she would manage somehow to get down in safety and probably has done so at some isolated place where she has been unable to get word to me of her safety."

Lancaster, meanwhile, expressed his fear that Jessie had been forced down at sea, and that she was now afloat somewhere between Cuba and Florida in the collapsible rubber boat she carried in her plane. Lancaster had been holed up in Pittsburgh awaiting Jessie's return, but now he rushed to Washington, D.C., intent on convincing the Department of the Navy to help find her. He also tried contacting the famous speed flier Captain Frank Hawks to request assistance. As Jessie remained missing for a second day, seaplanes scoured the Florida Keys in search of clues, and commercial and private pilots between Miami and Havana hunted for signs of her whereabouts. But as night came on with no additional information, nearly everyone accepted that Jessie was dead, her Bullet crashed in the ocean.

Lancaster, however, insisted that the search for Jessie should continue. He was backed in this opinion by none other than Laura Ingalls, who declared, from Miami, that it "would be a grievous mistake to give up the hunt" for Jessie. "It is possible she was forced to land on some isolated key or spot on the mainland with no communications facilities," Ingalls pointed out. Lancaster spent the day making the rounds of the Navy Department, pleading for help, despite protests from officials that the weather was too foul to fly in, with high-speed winds thrashing the Atlantic from the eastern seaboard to the Gulf of Mexico. Nonetheless, the navy finally agreed to supply Lancaster with a plane. He left immediately for Miami, his aircraft whipped by the same powerful winds that pilots in Florida now assumed had downed Jessie's plane. It was two days after Jessie's disappearance, and the reports were conclusive: "Aviation officials today agreed in expressing the belief that Mrs. J. M. Keith-Miller perished in an attempted flight in adverse weather conditions from Havana to Miami," wrote *The Baltimore Sun.*

Soon after takeoff from Havana, Jessie had realized she was in trouble. She'd just reached her cruising altitude when the Bullet was assaulted by intense crosswinds that spun and tossed it like a rag doll, battering Jessie until her body was black-and-blue. Because the Bullet lacked instruments for flying blind, Jessie didn't know whether the prevailing winds were pushing her west, but she knew the Florida Keys, no matter her progress, were an hour away at best. She thought she might be drawing near when her view was suddenly arrested by a thick black line on the horizon, the sign of a massive approaching storm. She hardly had time to steel her body before the temperature dropped precipitously and the wind's fury intensified. Then a swarming black cloudbank consumed everything around her, flinging the Bullet into the storm's turbulent vortex.

Her muscles straining, Jessie tried to push the Bullet above the storm, but she couldn't escape the wind's roiling currents. Though she had enough fuel in her reserve tanks to return to Havana, she realized she was entirely without bearings. Terror lodged in her throat. She no more knew in which direction Cuba lay than she knew how to locate the American mainland. Jessie's panic increased to the point that it subsumed all hope. "I thought it was all over for me," she later recounted, "and I contemplated diving with the ship headfirst into the sea to get the agony over with quickly."

At last, off to the right, the ocean took on a greenish hue, the sign of approaching land. Within minutes Jessie spotted the coastline in front of her, though her maps proved unhelpful in determining her exact location. All she could see through her window were the thick trees and vines of a tropical forest. Maybe, she thought, she could trace the bottom of the coast until Miami appeared on the other side. And yet she didn't think Florida's western coast was so jungle-like. Was she mistaken in her bearings? She spotted a village down below. Her fuel was close to gone; there was no more time to gamble on Miami. The area around the village was her only hope, though every inch appeared covered in trees and shrubs. She aimed for the section that most resembled scrubland, the plane slowed by strong winds. After seven hours aloft, the Bullet skidded to a halt among the rough and tangled brush. Aside from a few bumps, Jessie, amazingly, was uninjured.

She sat in her cockpit, gathering her thoughts and nerves. She hadn't been there long when a line of village residents snaked around the plane. As they spoke to her in English, Jessie began to gain her bearings. She had landed on Andros Island, which lay east of Florida, in the Bahamas. She had been convinced the storm had blown her into the Gulf of Mexico, but her calculations were off by 180 degrees. Without her reserve fuel tanks, Jessie would have died in the Atlantic's frigid waters. The sympathetic locals guided her on a fifteen-mile hike through the jungle to where, much to her shock and delight, a fellow Australian, the world-champion swimmer Percy Cavill, had his residence.

Jessie was well aware that a major search for her whereabouts was likely under way, and she was desperate to contact the United States in case pilots were needlessly risking their lives to find her. She knew Lancaster, too, would be frantic at her disappearance. But the lack of a ready communications system on the island meant that two full days passed before she was finally able to reach, via Percy Cavill's fishing boat, the nearby island of Nassau, which had a working radio station. Jessie's mother, in New York, received the first telegram, which read simply, "I am at Nassau. Safe. Notify friends. Love. Jessie." In Miami, an immensely relieved Lancaster immediately jumped in a chartered seaplane to go meet Jessie. The two of them patched up the Bullet as best they could and sped back to Miami. Jessie was deluged with admiring telegrams, one of which, to her great pleasure, proposed a $1,500 payment for the tale of her treacherous flight.

Jessie had little time to relax in celebration. She needed to fly the Bullet back to Pittsburgh if she wanted to heal her wounded pride and also collect the $1,000 prize from Aerial Enterprises Incorporated. On December 12, two full weeks after she'd first set off from Havana, Jessie departed Miami. But the prize money was not to be hers. As she took off from a stopover in Jacksonville, a broken fuel pump killed the Bullet's engine. Jessie tried frantically to veer away from a clump of trees in front of her, but the plane went down hard. The airframe was destroyed. Jessie was badly shaken but once again, rather miraculously, unhurt. Still, the flight was officially over. In a few unceremonious instants Jessie's fortunes had dramatically changed.

8

TO MIAMI

The next twelve months—all of 1931—proved an unsatisfying grind, though both Lancaster and Jessie found paid work. In aviation, the big news centered on Wiley Post and Harold Gatty's attainment of the first round-the-world flight in a single-engine plane, along with Clyde Edward Pangborn and Hugh Herndon, Jr.'s record-setting nonstop flight across the Pacific Ocean. Lancaster and Jessie's old acquaintance Bert Hinkler received acclaim, as well, for being the first person to fly solo across the South Atlantic. But these were exceptions; far fewer aviation records were being set or broken than in previous years, and most available jobs proved a far cry from the media's glamorous portrayal of the world of flight.

As a case in point, Lancaster headed to Los Angeles to work as personal assistant to Jack Maddux, the president of Transcontinental Air Transport, a precursor to TWA. Desk-bound work was not Lancaster's forte, and his carelessness and absentmindedness made him a hapless secretary. Not that Maddux was surprised: he had hired Lancaster as an act of generosity for a down-on-his-luck aviator, not because of his administrative skills.

In June, Jessie began the lengthy process of applying for American citizenship, hoping that it would increase her chances of finding employment.

"America gave me an opportunity in aviation that I was unable to get in England," she informed the press. "I want to become an American because I really want to get somewhere before I die." As it happened, her greatest success that year was a three-month contract with the Redpath Chautauqua lecture bureau in New York. Though initially a reluctant public speaker, Jessie had grown over time to relish the experience of regaling audiences with tales of her aerial adventures, and she was happy to lease her Upper West Side apartment and head out on the road, hopscotching to a new town every day.

Her most memorable incident that summer occurred at the end of July, in the small town of Fort Plain, New York, when she awoke to the smell of smoke seeping beneath her hotel room door. Jessie ran into the hallway and discovered that her floor's storeroom was on fire. Still in her nightgown, she sprinted down the hallway, banging on every door to awaken the other guests. She also roused the night clerk, who rang the fire alarm and then dashed outside to clang the town's alarm bell. Jessie's quick-thinking actions ensured that everyone in the hotel escaped safely, and she was afterward hailed for her bravery by the local fire department.

But lifesaving heroics and her fondness for public speaking aside, by the tour's end Jessie was utterly depleted, the frenetic pace having wreaked havoc on her health. Yet there was little time for rest, as her financial needs overwhelmed any personal concerns. Hardly had she settled back in New York City to recuperate before the next potential moneymaking enterprise presented itself.

While she had been crisscrossing the country, Lancaster and Maddux had dreamed up a promotional scheme in which Jessie would fly the actress Mary Adams and her dog from California to New York. Now, despite Jessie's fatigue, Maddux flew her out to Los Angeles to discuss the plan. But the promotion was not to be: Jessie had barely touched down in the city when her appendix ruptured. Coupled with her already-weakened state, the resulting difficult operation forced her into a long period of convalescence, during which she stayed in Adams's Spanish-style villa.

The hard luck didn't end there. Not long after Jessie's operation, Maddux was forced to fire Lancaster, whose administrative incompetence had finally proved too great a liability given Transcontinental Air Transport's declining fortunes, another effect of the continuing Depression. As a sign that there were no hard feelings, Maddux gave Lancaster a large black Lincoln car as a parting gift.

Lancaster and Jessie were now broke, with no immediate financial prospects, just two of thousands of unemployed pilots trapped in the throes of the Depression. They agonized over whether they would ever be able to fly again. "I spent days discussing impossible plans with Bill," Jessie later recalled, "until my head ached with the futility of it all."

Just when matters seemed at their bleakest, a possible solution arrived in the form of aviator William Gentry Shelton, Jr., whom Lancaster knew from his Ford Reliability Tour days. The ruddy-cheeked, pudgy Shelton, a thirty-five-year-old St. Louis native with an aquiline nose and thick wavy hair, was known in aviation circles for his attempted endurance flight above Lambert–St. Louis Field, during which he and a copilot had remained aloft for five days. Shelton hailed from a privileged background, and he was driven by an enthusiasm for adventure, which had often led him into scrapes—breaking a leg during a parachute jumping contest, being slapped with a thousand-dollar fine for buzzing too low over Garden City, New York—from which his wealthy father, the owner of a company that produced beauty shop electrical equipment, had rescued him. But while Shelton may have been irresponsible, with the broken marriage to show for it, his charm, humor, and intelligence were as genuine as they were refreshing. It was only an added bonus that Shelton, courtesy of his father, owned a Lockheed monoplane.

One night, when Lancaster and Jessie were at their lowest, Shelton suggested that the three of them use Lancaster's new car to drive to Florida for the upcoming Miami All-American Air Races, which Lancaster had attended with Kiki back in 1929. The Miami air races were one of the nation's largest such annual gatherings, with hundreds of participating aircraft. Not only might Lancaster, Jessie, and Shelton be able to participate in the races, but they could also network in the hopes of finding jobs. Even better, they could potentially use Shelton's Lockheed to set up a small charter business in the tropics, one that would transport customers from the Florida Keys to Cuba and the Bahamas. Shelton had previously owned a charter company in Missouri, and though that company had failed, he was keen to try again.

Only the briefest of discussions was required. At the end of December 1931, the trio hopped in Lancaster's black Lincoln town car to set off for

Miami. Along for the ride were Lancaster and Jessie's fox terrier, Mickey, a "perfect house dog," in Lancaster's words, and their thoroughbred British bulldog, Bozo, a "delightful old fool." Shelton would travel with them as far as New Orleans before boarding a train to New York to reclaim his Lockheed. Lancaster, Jessie, and Shelton hadn't drawn up a contract; they were relying on the bonds of friendship instead.

As the group sped on its way, Jessie began to think of Miami as an almost magical place, like Oz, where all their problems would be solved. Their planned charter company would provide them with enough money to survive in the current brutal economy, after which they could return to the more glamorous business of setting world records and basking in the public's adulation. Bursting with anticipation, they stopped in the middle of the blazing Arizona desert to formally shake hands in acknowledgment of their new partnership. In Miami, Jessie imagined, the three of them "would ride out the Depression until the flush days came again with the blue skies above us and glorious days."

When they parted at the New Orleans train platform, Shelton pledged to meet Lancaster and Jessie at the Miami air races, with his Lockheed in tow. Following another round of handshakes, Lancaster and Jessie climbed back into the Lincoln for the final stretch of their journey.

As soon as they arrived in Miami, Lancaster and Jessie joined up with Major Jack French, Jessie's old booking agent in the city. Years earlier, French had been the first person to invite the couple to Miami; now, to help out with rent, he would serve as their housemate. On January 2, 1932, the three moved into an airy white terra-cotta-roofed house in Coral Gables, obtaining a twelve-month lease at forty-five dollars a month. It was, rather astonishingly, the first time that Lancaster and Jessie had ever lived together—though, ironically enough, their relationship had over the past twelve months morphed into something almost wholly platonic, not romantic, a fact that somehow failed to register with the always unmindful Lancaster. Their emotional connection remained as cherished as ever, and they were occasionally still physical, but the truth is that their life as a couple had grown stagnant, regardless of their intentions. Economic circumstances during the previous few years had forced them to spend so much time away from each other building—or attempting to build—their separate careers that they had never had a chance to properly create a life for themselves, in the same place, as a couple. The fact that their relationship remained a secret was, of course, an even more dominant factor, along with the concerted efforts of Jessie's mother. Jessie was belatedly coming to realize that some major part of herself felt unfulfilled, even if Lancaster didn't recognize it. With the romance gone, what remained in its place was the inexpressible but wholly unbreakable bond that had initially been forged during their England-to-Australia flight. That bond, which their series of near-death escapes had hardened, existed on a far deeper plane than mere romance—which the traumatic events of the coming months would all too soon prove.

In Miami, their two-story property, at 2321 S.W. 21st Terrace, was surrounded by an acre of lush foliage. The setting was as peaceful as it was attractive, with the closest neighbor barely visible through the greenery. As Jessie later described the residence, "The windows were framed in purple bougainvillea and the trailing jasmine vine. At night time, [the] scent would drift through the open windows and fill the upstairs sleeping porch . . . with its overpowering sweetness." Jack French occupied the lower bedroom, Lancaster the upstairs sleeping porch, and Jessie a main bedroom just steps away from the sleeping porch.

After so many years in transit, with countless hours spent in apartments and hotel rooms, Lancaster and Jessie were delighted at their find. The night they moved in they celebrated by pretending that their moonshine was Bacardi and gin. "This time I really believe it will be for a lasting period," Lancaster wrote joyfully in his diary. "For once we have had the best of a bargain. Chubbie seems so happy over the house. She is her old sweet self again." (Lancaster always called Jessie by her childhood nickname, "Chubbie," which her family had originally dubbed her because of her chipmunk cheeks.)

One wrinkle in their happiness, however, was lack of news from Gentry Shelton, which served to compound their money worries. Shelton cabled from Ohio the night they moved into their house, but he offered no real information. "Damn Gentry!" Lancaster jotted in his diary, calling him a "blighter." "Am keenly disappointed. . . . We telegraph him imploring him to communicate—but no reply." Still, the couple didn't lack for friends. With the Miami All-American Air Races only days away, pilots from several countries, many of whom they'd known for years, descended on Miami. On January 4 Lancaster and Jessie threw a party at their house, where the drinking started early and vigorously. Their friends were "here for a good time and [got] very tight," Lancaster noted. In varying states of collapse, many of these friends crashed for the night in the enclosed second-floor sun porch that housed Lancaster's bed.

When the revelers awoke the next morning the drinking picked up where it had left off. By evening Jessie was swimming in alcohol, and when she tried to drop one of their friends back at the Columbus Hotel, she smashed the Lincoln into another car. Lancaster, in the backseat, immediately switched places with her and pretended to have been the driver when the police came. As a result, his driver's license was suspended and he received a $50 fine, leading him to grouse, "American justice is all wet." At least, Lancaster hoped, Jessie had learned a valuable lesson about drinking and driving.

The 1932 Miami All-American Air Races, meanwhile, proved far less successful than in previous years. Trapped in the throes of the Depression, few potential audience members were willing to pay the required attendance fees. Competitive aviation was also becoming old news, and it no longer possessed the ability to surprise. Even a performance by a Jimmy Doolittle–led contingent of military aircraft couldn't quite make up for the gloom. In his diary Lancaster wrote that he and Jessie felt "out of things" at the meet, since they "had no ship to race," thanks to Shelton's continued absence.

Only a single business contact at the air races proved hopeful: two men from a new company called Latin-American Airways told Lancaster and Jessie they might be interested in employing them as charter pilots if they could procure an airplane. The men, Mark Tancrel and Jack Russell, announced they were about to travel out west to investigate potential flight routes between the United States and Mexico. Lancaster thought the idea had potential, and he told Tancrel and Russell about Shelton's monoplane. He couldn't help feeling slightly suspicious of Tancrel, however, who was decked out in a naval uniform and claimed to be a former captain in the U.S. Navy. Lancaster was dubious: the skinny, dark-haired Tancrel, who had a sunken chin, wide cheeks, and a prominent nose, seemed more like a disreputable salesman than like a former military officer. He found Jack Russell, a rugged, solidly built man with large ears and an expansive smile, to be more reassuring.

Between setting up their new house and the social activity surrounding the air races, Lancaster and Jessie's first days in Miami passed in a whirl. But with no work lined up and no sign of Shelton, financial worries ate at them. They loved their house, and they loved the warm Miami weather, but Lancaster's diary entries reveal the depth of their anxieties. "Cash getting low!!! . . . The outlook for the immediate future is none too bright. I cannot see daylight yet. Chubbie very depressed. . . . It's a sort of helpless feeling, this utter lack of cash. No sign of work, either! . . . Chubbie still the best little sport over matters, but she is blue, too. . . . Money seems to be getting scarcer every day." At the rare times when they scrounged up enough cash for fuel, Lancaster would fly them over Miami while they basked in the sights of their new sun-splashed metropolis.

Though Lancaster and Jessie were both by nature spirited and upbeat, their savings were nearly gone, and their moods couldn't help but be affected. They still owed their landlady half of a six-month advance. Their housemate, Major Jack French, despite his pledges to the contrary, proved unable to scrounge up any money for rent, and he was a lazy, inconsiderate cohabitant. Lancaster was reduced to "hunting" for dinner with Mickey, the fox terrier—which, in reality, meant stealing chickens from neighbors' yards. Lancaster and Jessie's only success came in selling short articles about their flying adventures to magazines like *Adventure* and *Liberty.* A story about the venomous krait snake that had invaded their plane in Burma; a how-to article by Lancaster titled "If You're Fit, You Can Fly": these were their specialties.

Jessie, the primary breadwinner for the past several years, knew how doggedly Lancaster was searching out work. But her nerves were growing frayed by their near-poverty existence, and, unfairly or not, she sometimes begrudged his failed efforts. None of his harebrained schemes for success ever seemed to pan out, while his signature heedlessness had, if anything, only grown more pronounced over time. Not that she thought for a moment of breaking up their partnership. But despite her best efforts, her frustration with Lancaster increased. Irritated, she would retreat to her room, which soon became her coveted private space. "I was able to lock myself in away from everything whenever I wanted to," she later recalled. "I would read or write or just go there to get away from all the flying talk for a little while."

The truth is that, from a business standpoint, Jessie no longer needed Lancaster. She had become the more celebrated pilot of the two, and indeed, many people had advised her that Lancaster's presence was actually a drain on her career. Repeatedly, she had been urged to cut him loose, though she was far too loyal to ever consider that an option. But after so many years of drifting in America, and still nothing to show for their once-ardent affair, Jessie's sense of their relationship was undergoing a significant transformation. "I was cooling off," she later admitted. "I thought there was no future for us."

In mid-January, Lancaster finally talked with Shelton, who called from Floyd Bennett airfield in Queens. Shelton had gotten his hands on a Curtiss Robin monoplane, which he promised to fly down to Miami. By this point Lancaster had little faith in Shelton's promises; he was therefore disappointed, but not surprised, when Shelton phoned the next week to say that Lancaster should come to New York instead.

Though Lancaster had misgivings about the trip, he and Jessie desperately needed a plane if they were to earn a real living. So Lancaster reluctantly sold his watch, bid a sad farewell to "little Chubbie," and took a train to the Jacksonville airport, where he hoped to hitch a ride to New York. His efforts failed. The airport manager and the manager of the hotel where Lancaster stayed were "kind, but not helpful," Lancaster wrote, but "(w)ho is, these days?" He hopped on a bus instead, using the money from his watch to buy a twenty-five-dollar ticket to New York City. He spent a rough two days stretched out in the bus's backseat, feeling "as dirty as a chimney sweep."

When he arrived in New York, Lancaster quickly rounded up Shelton, who was getting drunk with an old friend. Shelton and his friend had dates with two young women that evening, but early the next morning, Lancaster shook Shelton awake, and they headed out to Floyd Bennett Field to examine the Robin. The plane, Lancaster grimly reported, was "not new by any means." One day later Shelton left New York to visit his father in St. Louis. He promised to wire Lancaster money to fly the Curtiss Robin to Miami, but, as Lancaster had half-expected, the funds never materialized.

That night, Lancaster telephoned Jessie, but the call went poorly: "She disappoints me greatly by her failure to be her sweet self for a few minutes," he dejectedly wrote afterward. "(D)id so want cheering up as things are still black. . . . Oh, it's vile." Two nights later, still in low spirits, he wrote, "Miss Chubbie more than anything. . . . A dog's life!" Lancaster spent his time in the city visiting old friends, many of whom owed him money but were far too broke, in such dire times, to pay him back. "Everyone is very nice to me," he wrote. "Have no money, but what the hell!" The Depression had its cold fingers into everybody. Stress, desperation, hopelessness: these were the overriding emotions of the men and women in Lancaster's aviation circle. Everybody owed everybody money, and no one had a penny to pay.

By February 1, Lancaster had grown "heartily sick" of New York, so it was all the more unexpected when, two days later, he received a mysterious reprieve: a Miami attorney named Ernest Huston wired him a hundred dollars. Lancaster didn't know what the money order was for; he only knew it was enough to cover his debts in New York, and to pay for his return to Miami. But this good news was briefly overshadowed when he returned to the Aberdeen Hotel to find two telegrams from Jessie imploring him to call right away. "Am in a cold sweat . . . What can it be?" he wrote in his diary, after his first calls didn't go through. "[T]his urgent request to telephone Chubbie has knocked me flat. God, if anything has happened to her I shall suffer as I have never suffered in my whole life."

Unaware of Jessie's waning feelings, Lancaster's obsession with her had, by this point, become the overriding factor in his existence, with his own well-being now entirely dependent on his perception of Jessie's happiness. Though his diaries are filled with details of regular social interaction with a wide swath of friends, he offers no evidence that these brought him much pleasure. Instead, his thoughts return constantly to Jessie—what she might be thinking or doing at any particular moment—and how he might further sacrifice himself for her. When, late on February 3, he finally got through to Miami, he wrote, "Just talked to Chubbie. Gee! It was wonderful to hear her voice. I love her more than my very life. I think she needs me. If I did not think this I would give my life to make her happy. . . . Longing to hold [her] once again."

In fact, Jessie had wanted to talk with Lancaster to deliver good news. The hundred-dollar money order had come attached to a job offer: Jessie had been approached once again by the men from the Miami All-American

Air Races, Mark Tancrel and Jack Russell of Latin-American Airways, who remained interested in hiring her and Lancaster as pilots. There was additional good news, as well: a New York publisher had contacted Jessie to express interest in a book about her life, provided she could write one. But as evidenced by Lancaster's diary, neither of these facts particularly registered with him; he was relieved only to hear Jessie's voice. So great was his excitement at returning home to see her that he rolled out of bed at 6 a.m., having not slept a wink.

Much to his chagrin, poor weather kept him grounded in New York for the day. Killing time, he met George Morris, a literary agent who had sold one of his stories to *Liberty* magazine, for lunch. They kicked around ideas for additional articles and stories. Lancaster then headed to the Army and Navy Club, where he won six dollars in a game of bridge, improving his mood. (A few days earlier he'd tried to cancel his club membership for financial reasons, but they had waved him off, saying that many of their members could no longer afford to pay club dues.) He spent the rest of the day trudging around Manhattan, up to West 97th Street and down to East 47th Street, saying goodbye to friends and repaying the small loans that he had racked up during his visit.

The following day he managed to fly the Curtiss Robin to the Washington, D.C., naval field, but the plane engine's cylinders misfired the entire way, forcing three emergency landings. Navy mechanics fitted the Robin's engine with twenty-four dollars' worth of spark plugs, which vastly improved the plane's performance, but rendered Lancaster effectively broke. He flew to the small, impoverished town of Florence, South Carolina, where Jessie wired him money. *Liberty* magazine had just published his article "If You're Fit, You Can Fly," and a Standard Oil Company man at the airport who had read it treated Lancaster like a celebrity, bringing him home for dinner. For a "brief time," Lancaster noted in his diary, the article had put him "to the front again." It was a nostalgic taste of the old life.

When he finally made it back to Florida, he landed at Jacksonville, where the friendly airport manager fronted him ten dollars' worth of fuel. His subsequent flight down the coast to Miami was "delightful," but, to his great disappointment, neither Jessie nor Major Jack French had come to the airport to greet him. He found himself shaking hands instead with Mark Tancrel and a woman who introduced herself as Jack Russell's wife. Latin-American

Airways was, it seemed, chomping at the bit to hire him and Jessie for their proposed charter route between the United States and Mexico. In his dismayed, rumpled, travel-weary state, Lancaster had no way of knowing that this unexpected meeting would kick off the final, tragic act of his and Jessie's time in America.

9

FUTURE UNKNOWN

Tancrel, still decked out in his naval captain uniform—which looked as ill-fitting on him now as it had at the Miami air races—wasted little time on pleasantries. Latin-American Airways' planned charter business was finally ready to launch. After greeting Lancaster, Tancrel announced, "We want you to fly to Mexico almost immediately—in the next couple of days." Lancaster, haggard and drained from his trip to New York, was taken aback, and somewhat unsure how to respond: in his diary that night, he confessed that he found himself "dazed" at the conversation with Tancrel and Russell's wife. After leaving the airport, they ventured back to Coral Gables to discuss the offer with Jessie. In addition to his unsettled state, Lancaster was, as usual, more concerned with Jessie than with business. Her welcome-home greeting hadn't been nearly as enthusiastic as he had anticipated during his journey down the coast. "Chubbie sweet," he wrote gloomily that night, "but fear I expected too much!"

The next morning Lancaster and Jessie visited the office of Ernest Huston, a respected Miami attorney, for a follow-up meeting with Tancrel, this time accompanied by Jack Russell. Lancaster couldn't help but remain suspicious of Tancrel; he found him a "terrible storyteller (all lies)." His doubts were further compounded by Tancrel and Russell's description of the Latin-American Airways charter work as involving, in Lancaster's words, "(r)unning cash belonging to Chinamen in Mexico." What, Lancaster wondered, could this mean? He understood that Tancrel and Russell were initiating a charter business between Mexico and the United States, but the specifics of that business remained frustratingly murky. Still, Ernest Huston, the attorney, certainly appeared trustworthy, as did Russell and his wife, and Huston's law office provided the proceedings with a veneer of respectability. Lancaster and Jessie were also desperate enough for cash that they needed to pursue all potential sources of income. Whatever doubts Lancaster harbored were outweighed by a basic need to put food on the table. Compared with growling stomachs, and the utter absence of any alternative prospects, the air of mystery surrounding Latin-American Airways would have to be endured.

Putting aside any qualms, Lancaster and Jessie signed an agreement in Huston's office: "Captain Lancaster and Mrs. J. M. Keith-Miller, on behalf of themselves and Captain Shelton, agree to furnish for the uses and purposes of Latin-American Airways Incorporated . . . two airplanes of the type which they now possess. . . . Said planes to be used and piloted by Captain Lancaster." The agreement's execution depended on Gentry Shelton, whom Lancaster and Jessie needed in order to finance a second plane. Shelton was due in Miami soon; without his endorsement, the agreement would be annulled. If the deal went through, Lancaster, Jessie, and Shelton would each receive one-sixth of the venture's net profits, along with travel expenses.

The following morning Lancaster brought Tancrel out to the airport for a test flight in the Robin. "Feel safe," Lancaster noted in his diary that night, "that he knows little or nothing about flying." But Tancrel authorized repairs for the Robin on the company's bill, and Huston provided twenty-five dollars to back him up. Still, Lancaster pressed Tancrel for more specifics regarding the venture. Were there any plans to break the law? Aside from cash, what type of goods would Lancaster be ferrying? Would there be any passengers? All flying would be done in Mexico, Tancrel assured him, so U.S. law was not a factor. Otherwise, Tancrel remained vague. Russell would be heading to Mexico the next day to set up business, Tancrel said, and his activities would determine the exact cargo. Lancaster, with other opportunities nonexistent, resolved to play along, at least for the moment.

He was much less conflicted about another potential moneymaking project: the writing of Jessie's autobiography. As Jessie had told him on the phone, a New York publisher had contacted her with just such a proposal, though no money would be offered until the book was actually written. Taking her friend Amelia Earhart's best-selling books as an inspiration, Jessie felt sure her adventures could make for a compelling read, but although she'd written numerous articles, the thought of composing a full-length book intimidated her. In a rare display of insecurity, she was convinced she couldn't do it alone.

As it happened, when Lancaster was in New York City, Jessie had spoken at a local Miami function about her life in aviation. Afterward she had fallen into conversation with a beautiful, fiery woman named Ida Clarke, who was the widow of a Nashville newspaper editor and the descendant of a long line of newspaper workers. Ida Clarke had worked as a journalist since graduating college, and she was now a powerful, and powerfully connected, advocate for women's rights, as well as a professor of journalism at the University of Miami. When, in a follow-up meeting, Jessie had mentioned her anxiety about writing an autobiography, Ida Clarke had excitedly suggested that her son Haden, himself a published writer, might make the perfect collaborator.

Charles Haden Clarke was a towering, darkly handsome thirty-one-year-old Columbia University graduate whose unforced confidence was coupled appealingly with an earthy charm. When Jessie met him a few days later, she found him bright, witty, and easygoing, his considerable allure magnified by his strikingly blue eyes. Still, she remained uncertain about hiring him to be her ghostwriter, and passed the final decision on to Lancaster, who, with genuine enthusiasm, declared his first impression of Clarke to be "very good," though he had done little more than shake his hand. So excited was Lancaster about the idea of Jessie collaborating on a book with Clarke, in fact, that he immediately whisked her off to a Lionel Barrymore film to celebrate. On that heady Miami night, as they sat together in the darkened theater, their spirits high, neither took particular notice of the film's grim title: *The Man I Killed.*

The next day Clarke swung by the house for a more detailed conversation with Lancaster. Clarke claimed his writing credentials included a stint at *Good Housekeeping* magazine, along with various newspaper jobs, but now that the journalism market had dried up in the Depression, he was unemployed and penniless, despite his master's degree. He had a wife in California, Clarke added, but they were divorcing. He also described his vision of a ghostwriter's role: to present a book in the subject's own voice. "Like him very much," Lancaster affirmed in his diary that night, an impression likely fostered in part by the fact that he recognized so much of himself in Clarke's current situation.

Lancaster told Clarke that he and Jessie couldn't afford to pay any money up front, but if the book sold, Clarke would receive half the profits. To ease Clarke's immediate financial difficulties, Lancaster proposed that he move into the house in Coral Gables. (He also suggested that Clarke's mother could join them, replacing the freeloading Major Jack French, but Clarke refused, saying he could only tolerate his mother in small doses.) Rent would be free, and Clarke's access to Jessie would be total. Clarke leaped at the opportunity. He moved in the following day. Once he was settled, Clarke and Jessie proceeded to get "cock-eyed, but not unpleasantly so," Lancaster wrote in his diary. During the languid Miami days and nights, alcohol was as robust and constant a presence as the salty ocean air.

Not long after, Lancaster turned thirty-four years old. To celebrate, he, Jessie, Clarke, and Mark Tancrel, of Latin-American Airways, drove over to Miami Beach to fish—although, Lancaster later wrote, "Chubbie and Haden drank instead." Tancrel, hoping to ease Lancaster's financial anxieties, advanced another fifty dollars to help with rent in Coral Gables. Lancaster appreciated the gesture, but admitted that he felt "more mystified than ever over the whole [Latin-American Airways] affair." Still, that day, and the following two days, passed happily, with Jessie acting sweetly and the "ideal" Miami weather a constant boon. But by midweek Tancrel appeared to have blown through all of Latin-American Airways' cash, and Lancaster and Jessie decided it was high time to investigate his difficult-to-swallow claim of being a U.S. naval captain.

Lancaster contacted an old acquaintance in the Navy Department, who reported that Tancrel's name did not appear anywhere in their files. Confident that Tancrel was indeed a fraud, Lancaster showed him the Navy Department's letter, and demanded to know the truth. He also informed the lawyer Ernest Huston, whom he trusted, of his discovery. Tancrel, however, appeared unperturbed, telling Lancaster, "They lost my records at Washington when the Bureau of Records burned." There actually *had* been a Bureau of Records fire, and yet Lancaster couldn't shake his conviction that Tancrel was a phony, even after Tancrel provided documentation from the U.S. Navy Reserve. But by this point Lancaster felt financially indebted to Tancrel—not to mention that he'd signed an agreement with Latin-American Airways—and he lacked the resources to simply repay the money and walk away.

Meanwhile, Gentry Shelton had wired with some welcome news: he would be arriving in Miami that Friday. When Lancaster and Clarke met him at the train station early Friday morning, Shelton was nursing a terrible hangover, and yet he still, undaunted, proceeded to get drunk before lunch. Clarke, obviously sensing a fellow enthusiast, eagerly joined Shelton on a drunken bender that ended up lasting seventy-two hours. The scene that weekend was chaotic: the Coral Gables house's landlady was "raising hell" about rent; Major Jack French had accused Jessie of rudeness, infuriating Lancaster; and Lancaster and Clarke had to resort to poaching two rabbits and two ducks, with Mickey the dog's help, for meals. Yet Lancaster confessed, "This place is getting into my blood! . . . Here it is in the middle of New York winter and we can swim and bathe in the sunshine."

Over the next week Lancaster, who was responsible for test-flying the Robin, mostly refrained from drinking, but Clarke and Shelton, with assorted hangers-on, continued their partying. Jessie often joined them, though she was drinking as much from boredom as anything else. Still, she harbored a growing resentment of the young, healthy men who, instead of working, were lolling around her house all day getting smashed, and not lifting a finger to help her. "I was pretty acid about the whole thing," she later admitted. Lancaster, displaying his customary obliviousness, appeared not to notice. "Chubbie adorable, as usual," he wrote in his diary. "Future unknown! But what the hell!"

Clarke shared Lancaster's room in the second-floor sun porch, an arrangement that enabled them to become fast friends. They spent long hours making up wild tales of heroic sea adventures, and trying to penetrate the veil of mystery that hung around Tancrel, Russell, and the entire Mexican venture. They played afternoon cards at the Miami Beach Club, winning almost seventy dollars in a few short days, though this didn't stop the Florida Power and Light Company from shutting off the electricity at the house due to nonpayment of bills. But when the landlady showed up early one morning demanding the remaining fifty-dollar rent balance, she was shocked to discover that

Lancaster had the money. He and Jessie were now set in the house until June, when the next rent came due.

"Chubbie quite sportful about everything," Lancaster wrote in his diary, but his perception was wrong; in fact, Jessie's frustration with the situation in Miami continued to increase. Yes, the rent was now covered, but the electricity was still out—Lancaster had to boil water for his coffee over a backyard fire—and Jessie didn't like the way Lancaster and Clarke squirreled themselves away for hours, with seemingly nothing to show for it. Clarke had yet to produce a single sentence of the book. Every day, it seemed, Jessie had to remind Lancaster that they were offering Clarke free lodging so that he could work on her autobiography, not so that Lancaster could take him gallivanting around Miami like some freeloading party companion.

In the first week of March, Mark Tancrel swooped back into the picture to demand that Lancaster leave immediately for Mexico. Tancrel's Latin-American Airways partner, Jack Russell, had just confirmed from out west that the company's planned charter routes were fully in order. Despite Tancrel's brash insistence, however, Lancaster refused: he was unwilling to abandon Jessie before the electricity and telephone bills had been paid. He also wanted to leave Jessie with a nest egg that would last for several days. *Liberty* had just rejected her story "Flying for Fun," and she needed income. An irritated Tancrel lashed out heatedly at Lancaster, claiming the airline would lose money unless they departed at once. Lancaster, standing firm, wrote in his diary that while he hated "to appear hard-boiled," his concern for Jessie trumped everything else. Tancrel, despite his aggravation, pledged to secure twenty-five dollars for her.

Soon after, Lancaster sat down with Clarke for an intimate discussion. Clarke had heard wild tales of Lancaster and Jessie's flying escapades, but now, as daylight streamed through the sun porch's open windows, Lancaster confessed the truth: he was profoundly in love with Jessie, and had been for the past five years. If anything happened to her, Lancaster said, he would have no reason to carry on living. With his trip to Mexico, Lancaster was taking a marked leap of faith that he could trust Clarke to protect Jessie's well-being. With similarly patriarchal solemnity, Clarke pledged to be Jessie's caretaker, to curb his drinking and his partying, and to make progress on the book.

That afternoon, Lancaster and Clarke won $17.50 in a Miami Beach bridge game, prompting merriment when the two returned to Coral Gables. With the bill now paid, the house's electricity was turned back on, and Lancaster gathered himself to leave for Mexico in the morning. Tancrel had informed him that their ultimate destination would be the city of Nogales, located on the Arizona-Mexico border. Lancaster studied maps of the route, predicting that that the journey would last no more than four days. In addition to clothing, Lancaster packed a loaded .38 revolver that Ernest Huston, the lawyer, had given him, after Huston suggested obliquely that it might be a useful item to carry on his journey to Mexico. Gentry Shelton, true to form, headed out to the bars for a last round of drinking before the trip commenced. As Lancaster slept, a heavy rainstorm pounded the house until the early morning hours.

10

MENTAL AGONY

Vestiges of the overnight storm remained in the morning, but Lancaster, Shelton, and Tancrel were too keen to begin their journey to wait for the weather to settle. The Robin had hardly left Miami, however, when the blustery conditions transformed into a full-force gale. Lancaster worked hard to keep the plane on course, but the Robin's pace remained glacial as it steered its way through heavy winds. Yet even as Lancaster's shoulders ached from his tight grip on the plane's controls, his passengers appeared unmindful: Shelton, badly hungover, slept for hours on end, while Tancrel blithely ate fruit and rambled on about nonsense. After touching down at last in St. Petersburg, in the middle of high-speed winds, the trio checked in to the Commodore Hotel. "Feel as if I had been drinking myself," Lancaster noted in his diary, describing his wobbliness after the taxing flight.

Lancaster tried to ring Jessie from the Commodore, but the unpaid phone bill at 2321 S.W. 21st Terrace had come due, and service had been shut off. He cabled Jessie instead, then dispatched a letter prodding her to tie up a few loose ends, including restoring phone service. He gently chided her and Clarke to "keep sober and write the book," before concluding with his usual proclamations of love.

Lancaster, Shelton, and Tancrel departed St. Petersburg at daylight, spending an exhausting eleven and a half hours in the air, but the Challenger engine threw oil the whole time, a worrisome sign, and Tancrel continued telling bad jokes, an ordeal Lancaster described as "hell!!!" When they finally landed in Beaumont, Texas, a mechanic diagnosed a thrust bearing gone on their engine. That night Lancaster wrote Jessie an apologetic note: "Tancrel has only just got enough to get the troops to Nogales, so have not been able to get any cash to send." He enclosed what little money he had—a single dollar—in the envelope. "Don't laugh," he wrote, "[the dollar] will put five gallons of gas in the Lincoln."

The Challenger engine was still throwing oil the next morning, forcing a delay while Shelton phoned Dallas for replacement parts. The wet day passed drearily. Tancrel, much to Lancaster and Shelton's annoyance, continued his babbling, spinning a string of fanciful yarns. Lancaster was dealing with other stresses, as well. "No news from Chubbie," he wrote in his diary, "which worries me far more than flying in this bad weather." Eager to reach Nogales—in part to escape Tancrel's yammering—Lancaster instructed the Beaumont mechanic to warm the Robin's engine for a 6 a.m. departure.

When Lancaster, Shelton, and Tancrel arrived at the airfield, they were horrified to discover the Robin flipped on her nose, her propeller blades broken. The mechanic had made the mistake of warming the engine with the plane's tail facing the wind. Lancaster borrowed a replacement propeller from the Orange County airfield, and then wired Jessie to send her own spare propeller straight to Nogales. Funded by Huston, Jessie promptly did so, and by noon the Robin was in the air. Lancaster, eager to make up for lost time, flew to the Chihuahuan Desert's northeastern edge.

Overnight the temperature dropped to a frigid six degrees below zero, freezing the Robin's engine. When the sun rose, Lancaster and Shelton exhausted themselves trying to turn the engine over, until a midday snowstorm, an infrequent West Texas occurrence in winter, rendered their efforts moot. Returning to the Hilton Hotel, they ran into an ex-navy pilot named Lon Yancey, who offered them drinks. Shelton, to Lancaster's "surprise and delight," declined. Shelton was determined to stay on the wagon—beer excluded—until the journey was complete. As Lancaster wrote to Jessie that night, "Old man Gen has been a brick; he has not taken a drink since leaving Miami." Lancaster's largesse even extended to Tancrel, who was acting "well subdued and not so annoying. The cold has frozen him up." Lancaster confided in his diary his main excitement of the day: "Wire from Chubbie, thank God. God bless her, how dear she is to me."

The next morning's weather was still poor, but Shelton was eager to push on. This was fine with Lancaster, who was deeply frustrated with the amount of time they'd already lost. They were nearly out of money, and they could no longer afford to be picky about the conditions in which they flew. After refueling, the trio set off on a direct compass course for El Paso, but they hadn't gone far before the weather turned even worse. Snow began to fall, hampering their view. When they were halfway to the 8,500-foot peaks of the Guadalupe Mountains, visibility became nil.

Just as the Robin approached the mountain ridge, the Challenger engine belched forth all the oil in its tank, completely dousing the forward windshields. The oil pressure plunged; the oil temperature needle flatlined to the right. The engine, Lancaster wrote to Jessie the next day, "thumped like a thrashing machine." Shelton, who was piloting the plane, handled the emergency like a pro. With the Guadalupe's peaks only twenty feet below, Shelton carefully reversed course, then flew twenty miles back to an emergency landing field at the foot of El Capitan. Due to the oil-covered windshield, Shelton was flying blind. Lancaster opened his window, stuck his head out into the cold, and shouted instructions. Tancrel panicked; in his wild fear, he attempted to jump out of the plane, and had to be restrained by Lancaster. The twenty miles to the emergency field seemed to last ages. When the Robin finally landed, the three spent men staggered out into the field. Lancaster called it his "narrowest escape since [his] crash in Trinidad."

The group drove the plane's engine to El Paso for repairs, where Russell met them, spinning tales about lucrative flight opportunities on Mexico's west coast. Lancaster derided Russell's claims as a "waste of time." The most they could hope for, Lancaster estimated, was a hundred dollars a day, far less than Tancrel and Russell had promised. He also wanted their activities to remain strictly within U.S. and Mexican law.

Lancaster, now stuck in El Paso, was wracked with guilt at his inability to provide for Jessie. "Darling, you know how much I love you, so you must realize what a ghastly thing it is for me to have no money to send you," he wrote, adding, "Nothing I hope can ever take you really from me." Lancaster never handled idle time well, and the feeling of limbo that now entrapped him was made worse by Tancrel's unending stream of tall tales and jokes. The two men were staying in the same room. "I am tired of his opening phrases: 'When I was master of so and so' or 'When I was bullfighting in Mazatlan and had killed three bulls with one sword,'" Lancaster complained to Jessie. "He will look well walking down to the hotel lobby dressed as a U.S. Navy Captain, when the desk clerk calls over and says no more telephone calls or wires until the bill is paid, 'Captain!'"

Lancaster confessed that he'd felt "much better mentally" when he had "work to do, such as flying here, and working on the engine." He confided to Haden Clarke that he no longer trusted Russell, who was pressuring him "to run two Chinamen over the border" in a borrowed aircraft. Despite Lancaster's pledge not to break any laws, the prospect of making a few hundred dollars, which he could pass on to Chubbie, was difficult to resist.

Lancaster remained fairly positive that Tancrel was a fraud, but Tancrel's seeming lack of shame could be entertaining in its way, as when the manager of their El Paso hotel pressed them to pay their room bill. Tancrel, unflustered, responded by suggesting the manager should give *them* money instead to invest in Latin-American Airways. Lancaster and Shelton also found hilarious an incident in which Tancrel critiqued the poor wallpapering job in the hotel's hallway. "I've hanged thousands of square miles of wallpaper," Tancrel huffily declared, after Lancaster and Russell ribbed him about his comment. They mocked this statement, too, until Tancrel produced a Wallpaper Hangers' Union of Washington, D.C., card bearing his name. This produced further laughter: Why would a U.S. Navy captain belong to such a union? Tancrel's claims of captaincy were obviously false. He also told Lancaster that he was a Freemason, and attempted to prove it by giving the secret handshake. "It was as far from the Masonite [handshake] as it could be," Lancaster chortled in a letter to Jessie.

The most amusing incident occurred one morning at 4 a.m., when Tancrel frantically shook Lancaster awake because of shouting in the hallways. When they opened their hotel door they were confronted by billowing smoke coming from a fire in a lower-floor room. As Lancaster described the scene to Chubbie:

> Our gallant Captain M.G. Tancrel seized the hose manned by the bellhop and night clerk and after the door of the room had been opened he shot several tons of water in. The smoke was terrible. "It's life and death," said he, gallantly entering room 438 with chocking breath. Hell! The room was empty! The room clerk then remembered that a man and woman full of booze had checked out but an hour previously. Lights were turned on, the smoke cleared, and there was a hole in the center of the bed. Tancrel had shot the windows out with the hose stream, brought down five plaster ceilings-rooms underneath, and put . . . an inch of water on the fourth floor. Then he was mad because the hotel manager did not send him a bouquet and a receipted bill for his gallantry.

On another memorable morning, Tancrel and Lancaster were awakened by a sharp knock on the door. When they opened up, a sixty-year-old Australian man strode into the room. "I'm Billy Smith," the man announced, "sergeant of detectives for this city, boys!" A panicked Tancrel blanched. But Lancaster, thinking quickly, announced, "I'm a digger [Australian], too," forging with the detective an instant bond. Smith produced the telegram that had brought him to the room: "Chief of Police, El Paso, Texas: Arrest Gentry Shelton in care of Captain W. N. Lancaster, Hotel Hussman, for felony, theft. W. A. Ovington, Sheriff, Beaumont, Texas." Lancaster was briefly confused, until he realized, to his ire, that the Beaumont airport officials who had lent him and Shelton a propeller—to replace the propeller their errant mechanic had been responsible for breaking—were upset that it hadn't yet been returned. Lancaster and Tancrel telephoned Shelton in Nogales to tell him the news, taking mischievous delight in his traumatized reaction. Detective Smith was "quite won over" to their cause, as his sarcastic response to Beaumont indicated: "W. Ovington, Beaumont, Texas. Gentry Shelton left some days ago for California and points North, suggest you line up a dog team and requisition some woolen [underwear]." Lancaster roared with laughter at Smith's words. He found it delightful that El Paso was filled with "cattlemen" who were "for the most part a cheery and picturesque crowd."

Still, these incidents were an exception. Lancaster was far too distressed by the lack of communication from Jessie to be in good humor overall. As he admitted in his diary: "Tonight I am more than just worried, I am plumb crazy because of no news of Chubbie." Shelton was in Nogales, where Jessie was supposed to be mailing her letters, but nothing had arrived there. "Am terribly worried on [Chubbie's] account," Lancaster wrote Clarke. "Haden, old man, the knowledge that you are 'standing by' the fort and looking after Chubbie has meant more to me than you will ever know. As soon as you get this tell me frankly if I should beg, borrow or steal my way back to Miami." Even a chance meeting with an old RAF buddy, Joseph Ince—who had witnessed one gangster murdering another at his hotel the previous night—couldn't fully distract Lancaster, although he was grateful for the company.

But his love for Jessie overrode all else, to the point of obsession. "I love you and long for you, my sweetheart," he wrote her. "I lay in bed at night and pray you are not suffering too great a hardship. I want to have you in my arms again, Chub. I love you more and more each moment of my life." The more isolated Lancaster became, the more he retreated into an idea of Jessie as a kind of savior, an island of purity in the sea of moral and financial uncertainty that surrounded him. Jessie's cooling feelings, to whatever extent Lancaster suspected them, only fueled his dedication. "Do you still love me?" he inquired in a letter, but the answer seemed irrelevant to his ardor.

Finally, on March 20, Lancaster received three letters from Jessie and one from Haden, all written two days earlier. He was relieved, but he didn't hide from Jessie his precarious financial situation: he and Tancrel now had precisely forty cents between them. Lancaster was distressed to learn that Jessie hadn't received the five dollars he'd mailed days earlier. He realized with fury that Russell was the likely thief, since Russell had seen him place the bill inside the envelope, and Russell had also delivered the letter to the post office. Compared to the brazen Russell, Lancaster felt, Tancrel was actually "quite generous hearted." Russell had also proven himself devious by diverting Latin-American Airways' money for his own uses: he'd sent money to his wife that Tancrel had given him to spend on traveling to Nogales, Phoenix, and Tucson. He then wired Tancrel with a "cock-and-bull" story about his car breaking down, and pleaded for more cash. Yet Russell's crookedness now came in handy.

Desperate to get his hands on money to send to Jessie, Lancaster searched for items to sell. (He had already sold his watch.) He opted to pawn the loaded .38 revolver that Ernest Huston had loaned him back in Miami. With the gun in his pocket, Lancaster prowled through El Paso searching for a buyer. Pawnbrokers unanimously turned him down; Texas stores, it seemed, were already filled with firearms. So Lancaster met with a "gangster" friend of Russell's, who gave him a five-dollar loan on the gun. If Lancaster couldn't pay the money back by Tuesday, the gangster would own the gun.

"I have completely lost faith in the ability of Russell and Tancrel to produce any legitimate business worth while," Lancaster fumed in his diary, while reaffirming that he had "not the slightest intention of doing anything dishonest or breaking the laws of the U.S.A." But he and Shelton had gone too far, and had too few other options, to abandon the trip just yet. "Until Gent and I get on the spot we can't tell whether any of these Latin-American people are speaking the truth," Lancaster rationalized to Jessie. At least Shelton himself had proved trustworthy, remaining sober and focused for the entire trip. But Lancaster's law-abiding resolve, however firmly held, was wavering in the face of his potentially hopeless financial situation. Tancrel was dropping regular hints about illegally transporting Chinese citizens from Mexico to the United States, as per Russell's offer, and even Shelton seemed to feel that a onetime deal might be worth the risk, considering the money to be made.

Lancaster was tormented, unable to make up his mind. He had promised Jessie that he wouldn't break any laws, and a promise to her meant more than anything. But what if Jessie agreed with Shelton? He tossed in bed all night, until, at 5:30 a.m., he threw off his sheets and went to his desk to write a letter to Haden Clarke:

> Forgive what appears to be dramatic and believe in the absolute sincerity of this note! I am faced with quite a problem. You know I am devoted to Chubbie. For her I would do anything, if necessary risk anything. [At the present time the economic situation is so acute that I must in some way remedy matters.]
>
> This Mexican venture so far has been painful. . . . Now we are within reach of some cash if I take a chance and make a little trip with unmentionable cargo. Gent has weakened and thinks we must go ahead in the manner "R" [Russell] suggests. . . .
>
> If I return to Miami, bringing with me just my body and the

> few garments I left with, the strain on Chubbie is going to be great. Whereas if I am able to send back in the course of a few days several hundred dollars, the child will be happy and it will brace her for the future.
>
> Because of our newly formed friendship for each other, I am asking you to assist me as far as possible. Write me, as fully as possible, your ideas after going over such evidence as you have. There may be a way of obtaining Chubbie's reaction without fully disclosing the hand.
>
> For me, life would be very empty if I lost Chubbie. For me, she is the all-important thing. If I thought my return to Miami in a penniless condition would mean the possibility of losing the kid I would take even greater chances to return with money than might be prudent.

That same day, Lancaster wrote to Jessie, describing the day as "ghastly," with forty-five-mile-per-hour winds churning up dust and sand, covering anyone who ventured out. He informed her of Russell's plan to smuggle Chinese nationals, but added, "[D]o not worry. I am not going to take any chances." He also urged her to keep Russell's news confidential from anyone in Miami until "such time as we might want to produce it." Lastly, he reiterated his hope that Clarke was making progress on the book, as that seemed to offer "the greatest opportunity for the future."

Still, messages from Jessie arrived far too infrequently for Lancaster's taste; his writings were soon filled with remonstrations regarding her seeming neglect. Jessie argued that there was no point in her writing him regularly, since she never knew where he would be staying, but this did little to placate Lancaster. "Cannot understand why Chubbie does not write," he wrote in his diary. "This is my greatest hardship, the lack of news from her." And the next day: "No news from Chubbie. She has disappointed me far more than this damned expedition." And again: "No letters—Chubbie, you wretch!" Every day he poured out his love for her, but to little avail. "I miss you, Chub, terribly. Have wanted you more than I can describe," he proclaimed in one typical message. "Oh! To give you a great big hug and feel you close to me once more," he ended another. "I love you more and more each moment of my life," he pledged. But the few replies he received from

Jessie seemed brief and tossed-off, and he described to her his bruised feelings: "Last night I received a typewritten letter from Haden, which had a short note from you written on the bottom. . . . This is all I have had from you since Friday. As a result, I am terribly blue tonight. Maybe the morning will produce a sweet letter from you. But I am getting accustomed to disappointment."

The lack of news from Jessie only increased Lancaster's anxiety at not having money to send her. He was so broke that he and Tancrel had eaten only one thirty-cent meal per day for the past four days. His clothes were filthy, but he had no money to dry-clean them. Ernest Huston's gun was gone, too, since Lancaster couldn't raise the funds to repay the gangster who was holding it. He had reached his nadir: he was starving, dirty, broke, and surrounded by likely criminals.

Though Tancrel still kept up the fiction that Latin-American Airways was a legitimate enterprise, he again suggested that smuggling Chinese nationals—at a thousand dollars a pop—from Mexico to America could be a lucrative short-term fix. Despite the offhand manner in which Tancrel made his pitch, Lancaster had a strong hunch that this had always been his and Russell's plan. This seemed confirmed when Tancrel, still playing the naïf, said he had just discovered that Russell was a drug smuggler. According to Russell, Tancrel reported, flying a single marijuana-filled suitcase from Mexico to San Francisco would net thirty thousand dollars. Lancaster felt sure that Tancrel's ignorance was feigned, and that Latin-American Airways had been set up as a front for criminal activity. Tancrel was obviously probing Lancaster to find out if he was on board.

On March 24 Lancaster cabled, complaining that he was "terribly disappointed and worried" that he'd had no news from her, adding "this period of waiting has been worst ever experienced." Hours later, Lancaster's letter to Clarke about the possibility of illegally ferrying aliens across the border received a firm response. Despite Lancaster's plea to keep the matter hush-hush, Clarke had gone to Jessie anyway. Now they cabled: "Both advise against contemplated move most emphatically. Abide by original decision to letter. This no time to take chances. Situation not so hot but such steps by no means warranted. You are in dog house on chain if you ignore this regardless of outcome. Writing El Paso, love, regards. Chubbie and Haden."

Lancaster was already wary of breaking the law, and the cable from Jessie and Clarke only strengthened his resolve. He informed Tancrel that he wanted no part of smuggling drugs or people. He wrote back to Jessie, promising, "Alright, my sweetheart, I will abide by your decision. . . . I will not take any chance at all. . . . As long as you stick by me, Chub, in this worrying time I don't care a damn. You alone are the one thing that matters to me."

He also told her to thank Clarke for his kindness and his help. "I somehow felt I could trust him more than anyone else I have met for a long time," Lancaster confided. "I hope this has turned out to be so."

Lancaster received a lengthy, caring letter from Clarke several days later that seemed to vindicate his trust in him. Because Jessie already suspected that Lancaster was contemplating breaking the law, Clarke began, he had disregarded Lancaster's instructions and "put the whole thing to her squarely." Clarke then elaborated on the many reasons why Lancaster should steer clear of illegal activity:

> The risk involved is entirely out of proportion to the gain you can anticipate. The slightest slip would result in your being deported, the loss of all the prestige you have worked 16 years to gain, and an awfully tough road to the future for you. The amount of money you would make would furnish only temporary relief at best, and would in no wise help you to become permanently established. You should not let the fact that you are in a tough spot influence you to take a step that you know to be unwise. The worst time in the world to make a foolish decision is when you are down to your last stack of chips. . . .
>
> [Y]ou are surrounded by people who are using every argument in their power to convince you and put the matter in the best possible light. . . . Regardless of what your associates say, and of how rosy the chances may seem, I know perfectly well that there is a very big chance of things going wrong. . . .
>
> You promised Chubbie that you positively would not swerve from your original intentions and I am convinced for you to do so would make her most unhappy regardless of the outcome. I appreciate that your one idea in the whole matter is her welfare and happiness, so

> since the move must defeat this purpose, what possible argument is there in its favor? I agree that it would be a bit tough to come back absolutely empty-handed, but I strongly advise this in preference to the move you contemplate. Frankly, I think she has been convinced you were on a wild goose chase from the very beginning and I assure you she will in no wise blame you if the thing is a flop.

Clarke admitted that his and Jessie's finances were "precarious," but said he planned to write short magazine articles and continue playing bridge as a means of bringing in cash. As long as their neighbors kept raising chickens, Clarke noted, he and Jessie wouldn't starve.

Clarke then added a touchingly personal note: "Bill, I can't begin to express my appreciation for the friendship you have repeatedly shown for me. To say that the feeling is mutual is putting it mildly. Nothing in the world would make me happier than to do everything in my power for you and Chubbie." They were all "playing on the same team from now on," Clarke concluded, and "whatever I have or can get goes into the pot."

When the replacement Challenger engine finally arrived in El Paso, neither Tancrel nor Lancaster could afford the collect charges on it, so the generous local mechanic with whom they were working paid the fee himself. Another stroke of luck occurred at the Hotel Hussman, where Tancrel managed to charm the manager into letting him and Lancaster depart without paying their ninety-five-dollar hotel bill.

After driving out to the Guadalupe Mountains to install the plane's new engine, Lancaster flew back to El Paso, where Tancrel was bickering with the staff of their new hotel. The so-called captain seemed "to rupture his credit" wherever he went, Lancaster drily noted in his diary. From the hotel, Lancaster phoned Shelton in Nogales, who told him some discomfiting news: Russell's wife claimed that Jessie was having a "gay old time" in Miami. In Lancaster's stack of mail sat a letter from Chubbie and Haden, but it did little to ease his mind. "Very disappointed. Looks as though Chub has dashed off a note as a sort of duty," he wrote that night in his diary. "Haden a little more enlightening. Hope he is keeping his promise to me, feel sure he is. But Chubbie—Hell!!"

In the morning Lancaster and Tancrel snuck away from El Paso "under great difficulties," still owing money to the Hotel Hussman for lodging and to the Guadalupe Pump Station for gas. Once in the Robin, they flew to Nogales, their long-planned final destination. The journey from Miami had taken three weeks longer than Lancaster had anticipated. Despite everything he'd learned, Lancaster still somehow clung to the faint hope that Latin-American Airways might have legitimate business to offer. His reunion with Shelton in Nogales was a happy one, although Shelton, with Russell in tow, had been drinking. "Gent seemed so glad to see me . . . that I forgave him," Lancaster wrote in his diary. Shelton had rented an apartment in which the group all stayed.

The next day Lancaster paid a visit to Mexico, where, he wrote, he talked with several "interesting people," but ultimately came to the conclusion that there was "nothing legitimate here." It was finally time, he felt, to "put [his] foot down and call a showdown all around." As it happened, he didn't need to. A day later Tancrel convened a meeting in which he and Russell laid out a concrete plan for drug and human smuggling. Their chips were finally on the table. Operating under cover of darkness, Lancaster would fly the Robin to Mexico, where a group of Chinese nationals with drug-filled suitcases awaited him. Lancaster would fly these men to an isolated location, chosen by Russell, in the Arizona desert. All the groundwork had been laid, Russell assured Lancaster. The drugs would be sold in buyer-friendly San Francisco, where demand was heavy. The reward would be massive: within a scant ninety days, Tancrel, Russell, Lancaster, and Shelton stood to make a hundred thousand dollars each.

Lancaster couldn't believe he had been so gullible for so long. Angrily, he announced to Tancrel that he was going home to Miami. Shelton agreed. But Tancrel and Russell weren't ready to give up. How, they asked, could Lancaster and Shelton fly back to Florida when they were completely broke? Their only hope of getting money resided with Latin-American Airways. "I can raise funds in Los Angeles," Russell told them. He and Tancrel had just enough money to buy gas and oil for a flight to Los Angeles. Lancaster thought Russell was lying, but, being utterly penniless, his options for exit were few. "The whole bunch . . . are a complete wash-out," he wrote disgustedly in his journal. "Dope-running was the game. Had to have turned down any proposition of this nature. Money or no money. Promise to Chubbie is coming first." Not that he felt content on that front. "No news from Chubbie. . . . The little devil! I should not think of her so much. She does not deserve it."

On April 1, Lancaster flew Russell to Los Angeles, where they took a room at Hollywood's Padre Hotel. Still determined to tie Lancaster to Latin-American Airways, Russell tried a new form of manipulation. Russell, Tancrel, and Shelton had all heard rumors surrounding Jessie and Clarke, suggesting that the two were becoming physically intimate with each other. Lancaster had been intentionally kept in the dark. But now, in their Los Angeles hotel room, Russell attempted to use this knowledge to his advantage. He pulled out two of his wife's letters from Miami and handed them to Lancaster. Russell pointed to the sections of the letters describing Jessie's behavior. "Chubbie and Clarke came round tonight," Russell's wife had written in one. "I really think now that Clarke has gained Chubbie's affections, and Bill lost them." In the other letter she wrote, "Was round at Chubbie's tonight. She and Clarke got all ginned up together. Don't tell Bill but I believe she is well satisfied." The last two words were underlined.

Why hurry back to Miami now? Russell asked Lancaster. He should earn all the money he could, and return to Florida when he was flush. It would only take one flight from Mexico, Russell prodded Lancaster; they could even cut Tancrel and Shelton out of the deal. Despite his vulnerable position, Lancaster flatly rejected Russell's proposal. Instead he wired Jessie, "Flew Russell here yesterday but fruitless trip. Expect to fly Nogales tomorrow. Shelton's father telephoned Nogales is willing to help with amphibian. Seems best thing. No news from you before leaving Nogales. Terribly anxious. Tell Haden stand by, I trust him." In his diary that night, he revealed the intensity of his suffering. "Mental agony," he wrote, before jotting: "Hell!"

11

EAGER, DRUNKEN LOVE

Ever since moving to Miami, Jessie had found unexpected joy in having a house to call her own, and even small things like arranging the furniture brought her a sense of security, financial worries notwithstanding. During her five years of flying the thought of a house had seemed stifling, reminiscent of the confines of her old life in Australia, but now that feeling had dissipated, to be replaced with an air of satisfaction.

Jessie's life was evolving on the personal front, as well. Keith Miller had at last filed for divorce on the grounds of desertion, just one day after the three-year period required to file such a claim ended. He argued in his claim that, beginning in 1927, Jessie had "absolutely declined to be a wife except in name," a coded reference to the fact that she had stopped having sex with him. Jessie unconcernedly told reporters that she welcomed the news: "He's done me a favor and that's fine of him. He had home and fireside ideas. I had others. I chose flying and demanded the right to live my own life."

The divorce itself was friendly enough, however, since both partners had long realized that they made an imperfect match, though Miller had tried harder than Jessie to salvage their marriage, pleading with her repeatedly to return home. In response to one of Miller's earnest letters, Jessie had written, gently but firmly, "I am afraid that my career in aviation means too much to me to give it up. I am sorry to have to say that, but I feel as if I cannot live with you as your wife again, and I hope you will forgive me. I hope you find happiness and wish you the best of luck."

Jessie's newfound freedom put her relationship with Lancaster into starker relief. Kiki, despite pressure from Lancaster, remained dead set against granting a divorce. Jessie and Lancaster's romance would have to plod along in secret. How then, Jessie pondered, would she ever attain with Lancaster the kind of comfort that she yearned for? The two had been leading double lives for nearly five years now; Jessie was heartily sick of it. Social expectations for the two were different, as well. If Jessie remained single for the rest of her life, she would be denigrated as a spinster. Despite all she'd shared with Lancaster, the thought of living out her life as the "hidden woman" depressed her. Over the previous years, her love for Lancaster had gradually shifted, almost before she'd noticed, from passionate to platonic. But even though she no longer felt romantic toward him, she valued his faithful presence in her life; occasionally they even still made love, though for Jessie this was more from habit than passion. "We were such good friends," she remembered later. "We really got on well together; we were pals. We had great fun together."

Lancaster, needless to say, had a different view of their relationship. As much as he claimed to want a divorce from Kiki, he never worked up the initiative to actually do so, and he never gave serious thought to—or he was simply incapable of imagining—Jessie's emotional needs. His adoration of her was such that he appeared wholly satisfied just to be in her presence. At no point did he seem to grasp that Jessie was no longer in love with him, and that her attitude toward him was simply that of an intensely devoted friend.

Jessie found the days after Lancaster's departure for Nogales to be an unpleasant slog, owing in large part to a crushing lack of funds. She begged Lancaster not to send his wires collect, since she and Clarke had to pay cash for them. Matters were worsened by the fact that Jessie and Clarke were completely out of alcohol, and too broke to replenish their stock. As a result, friends no longer came to see them. With no drinks, no company, and no car, the two were "bored to sobs," Jessie moaned, and had "nowhere to go in the evening—it's hell!" She hocked her watch, but the money didn't last; days later she was down to twenty cents again. "I do hope you can come back soon," she plaintively told Lancaster, "as I'm so lonely here without you."

To Jessie's strain was added the pressure of trying to coax Haden Clarke into the difficult business of actually writing the book. Clarke kept insisting that writing depended on inspiration—which in his case meant smoking a great deal of marijuana, though Jessie was too naive at the time to realize this. Once the proper moment arrived, Clarke assured her, the book would be completed on time. Jessie was briefly sympathetic, acknowledging, as she told Lancaster in a letter, that it was "hard to write in a light and airy fashion when you don't know where the next meal is coming from and you can't get the laundry out."

Jessie knew, of course, that Lancaster was working assiduously to get his hands on some money, and that his flying skills were his most promising asset. As much as she distrusted Tancrel and Russell, she also knew that Lancaster couldn't evaluate the situation in Mexico without seeing it firsthand. She genuinely missed his presence, and her concern for his welfare was sincere. "I can't tell you how worried it made me to know of the awful times you are having," she wrote to him, before reminding him to "[k]eep away from Chinamen!"

Still, Jessie couldn't keep her increasing frustration with Lancaster's Latin-American Airways jaunt from rising to the surface. She was gentle at first: "Darling, I hate to nag, but maybe [this] will teach you a lesson," she wrote. "We all begged you not to start off unless there were enough funds to get you back again." But soon the tone of her letters grew more brittle: "I simply can't understand why you give checks when you know they are no good. I think it's dishonest and it makes people very suspicious. . . . The best thing is to burn your check book if you can't resist giving bad checks." Nor did she shy away from calling Lancaster to account as a supposed provider: "I am sorry to have to write this, but I told you when you cleaned me out of the little reserve I had in the bank that I would be stranded in the end. . . . Is there any chance of you being able to send me anything soon? I am feeling quite desperate. . . . I have used every cent I have in the bank and am completely penniless."

Jessie grew gradually more annoyed at Lancaster's complaints that she wasn't writing him enough. "I have been unable to wire you for days as I didn't know where you were," she admonished him. "I wired you twice before and the wires came back to me." In the meantime, the letters she *did* write to him were held up in the mail for more than a week. To make matters worse, she kept receiving conflicting (and confusing) reports of what Lancaster and the others were up to in El Paso and Mexico. "There is just one thing I wish you would do and that is please all get together and decide what you are going to wire us in Miami and stick to the same story," she complained. "Tancrel wires one thing . . . Gent tells Helen something different and you tell me something different again. They all phone me up when they get a wire and I simply don't know where I stand." Jessie apologized to Lancaster for sounding so depressed, but confessed that she *was* depressed.

Jessie's aggravation with Clarke's lack of progress on the book continued to deepen. "He is without doubt the laziest and slowest writer I have ever seen," she informed Lancaster, "but for God's sake don't tell him I said so or he will walk out and leave me alone." When Clarke finally cobbled together a brief first chapter, it was riddled with errors, partly due to his refusal to read the material that Jessie had prepared two years earlier. "The only thing seems for me to write the whole [book] and then have him re-write it, so this I'm doing," she exasperatedly reported. "Am getting writer's cramp!"

In the third week of March, with Jessie's frustration—and, equally potently, her boredom—at their apex, she decided to confront Clarke about his procrastination. He'd retreated to the sun porch, where his desk and typewriter were, to take another stab at the manuscript, but after a few minutes the noise of the typewriter ceased. When Jessie went to investigate why Clarke had stopped working, she was incensed to see him staring dumbly out the window, a joint in his hands. She lashed out: Why wasn't he typing? Clarke yelled back that he was waiting for the proper inspiration; he couldn't just "write to order."

Rather than ratcheting up the tension, the brief eruption served to calm them both down. Jessie didn't quite regret her actions, but she realized that every penny Clarke had managed to scrounge up—whether from editing jobs or from gambling—he'd shared with her. And it was hard to stay irate at such a charismatic yet vulnerable man, especially one with those captivating blue eyes and mischievous smile. She and Clarke were also looking forward to a break that night in the relative isolation and monotony that had marked their past three weeks: they'd been invited to a party.

As they prepared to go out, Clarke asked Jessie a seemingly innocuous question: "What are you going to wear?"

"Oh, just the old black one I expect," Jessie replied.

"I'd like you to wear the one with the rose on it," Clarke told her. "I like you in that."

A small gesture, yes, but Jessie was floored. She couldn't remember the last time a man had commented on her appearance. Lancaster peppered her with professions of love, but he never mentioned her outfits or how she styled her hair. Now Clarke told her how nice she would look with the popular flapper hairstyle known as the "Eton crop." Flattered, Jessie wetted and trimmed her hair, then brilliantined it into the distinctive short bob. Clarke gazed approvingly at the result, producing in Jessie a surprising sense of gratification.

Though the moment was brief, it reminded Jessie how long it had been—Lancaster's attentions notwithstanding—since she'd felt physically appreciated. For years Lancaster had none-too-subtly steered away any men who exhibited potential interest in Jessie, operating in that regard as much as bodyguard as lover. "They used to call him my 'old man of the sea,'" she later recalled, in a reference to Samuel Taylor Coleridge's "The Rime of the Ancient Mariner." "I couldn't get rid of him." But despite his obsessive interest in her, Lancaster also seemed, in many regards, to take her for granted.

That night at the party Jessie and Clarke happily partook of the freely flowing alcohol. They stumbled home long after midnight and collapsed into their respective beds. But when Jessie opened her eyes the following morning, she found Clarke lying across the foot of her bed, asleep. Mortified, she tiptoed out of the room while he slept. When Clarke awoke, Jessie pretended that they'd agreed to change rooms for the night. Both of them were acutely embarrassed, if also secretly beguiled.

They received another party invitation that evening, which, still hungover, they willingly accepted. The night was lush and warm, with a bright moon in the sky. When Jessie and Clarke returned home, they plopped down on the lawn with some home-brew alcohol and drank in the verdant aroma of blooming fruit trees and vines. Clarke took the moment to finally mention his transgressive behavior the previous night. But rather than disavow it, he confessed to Jessie that he was fervently in love with her. Overwhelmed by the moment, they sought out each other's mouths and began passionately, if sloppily, kissing. A short time later they stumbled back inside the house, to the sun porch on the second floor, and made eager, drunken love.

All of Jessie's discontentment from the previous weeks—indeed, the previous several years—seemed to coalesce. Her yearning for passion and excitement, combined with her desire for the stability and safety of a proper relationship, seemed to find a valve in the way she and Clarke now physically exhausted themselves. And the attraction wasn't just sexual: Clarke was a highly intelligent and wide-ranging individual, who could talk as knowledgeably and ardently about poetry as he could about, say, politics or culture. Lancaster, by contrast, only ever spoke of aviation.

When they awoke the next morning, Clarke elatedly proposed marriage. Jessie had always been impulsive; it was one of the shared traits that had bound her and Lancaster together. Now, after last night's fervor, it wasn't difficult to persuade herself that she and Clarke should be together. Surely she loved him.

She accepted his proposal.

Jessie was acutely aware that Lancaster would be crushed, but she naively believed that, once he adjusted to the situation, their professional partnership would carry on as before. And she still loved him as a friend, and desired his presence in her life. But since Lancaster couldn't or wouldn't get a divorce, Jessie felt she had every right to seek out a proper marriage. A marriage that, among other things, was *public*. Clarke was radiant and adoring, and if he suffered from occasional mood swings, that only indicated his zeal. Jessie, in the throes of sudden love, thought he would make a wonderful husband.

But with Lancaster sending her daily proclamations of love, Jessie found herself in a bind. She knew the intense difficulties Lancaster was encountering on his journey, and the depth of his anxieties. She rationalized that she'd be doing Lancaster a kindness by waiting until he returned to Miami to break the news. But her letters also indicated a desire to postpone that occurrence for the longest possible time. After Lancaster informed her of the meeting in which Tancrel and Russell had proposed their illegal smuggling operation, Jessie's response was directly contradictory to her previous advice. Whether this was intentional or not, it was clearly slanted to her advantage:

> I can't understand what you mean by the whole thing being a wash-out. . . . Having spent so much time and money, not to mention hardships, it seems an awful pity to give up now. If you come back now I don't know what the hell we are going to do. I know you are worried about me, but there is no need to be.
>
> Haden has been a peach and the odd bucks that he earns criticizing manuscripts and playing bridge has kept the troops going. If you all come back broke I don't know how I'm going to feed you! Haden and I frequently make a meal out of half [the dog's] hamburger, but with you and Gent that wouldn't work so well. Also we are working very hard at the writing. . . . Haden simply can't work with you and Gent and . . . all the excitement that went on before. Of course I miss you like the very devil, but I do so want to get this book out and make enough money to buy a schooner, and then we'll all ride out the Depression in the South Sea islands. How does that appeal to you darling?
>
> If you could just make enough over there to keep yourself and stick it out until we get this book written I really think it would be better than us all being in a flat spin here. The season is almost over here and I'm certain you couldn't make enough for cigarettes. . . . The Robin isn't suitable for finding pupils, either—and where are you going to find the pupils?
>
> This house was a madhouse before and it was impossible to get anything done. You used to yank Haden downtown with you every day and he was just wasting his time. . . . Do weigh it up carefully, dear, and write me what you think. . . . Of course if you ever do have a buck or two weighing down your pockets I should be quite glad to keep them from pulling your suit out of shape!!

In Jessie's next letter she seemed her old caring self again, warning Lancaster, "Watch your step, my darling, as I'm certain you are dealing with a damn slippery lot. . . . I do want you to be on your guard." Her mixed messages accurately reflected the turmoil of her situation. But for Lancaster, they were a punishment that kept him wretchedly awake throughout the unforgiving hours of the night.

12

THE TORTURES OF THE DAMNED

On Sunday, April 3, the day after Russell showed Lancaster the letters hinting at Jessie and Clarke's affair, Lancaster paid a visit to the Los Angeles Metropolitan Airport in Van Nuys. A friend who worked there agreed to loan him the necessary fuel to fly back to Nogales. Russell had yet to deliver on his pledge to raise funds in the city; Lancaster was sorely tempted to abandon him and fly to Nogales alone.

That night his suffering reached new lows. From the Padre Hotel he phoned Jessie repeatedly but received no reply. "Why!!" Lancaster wrote in his diary. The torment was too intense for him to sleep. At 4 a.m. he jotted, "Ill with nervous worry." Desperate, he called Shelton for advice, but Shelton—who knew the truth about Jessie and Clarke—urged him not to do anything.

On Monday Russell and an acquaintance, who Lancaster thought resembled a "tramp," joined Lancaster at the airport in Van Nuys. He flew them up in the Robin for a tour of the city. "Russell says this man is putting $200 into Latin-American Airways," Lancaster wrote in his diary. "Poor fish!!!" Russell continued insinuating that Jessie was having an affair, but Lancaster, despite his hellish night, upheld her honor. "Russell finishes himself as far as I am concerned," he noted huffily, "because he talks about Chub in a nasty manner."

On their flight from Nogales to Los Angeles, Lancaster and Russell had been accompanied by a passenger named Mrs. Stewart, the wife of a mining engineer. Now Mrs. Stewart wanted to fly home. Lancaster, fed up with Russell's false promises in Los Angeles, pledged to leave the following day. Despite his dislike of Russell, Lancaster agreed to pick him up at Burbank Airport for the flight to Nogales.

The next morning, Lancaster and Mrs. Stewart drove to Metropolitan Airport to retrieve the Robin. But upon reaching the plane they were met by a federal agent who announced he was searching for Russell and Tancrel. The agent peppered Lancaster with queries about his recent travels before finally letting him go. Wary of becoming caught up in Russell's impending arrest, Lancaster told Mrs. Stewart they should avoid Burbank Airport and instead depart for Nogales immediately. Having abhorred Russell from the start, Mrs. Stewart was more than happy to leave him behind.

The pair flew six hours to Tucson, landing just before dark. They were picked up by Mrs. Stewart's husband, Charles, who drove the remaining sixty miles to Nogales while chatting amiably with Lancaster about gold mining. After checking in at the Casa Ana Maria, Lancaster set out into the night to find Shelton, whom he located, blind drunk, at a Mexican bar. Once Shelton heard the story of the federal agent in Los Angeles, he enthusiastically supported Lancaster's decision to cut all ties with Latin-American Airways.

The night before, Jessie had finally answered one of Lancaster's phone calls, right in the middle of a party. Caught off guard, she'd given the phone to Clarke. Surrounded by eavesdropping partygoers, Clarke had little choice but to reassure Lancaster that things were fine and the rumors were false. His soothing words failed to restore Lancaster's confidence. Now, back at his hotel, Lancaster opened two fresh letters from Jessie, which she had mailed the previous Tuesday. He found them difficult to analyze. "Much disturbed," he wrote in his diary, before repeating that he was "[i]ll with worry." The entry ended on a plaintive note: "Chubbie, darling, what is it all about?"

Lancaster and Shelton approached Tancrel the next morning and declared that they were through with Latin-American Airways. At first Tancrel wheedled and cajoled them, pleading for patience. When the two held firm, Tancrel furiously erupted, shouting insults and hinting ominously at violence. Following this "harrowing" (Lancaster's term) confrontation, Tancrel tried to take ownership of Jessie's propeller, but he had no money, and his efforts failed. After securing the propeller for themselves via a loan from Shelton's father, Lancaster and Shelton drove to Tucson, lifting each other's spirits by plotting their trip home to Miami. On the way they would visit Shelton's father in St. Louis to discuss purchasing an amphibian for their planned West Indies–based passenger transport company. Freed from the burden of Latin-American Airways, the pair reconnected as friends, and their drive to Tucson was a merry one, despite the morning's events.

In Tucson they picked up the Robin at the airport, but a bolt sheared as they steered it out of the hangar, and the right side of the landing gear collapsed. The propeller cracked in pieces; fortunately, they had Jessie's to replace it. But a great deal of additional damage remained, rendering Lancaster anxious about the delay and the steep cost of repairs. Shelton's father again proved their only hope for assistance.

That night Lancaster wrote to Jessie, "On our way back east, thank goodness. . . . Have been through hell, sweetie, but see daylight at last." He also included a warning: "Russell and Tancrel may try to be vindictive. Take no notice of anything until I get back." He was longing to see her and kiss her, he wrote, to take her on his knee and tell her everything. "Sweetheart, remember Port Darwin?" he pleaded. "We made it. Remember Andros? You made it. Well, I am going to make it this time. For us both, always."

That same night Shelton wired Jessie a blunter message: "Taking Bill to St. Louis. . . . Tell Haden keep both feet on ground. Bill trusts him, but Russell upset half the Lancaster-Miller organization by repeating scandal. Everything will be all right soon but remember Bill doing best possible for both."

Thanks to the skill of the Tucson mechanics, the Robin was fully repaired by Friday morning. But Lancaster and Shelton, to their great frustration, were stuck on the ground. Shelton's father had yet to wire money for the eighty-nine-dollar repair fee and the hotel bill. Forced to wait, they whiled away their days mooning about the city and seeing movies with their remaining pocket change. Shelton remained "sober and a peach," Lancaster noted in his diary. As Lancaster fretted and obsessed over Jessie, Shelton provided a genuinely sympathetic ear, proving himself to be "a true friend," Lancaster wrote. Yet Shelton also tried to steel Lancaster against the possibility that Russell's wife was correct.

On Saturday, Lancaster wired Jessie, but her noncommittal reply filled him with worry. "If only she would say something nice, such as: Don't worry, I still love you," he complained in his diary. Shelton's friendship continued to bolster him, leading to moments of decisiveness: "I have made a firm resolution to end all this mental strain—have it out! Then work for our common good. I adore her and want to see her happy." But then the doubts would creep back in: "If only she did not drink while I was away, I would feel okay. . . . Is Haden Clarke trustworthy, is my problem."

The next day, still trapped at the El Presidio hotel in Tucson, Lancaster's misery deepened. "Awakened with misgivings," he wrote. "Suffer the tortures of the damned." He had to get back to Miami. East, he bluntly wrote, "is where my life lies, everything I hold dear is there." For the first time, he mentioned suicide: "If [Chubbie is] gone from me I will end this life. I can't stand the strain much longer." But as he described them, Lancaster's emotions appeared more schizophrenic than suicidal; in the very same entry, he wrote, "I still have the courage to carry on. The uncertainty is hurting deep, though."

At Shelton's urging, Lancaster again called Jessie, but he found her answers to be evasive and unemotional. Jessie, for her part, felt the matter needed to be discussed in person, not on the phone, hence her ambiguous responses. She told Lancaster she had mailed a letter to St. Louis, in care of Shelton's father, explaining everything. "What is this letter in St. Louis?" Lancaster agonized in writing, regretting the phone call. "I don't know whether I can stand any more shocks." The year 1932, he wearily confessed, had been a disaster. "I love you, Chubbie—have done my best but failed."

The next day he wrote Jessie another letter in which he struck a more balanced tone. He admitted that the phone call had left him unhappy, and he protested that the "predicament in which I find myself now is not my fault. . . . You will remember Haden and you even urged me to commence that fatal Sunday when I left." Things were difficult in Tucson: without money, he and Shelton had been "going hungry." They hadn't eaten for forty-eight hours, and the already skinny Lancaster had lost another ten pounds. But Lancaster also said the journey might have a positive outcome if Shelton's father agreed to purchase an amphibian. In a moment of wishful thinking, he told Jessie that he knew she would never betray him. "Tell Haden I am not taking any notice of any scandal," he added. "I know in my heart he is a sahib." And, as always, there was the now-misplaced declaration of love: "You know, my sweet, the only thing in life that keeps me going is thoughts of you. I love you so sincerely that I will do anything I can to make you happy."

The days of endless waiting and the lack of food caused Lancaster and Shelton to get on one another's nerves, despite their close friendship. Shelton's promised funds had not arrived; not wanting to alienate his father before they discussed the amphibian, he had reached out to someone else, but this person hadn't come through. Frantic to return home, Lancaster wired his friend Dorothy Upton a request for $150, just enough money to cover the repair and hotel bills, and to buy enough fuel to fly the Robin to St. Louis, where Shelton's father awaited them. Upton, in a show of genuine friendship, immediately sent the requested money. After long days of frustration and hardship, Lancaster and Shelton were now free to leave.

"As long as I have you I can fight and will win through eventually," Lancaster wrote Jessie, in his final message from Tucson. "Courage will be required at this stage, more courage than I have ever been called upon to display—but am keeping the chin up. Hunger pangs are bad! . . . My sweet, when I see you I will tell you all that has happened."

13

A MAN OF MANY SECRETS

Haden Clarke was a man of many secrets, but none so potentially explosive as the one he admitted to Jessie after they had become physical: he had syphilis. In those pre-penicillin days, syphilis was a large-scale public health problem whose foul, painful symptoms and lack of effective treatment terrified the American public. Jessie was genuinely stunned by Clarke's admission, not to mention appalled. But Clarke was so obviously miserable, his hangdog expression so pathetic, that she couldn't help but feel sympathy.

Soon enough, Jessie's shock and disgust began to recede, to be replaced by the conviction that loving someone meant forgiving their past improprieties. It wasn't Clarke's fault, she reasoned, that he had been unlucky. In a firm but loving manner, she told him she stood by him completely, but that he had to quit alcohol while he sought medical attention. She would show her support by abstaining from alcohol herself. She insisted, however, that she and Clarke could not get married until the disease had been fully treated, and Clarke received a clean bill of health.

Clarke was grateful for Jessie's understanding, but the thought of delaying their wedding panicked him. He wanted to marry Jessie before Lancaster arrived in Miami to try to win her back. Clarke promised Jessie that his own divorce would be settled any day, and there was nothing to prevent them from marrying immediately. But Jessie held firm. Now that Lancaster had broken free from Tancrel and Russell, she needed to tell him the truth. She and Clarke would write detailed letters explaining their relationship and their recent engagement. The letters would be posted to Shelton's father's house in St. Louis.

When Lancaster and Shelton arrived in St. Louis, the letters Jessie and Clarke had composed were waiting. Lancaster was in a state of almost unbearable anxiety, whipsawing between hope and apprehension. But when he opened Jessie's letters, any hope that the rumors swirling around her and Clarke had been false were immediately extinguished. "The inconceivable has happened," Jessie wrote ruefully. "Haden and I have fallen in love." She and Clarke wanted to get married. "I know that your one thought has been for my happiness, and feel that you will take it in the right way," Jessie told Lancaster, with more confidence than she actually felt. But she didn't shy away from the hurt: "It's breaking my heart to tell you this, after all we've been through."

Clarke's lengthy letter, which he'd written one week earlier, was, like Jessie's, a mix of remorsefulness and resolve:

> You doubtless have read Chubbie's letter, so there is no necessity for my relating again what has transpired. I wish, however, to explain with absolute honesty my attitude toward the whole thing and I am hoping against hope that I may be able to justify my action in your mind and to regain, to some measure at least, the genuine friendship I am sure you felt for me. When you left you put a trust and confidence in me which I appreciated from the bottom of my heart. I considered your every interest my foremost duty, and my last thought was of anything that would harm or hurt you. . . .
>
> Please believe that no other power on earth could have moved me to fail you and that I would not have been swayed by this had I not been convinced beyond a shadow of a doubt that the thing was inevitable and unmistakably permanent.
>
> When this thing first dawned upon us a few days ago I weighed

it carefully from every angle. No matter how I looked at it, I could find no possible course but the one I have taken. I did my damndest to make friendship kill my love for Chubbie, but it was a losing fight from the very beginning.

No matter how I felt toward you this other thing was stronger.

We both tried to talk each other out of it, but we could convince neither each other nor ourselves. . . . I don't know what chance of happiness you and Chubbie had before this happened, but I am sufficiently sure of my ground to know with absolute finality that now it has happened neither Chubbie nor I can ever be other than miserable apart. I know it's going to be a hell of a blow to you, old boy, but I am faced with the obvious choice of hell for one of us and heaven for two of us. . . .

You have told me many times that your one aim was Chubbie's happiness. I don't know that my word means much to you now, but I give it that I will always do everything in my power to make her the happiest girl in the world. If I ever fail in this, I stand ready to answer to you for it. . . .

Nevertheless, your attitude is going to be a dominating factor in the happiness of both of us and I am extremely anxious to know what it is. I am far from hopeful in this direction, but please wire me immediately and write fully regardless.

Our reason for not writing this immediately was by no manner of means a desire on our part to deceive you. We talked it over repeatedly and inevitably concluded there was nothing to be gained by upsetting you while the Mexican project was hanging fire. The night you called us up from Hollywood I felt like a snake, but there was a room full of people playing bridge at my elbow and it was entirely out of the question to do anything but to deny everything in emphatic monosyllables.

. . . Needless to say, this has been entirely confidential. I have communicated with my wife and have made arrangements for an immediate divorce. Chubbie and I plan to marry as soon as it is granted. . . .

Please think it all over sanely, Bill, and try to see your way clear to help us get it over with as smoothly as possible. If do you lose your head, I'm afraid I can do nothing but meet you half way. It would break Chubbie's heart if either of us did anything violent, but the decision regarding this is entirely up to you.

Yours,

HADEN

The finality of Jessie and Clarke's vigorous declarations of love for each other, coupled with the heartsickening news that they were soon to be married, hit Lancaster with an almost physical force. He proceeded to, he wrote in his diary, "behave like a schoolboy," collapsing in sobs as he handed the letters over to Shelton. Shelton tried to bolster Lancaster's spirits, dragging him over to their friend F. Q. Watts's house to drown his sorrows in alcohol, but no amount of comforting could relieve the agonized Lancaster. "Drink pint of real scotch but it does not affect me," Lancaster wrote that evening, after phoning Jessie twice. *Do you want me to come back?* he had asked her. She assured him that she did.

Whatever agony Lancaster endured that evening he kept to himself. The following morning he wired Jessie and Clarke a telegram that betrayed no hint of his inner turmoil: "Am no dog in manger, but hold your horses kids until I arrive. Insist on being best man and being friend of you both for life. Happiness of you my happiness. Hope arrive tomorrow night or Wednesday latest. Love, Bill."

Was Lancaster being genuinely selfless despite the harsh personal toll, as it would seem from his frequent declarations that his life's priority was Jessie's well-being? Was he putting a brave face on the crushing misery he felt? Or was the message a feint, a calculated attempt to put Jessie and Clarke at ease while Lancaster plotted a darker turn of events? These were questions that would soon loom large—in the pages of America's newspapers, and in a Miami courtroom—over Lancaster's fate.

14

A TERRIBLE THING

Haden Clarke received no comfort from the letters he and Jessie wrote Lancaster. He lived in fear that Lancaster and Jessie's love would reassert itself upon Lancaster's return, and that he, Clarke, would be cast off. His self-doubt seemed to feed upon itself, resulting in increasingly frequent violent outbursts that alternated with periods of gloom and hopelessness. His spirits plunged even further when he received a telegram from his wife detailing the shocking news that their divorce, which he'd expected any day, had been delayed until 1933.

Meanwhile, in St. Louis, Shelton's father had agreed in principle to Lancaster and Shelton's plans to buy an amphibian, but he wanted to hold off on specifics until Lancaster's Miami affairs were in order. To that end, Shelton Sr. loaned Lancaster a hundred dollars for the flight back to Miami.

His homecoming imminent, Lancaster turned to his remaining errands in St. Louis. Having pawned Ernest Huston's gun in Tucson, he needed to buy a substitute weapon before returning to Florida. Searching the city, he found a .38 Colt revolver, for which he paid thirty dollars of Shelton's father's money. Lancaster spent his final day in St. Louis getting a license.

On April 19—the same day that Clarke received the surprise telegram from his wife—Lancaster flew from St. Louis to Nashville, where he woke at 4 a.m. the following morning. The skies were still dim as he departed for Atlanta, his last refueling stop before Miami. From Atlanta he wired Jessie to say that he would land in Miami by late afternoon.

Jessie and Clarke drove to Viking Airport, on the Venetian Causeway between Miami and Miami Beach, to pick Lancaster up. They arrived at 4:30 p.m., but the Robin had encountered strong headwinds, and Lancaster didn't touch down until almost 7. As he taxied to the hangar, Jessie and Clarke strode across the tarmac to greet him. The mood was tense all around, but with airport workers lurking in the background, a forced politeness was in order.

"Hello, darling, I've missed you," Lancaster greeted Jessie, as he stepped down from the cockpit. He turned briefly to Clarke and delivered a tight-lipped, "Hello, old man." As they headed to the car, Jessie thought Lancaster appeared weary, mournful, and ill.

The trio drove off in the Lincoln, stopping first to buy Clarke cigarettes. Lancaster handed him a five-dollar bill, telling him to keep the change. On Flagler Street they stopped at a market to buy cheap steak, again on Lancaster's dime, before heading to a Laundromat to gather Clarke's clothes. Clarke balked at the thought of Lancaster and Jessie enjoying even a moment of privacy in the car together. After talking it over, the three walked into the Laundromat as a group. Clarke pulled Jessie aside and said he was too embarrassed to let Lancaster pay for his wash, so Jessie handed him two dollars. "You pay for it; what's mine is yours," she told him. But in the meantime, Lancaster had paid the bill.

"I'm nearly dead for a drink," Lancaster announced after they had returned to the car. "Let's stop and get some." They headed for a nearby bootlegger's. But when Jessie and Clarke mentioned that they'd temporarily given up drinking, and explained the reason why, Lancaster changed his mind: "We won't bother then. I never drink alone."

As they approached Coral Gables, Lancaster finally broached the topic that was foremost in their minds. "Chubbie, are you sure you know your own mind?"

"Yes, Bill, I am," she replied, in a firm but gentle tone.

"Ever since I've known you my only desire has been your happiness."

Chubbie assured him that she knew.

Shifting his focus to Clarke, Lancaster asked, "Do you think you can make her happy?"

The reply was strident: "I'm damn sure I can."

"Why didn't you tell me all this before?"

"We didn't want to add to your troubles in Mexico," Clarke explained. "We thought you had enough to worry you already."

Seemingly reassured, Lancaster said that on their wedding day he would give them a check for a thousand dollars, though he didn't mention how he would raise the money. "I'm only going to ask one thing," he added. "To make absolutely sure that you're doing the right thing, I want you to agree not to get married for at least a month."

When they arrived back at the house, Lancaster grabbed the stack of mail that had accumulated for him during his absence, and then headed upstairs for a bath. Jessie and Clarke went into the kitchen to prepare the steak. The dinner itself passed uneventfully, with Lancaster relating tales of his adventures with Latin-American Airways, and Jessie and Clarke gossiping about the latest news in Coral Gables. At one point Lancaster raised the possibility of booking Jessie on a worldwide lecture tour, which would presumably generate attention for the book. No one mentioned the emotional discomfort that remained hidden beneath the surface cordiality.

They had finished their steaks and moved on to coffee and cigarettes when Lancaster returned to the real matter at hand. Giving Jessie and Clarke a mournful look, he turned in his chair, and asked, "Now, what's this really all about?"

Clarke was defensive: "Chubbie and I want to get married. It's as simple as that."

Lancaster's voice was more weary than accusatory as he responded, "Haden, old man, I trusted you and you did this to me. You haven't behaved like a gentleman."

Lancaster's composure did little to steady Clarke's sudden rage. He shoved his chair against the wall, rose to his feet, and bellowed, "I resent that!"

This was just the kind of moment Jessie had dreaded. "If you two are going to fight," she said, "I'm going to bed." Chastened, Clarke regained his self-control. Now that uneasy politeness had given way to true emotion, Chubbie felt the full burden of the situation. The three started to head into the living room when the high-strung Clarke experienced another abrupt mood shift, this time to regret. "I guess you're right, Bill," he admitted shamefacedly, acknowledging his betrayal.

Jessie went to the kitchen to wash dishes, where she was joined a minute later by an exhausted-looking Lancaster. "This is a mess, isn't it?" he asked, before uttering a humorless laugh. Jessie was so overcome with despair that she leaned her head on Lancaster's shoulder and began to sob. As Bill offered her a consoling hug, Clarke stormed into the room. His fury had returned.

"Leave her alone!" he shouted at Lancaster. "It's my right to comfort her now. I won't have you trying to break down my wagon!"

"I'll give you a year to make her happy," Lancaster replied, "and if you haven't, I swear I'll come back and take her away from you."

"Leave her alone!"

"She's always come to me in time of trouble," Lancaster said, but Clarke was not to be appeased.

"She'll come to me now," Clarke insisted, yanking Jessie to his side. "I won't have him talking to you alone," he petulantly told her. "Anything that's said must be said in front of all of us."

"I think it's only fair to let me talk to Bill alone," a still-crying Jessie said, but Clarke repeated that he wouldn't stand for it.

Lancaster tried to reason with him. "I've known Chubbie for five years. It's natural we should want to talk alone."

Again Clarke refused.

Jessie had heard enough. "Leave me alone, both of you," she said with disgust, and sent them out to buy more cigarettes. When they returned, Jessie was in her room. She took out a stack of newspaper clippings regarding Latin-American Airways and the three again discussed Lancaster's experiences with Tancrel and Russell. As they talked, Lancaster sorted through his unopened mail, which included several letters from the National Air Pilots Association insurance company. When Jessie told him that the company had gone bust just one day earlier, Lancaster looked stunned. Jessie was confused by his response, until a thought flashed through her mind: Had Lancaster taken out a thousand-dollar insurance policy? Was that where his promised wedding present would come from? She immediately asked if he was planning to commit suicide while flying so that she and Clarke would receive the money. Lancaster said no, but Jessie kept pushing, and he finally

Above: Bill Lancaster in the Royal Air Force
Below: Bill kissing Kiki goodbye just before he and Jessie depart on their record-setting adventure

Above: Jessie and Bill after landing on an unidentified Australian beach, 1928

Below: Bill and Jessie after arriving in Darwin, March 19, 1928

Above: Bill and Jessie greet an adoring crowd in Australia.
Below: The Powder Puff Derby participants at Parks Field, East St. Louis, August 24, 1929. Jessie is second from the left; Amelia Earhart is fourth from the right.

Above: Jessie in her stylish aviator outfit, 1930

Below: Jessie with her Fleet biplane during the Ford Reliability Tour, 1929

Haden Clarke

Above: A "Sensational Miami Love Triangle"

Below: A game-faced Bill shaking hands with Latin-American Airways' Mark Tancrel as Jack Russell beams his approval, 1933

Above: An unhappy Jessie on the witness stand, Miami, August 1932

Below: Vernon Hawthorne grilling Bill as Judge Atkinson looks on, August 1932

Above: The wreck of the *Southern Cross Minor,* February 1962

Below: A page from Bill's Sahara diary

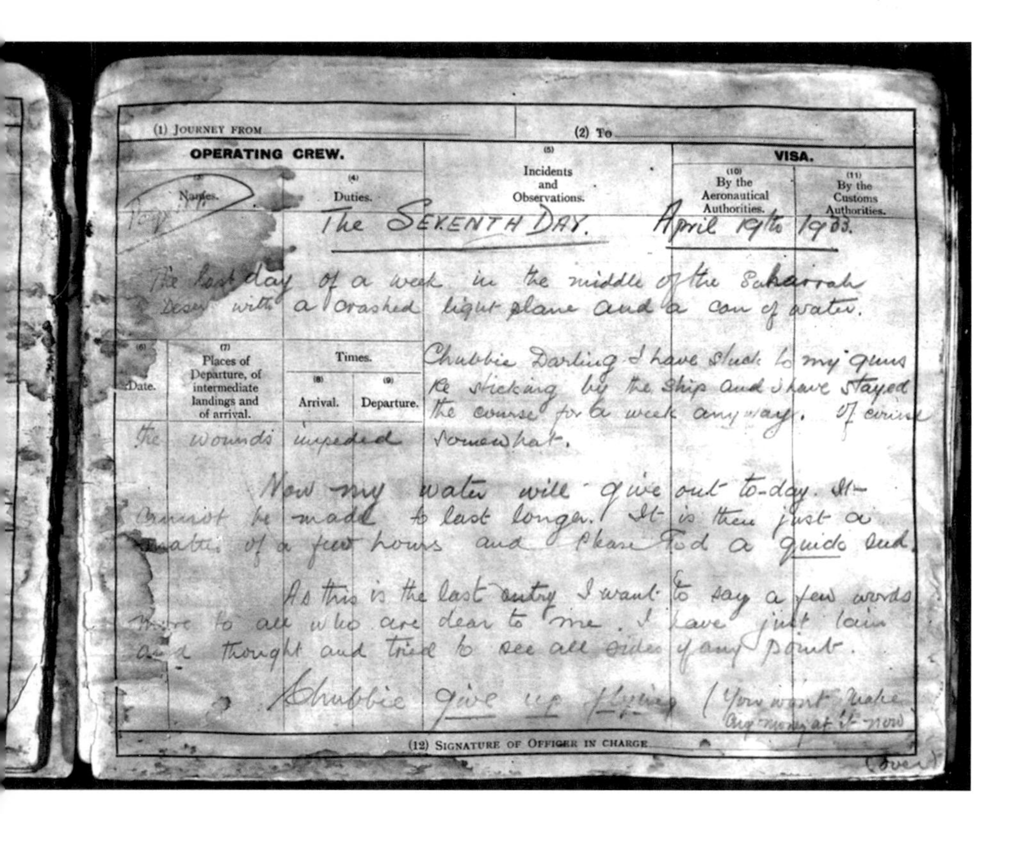

(1) Journey from (2) To

Operating Crew. — (2) Names. (4) Duties. — (5) Incidents and Observations. — Visa. (10) By the Aeronautical Authorities. (11) By the Customs Authorities.

The Seventh Day. April 19th 1933.

The last day of a week in the middle of the Saharrah Desert with a crashed light plane and a can of water.

(6) Date. (7) Places of Departure, of intermediate landings and of arrival. Times. (8) Arrival. (9) Departure.

Chubbie Darling I have stuck to my guns re sticking by the ship and I have stayed the course for a week anyway. Of course the wounds impeded somewhat.

Now my water will give out to-day. It cannot be made to last longer. It is then just a matter of a few hours and please God a quick end.

As this is the last entry I want to say a few words here to all who are dear to me. I have just lain and thought and tried to see all sides of any point.

Chubbie give up flying (You won't make any money at it now)

(12) Signature of Officer in Charge

(Over)

confessed. "No one would ever know," he told her. "If a ship spins, who is to know what happened?"

Eventually the conversation drifted back to Lancaster's trip out west. He described troubles he'd encountered on the various flights themselves, the poor weather conditions, how he had handled the Robin. Jessie, as a pilot, was engrossed by this information, which threw Clarke into another fit. He accused Lancaster of trying to win Jessie back through her interest in flying. "You can't blame me for trying to win her back any way I can," Lancaster replied. For the third time Jessie told them that if they continued to argue she would leave them to themselves.

The three went back down to the living room, where Lancaster plopped in a chair and Jessie and Clarke settled on the chaise longue. They talked about their precarious finances and of various ways they could make money in the future. Lancaster relayed Shelton's father's promise to buy them an amphibian. He also said he'd visit Ernest Huston in the morning to discuss the money Latin-American Airways owed him, though Jessie thought privately that Lancaster was pursuing a lost cause.

Clarke's temper continued to flare throughout their discussion, as he alternated between aggressiveness and surliness. Finally Jessie said that she and Clarke needed to talk alone. Lancaster whistled for the dog, headed out to the car, and went for a late-night drive around the neighborhood. "He'll try to get you back," Clarke complained to Jessie. "I know what he's up to." Clarke said he would never feel secure until he and Jessie were married. "I talked to Huston about it," he told her, "and he said we could probably get married legally here now, provided we stay out of California." In every other state they would be considered legally married. But Jessie was having none of it. Lancaster returned to the house after driving around for thirty minutes. When he walked into the living room he told Jessie and Clarke that he was leaving at once.

"Leave where?" Jessie asked, surprised.

"Back to St. Louis, where I can make some money and send it to you kids," Lancaster answered.

Jessie protested that he couldn't leave the house in the middle of the night, so Lancaster agreed that he would sleep there, and depart for St. Louis first thing in the morning. Pleading exhaustion, he then took his stack of letters and headed up to the sun porch.

Jessie and Clarke continued lying on the couch, awash in misery. The situation was far worse than either had imagined. Jessie, for her part, felt nearly suicidal with despair. "I wish we could end it all," she told Clarke. He said he felt the same way. They discussed Clarke's physical desire for her, and his dismay at not being able to have sex until his syphilis was cured. "I can't stand it any longer, I'm going nuts," he complained. A few minutes later he announced that he was going to bed.

"I want you to promise me to lock your door," he told Jessie, but she said she preferred to keep her door open for fresh air. Clarke protested: "I don't want that son of a bitch coming in to try to talk you out of our marriage." Jessie gave in.

After turning off the downstairs lights, Jessie headed up to her room, which was eighteen feet from the sun porch where Lancaster and Clarke slept. She saw them sitting on their respective beds, Lancaster still sorting through his mail. She walked into their room to set the alarm clock. "Yes, I want to get up early tomorrow," Lancaster said. "I've got lots of things to do." As Jessie left the room she said, "Good night, chaps," but Lancaster didn't respond, so she tried again. "Good night, Bill," she said with a little smile. This time Lancaster looked up and said, "Good night." Clarke shot her a disapproving look.

According to Lancaster, after Jessie left, he and Clarke began to talk. In Lancaster's telling, Clarke was suffering from syphilis-related pains, and he told Lancaster not to worry if he heard him pacing during the night: it was due to the pain, not because he was going to Jessie's room. He was almost in tears as he described to Lancaster his symptoms. Clarke also tried to justify his actions with Jessie. He'd had many affairs, he told Lancaster, but this was true love, and he was going to put all his efforts into making Jessie happy. He then showed Lancaster the letter his wife had sent from Los Angeles. It would cost him fifty dollars to obtain a divorce in Miami, Clarke complained.

Clarke also said his mother was having a difficult time because the University of Miami was withholding her salary, prompting Lancaster to remark that it would have been better for everyone if Mrs. Clarke had indeed moved into 2321 S.W. 21st Terrace. Clarke admitted further that he was concerned about finishing the book with Jessie. "I'm worried I won't make the grade," he said.

Finally Clarke moved on to some deeper confessions. He sheepishly admitted that he wasn't thirty-one, as he had pretended to be; he was only twenty-six. Nor had he graduated from Columbia University or worked extensively in journalism. "Do you think it will make any difference with Chubbie?" he anxiously asked Lancaster, who responded that Clarke should tell her the truth first thing in the morning.

Lancaster tried to lighten the mood by telling amusing stories about Latin-American Airways. Clarke reclined on his bed with his hands behind his head, laughing at the tale of Tancrel and the Wallpaper Hangers' Union. Shortly before turning off the light, Clarke said, "Bill, you are the whitest man I've ever met."

Jessie could hear Lancaster and Clarke laughing as she lay in bed reading. After leaving their room, she had changed into pajamas, washed her face, brushed her teeth, and wound her alarm clock. The time was 12:45 a.m. She locked her door, placed a pack of cigarettes on her nightstand, and got into bed, where she stayed up for nearly an hour reading a detective story about a man being pushed off the roof of a building. When she finished the story, Jessie turned off her light and went to sleep.

The next thing she knew Lancaster was banging furiously on her door, shouting for her to wake up. Groggily, Jessie rose to her feet and unlocked her door. Lancaster was standing in the hallway with a panicked look in his eyes.

"A terrible thing has happened," he said. "Haden has shot himself."

15

FORGERIES

That's ridiculous," Jessie said. "There's no gun in the house."

"Yes, there is," Lancaster told her. "I brought one back for Huston."

Jessie hustled to the sun porch, where Clarke lay convulsing on the bed, a gaping bullet wound in his right temple. Gurgling moans escaped his throat; blood coated his face and matted his hair. The full moon outside shone its radiant light through the porch screen, highlighting the creeping death-pallor of Clarke's skin. "Speak to me," Jessie urged; when Clarke didn't respond, she ran into the bathroom and grabbed a washcloth. She sat on the bed and began wiping the blood from Haden's face. "Call the doctor," she ordered Lancaster, who ran downstairs to the phone. She grabbed a bowl in which to rinse the washcloth, then continued bathing Clarke's face. Even as she washed him, gently lifting his head with her hand, blood continued to pour from his wound.

Downstairs, Lancaster banged the telephone receiver several times before remembering it was a dial phone. When he finally connected with the operator, he told her to send a doctor to 2321 S.W. 21st Terrace in Coral Gables. Returning upstairs to the sun porch, he went over to Clarke's bed, saying, "Haden, old man, speak to me." But Clarke only continued his guttural groaning, his body jerking and twitching. Lancaster went over to Haden's desk, where the typewriter was located.

"Look," Lancaster said, "Haden left these notes." He passed them over to Jessie. The first note read, "Bill, I can't make the grade. Tell Chubbie of our talk. My advice is, never leave her again." The second note read, "Chubbie, the economic situation is such I can't go through with it. Comfort mother in her sorrow. You have Bill. He is the whitest man I know." The messages were typed, with the two signatures—one reading "Haden" and the other just "H"—scrawled in pencil.

"We'd better destroy them," Lancaster urged, but Jessie disagreed. Lancaster protested: "There'll be a scandal if that note to you is made public." The notes gave all the evidence of a love triangle. But Jessie wanted to hold on to them; to do otherwise would be to invite suspicion.

The notes were only a brief distraction. Jessie's focus was getting medical attention for Clarke. The name of Clarke's personal doctor escaped her, so she decided to call Ernest Huston. As a prominent lawyer, he would know the town's finest physicians. Huston said he would call for help immediately and then meet them at the house.

Not long afterward the name of Clarke's doctor, Carleton Deederer, popped into Jessie's head. She rang him at once. "Haden has shot himself," she said. "He's bleeding terribly. Please come at once."

By now it was nearly 3 a.m. As Jessie hung up the phone, the front doorbell rang. When Lancaster opened the door, an ambulance driver named Ditsler from the W. I. Philbrick Funeral Home stepped in. Lancaster led Ditsler to the sun porch, where the driver looked over Clarke's wound. Because Clarke's feet kept striking the iron end rail of the bed, Lancaster grabbed a pillow from his own bed to place against the rail. But as he lifted Clarke's feet onto the pillow, Ditsler warned him that doing so would increase the flow of blood to Clarke's head.

"Do you think he'll talk again?" Lancaster anxiously asked. Ditsler said it was unlikely.

Jessie urged the driver not to move Clarke until the doctor arrived—it might exacerbate his injuries. Ditsler agreed, but as time ticked by with still no sign of a physician, he decided to check in with his office. Jessie asked him to also call the police, but he said the office had already done so.

When Ernest Huston arrived at 3:15 a.m., he found Jessie and Ditsler in the living room. Lancaster showed him Clarke's suicide notes. Should he destroy them? Lancaster asked. "No," Huston responded firmly. "They're important." Jessie was growing more sensitive to the scandal the notes might provoke, so she slipped the one addressed to her into the telephone desk drawer. She asked Huston and Ditsler not to mention it.

As the group waited still longer for a doctor to arrive, Lancaster said, "I wish that Haden would talk, so he could tell us why he did it." Frustrated and exhausted, Jessie called Dr. Deederer's house to ask when he'd left. Much to her surprise, Deederer himself picked up the phone. He had gotten lost on the way to S.W. 21st Terrace, he said, and driven back home to consult a map. He would be leaving in a minute.

In the hour since Lancaster had phoned for a doctor, Clarke had received no treatment, other than Jessie wiping the blood from his face. Finally the assistant manager from the Philbrick Funeral Home arrived and granted Ditsler permission to transport Clarke's body. Lancaster, mistaking the assistant manager for a doctor, agreed.

With difficulty, Ditsler and the assistant manager carried Clarke's body down the stairs. Jessie protested that a doctor was on his way, but to no avail. The assistant manager insisted on taking Clarke to Jackson Memorial Hospital. As the ambulance drove away, Dr. Deederer pulled up to the curb. He would take Lancaster and Jessie to the hospital, while Huston remained at the house. Shortly before leaving, Lancaster took Huston aside. "If it should be necessary, will you [represent] us?" he asked. Huston said yes.

Dr. Deederer had difficulty locating the hospital, and was forced to ask directions from the few pedestrians on the street. The car's progress was slow. Once at the hospital, Deederer was unable to treat Clarke because the attendants didn't believe he was a physician. When Jessie and Lancaster finally arrived at Clarke's room, they found a doctor, a nurse, and two policemen. As it happened, one of the policemen, Earl Hudson, was married to the sister of Clarke's old girlfriend Peggy Brown. "I know all about you and Jessie, [Clarke] told me," Hudson declared. Lancaster and Jessie were equally familiar with Hudson.

Hudson brought Lancaster and Jessie out to his police car for the drive back to Coral Gables. As they cruised through the darkened streets, Lancaster asked Hudson more than once if he thought Clarke would be able to talk and "tell why he did it." When they arrived at the house, Hudson and another police officer, Fitzhugh Lee, went straight to the sun porch. The gun lay in the center of the bed. Noting the blood-soaked sheets, Hudson picked up the gun and announced to Lee, "One thirty-two pistol." He wrapped the gun in his handkerchief and slipped it into his hip pocket.

Lancaster corrected him: "It's a thirty-eight Colt."

"No, it's a thirty-two," Hudson argued.

Lancaster picked up the gun's box and showed him the caliber on the label. Hudson, Lee, and Lancaster then gathered up the bedcovers, trying to locate the discharged bullet, but they came up empty. (The bullet was found the following morning lodged in Clarke's pillow.)

Following this unimpressive performance, Hudson inquired after Clarke's suicide notes, of which Ditsler, ignoring Jessie's plea, had informed him. Because Jessie wanted to keep Clarke's note to her a secret, she handed Hudson only the one addressed to Lancaster. But Hudson wasn't so easily put off. "There were two notes, weren't there?" he asked. "Where's the other one?" Jessie said the other note was personal, but Hudson wouldn't be dissuaded. Reluctantly, Jessie retrieved the note from downstairs. Having examined the scene, and still operating under the assumption that Clarke pulled the trigger, Hudson and Lee drove off.

After the officers left, Ernest Huston asked Lancaster whether the pistol Clarke had used belonged to him. Lancaster told Huston about pawning the original gun in Tucson and buying a replacement in St. Louis. "Technically it belongs to you," Lancaster argued. "Is it all right if I say it's yours?" Huston said no.

"Can I say it's the property of Latin-American Airways?"

Again Huston refused. He was no longer affiliated with Tancrel and Russell, whom he now knew to be criminals, and he was wary of being associated, however tangentially, with Clarke's shooting. The situation was far too messy for his liking.

Huston offered to drive Lancaster and Jessie back to the hospital. On the way they stopped at the Everglades Hotel to inform Clarke's mother of the tragic news, but they arrived too late—Dr. Deederer was already telling her the story. As Deederer described Clarke's wounds, Clarke's traumatized mother cut him off. Was there any chance her son would live? Dr. Deederer, answering honestly, said no. Hearing this, Mrs. Clarke opted to remain in her room rather than go to the hospital.

At Jackson Memorial Hospital, Clarke remained breathing, but he was still unconscious. No sooner had Lancaster and Jessie arrived than they were met by two detectives. "We'd like to question you at the courthouse," the detectives said. Lancaster and Jessie were driven to the immense Dade County Courthouse, placed in separate mouse-and-cockroach-infested jail cells on the nineteenth floor, and forbidden to talk. Jessie slowly realized, to her immense shock, that she and Lancaster were suspected of nefarious activities. As the hours crawled by, she was gripped by "desperate thoughts," she later recounted. "I realized that I was a woman, alone, ten thousand miles from my own country."

Having taken Lancaster and Jessie's keys to the Coral Gables house and the Robin, the detectives headed off to search the premises. At the house they gathered up Lancaster's diaries and letters, along with samples of Clarke's typing to which they could compare the two suicide notes. They collected, too, Lancaster's typewritten manuscripts of stories for aviation magazines. As they pored over the materials, they noted inconsistencies between Clarke's usual typing and that of the suicide notes. There were decidedly more parallels, the investigators realized, between Lancaster's typing and the typing on the notes.

As the detectives conducted their search, Lancaster and Jessie languished in their jail cells. Finally they were taken, in turn, to the office of their inquisitor, State Attorney N. Vernon Hawthorne, who two years earlier had made a name for himself by leading the unsuccessful fight to kick Al Capone out of Miami. The forty-two-year-old Hawthorne was a Florida native with a richly dramatic voice and an elegant manner that belied the fierce determination with which he tried his cases. Small but sturdy, his thinning hair still dark, Hawthorne had been state attorney since 1927.

When Jessie entered Hawthorne's office she found a group of five attorneys who deluged her, albeit politely, with questions about the previous night's events. Hawthorne, leading the charge, took her step-by-step through the hours from Lancaster's return to the time she went to bed. When she had finished, Hawthorne made her start from the beginning and repeat the sequence multiple times. The exhausted Jessie found the experience somewhat bewildering, though Hawthorne's manner was gentle and supportive. When Lancaster entered the office he experienced much the same treatment, with Hawthorne focusing most of his attention on the suicide notes. When they returned to their cells, they were provided with foul, inedible food and coppery water.

Around 11 a.m. Hawthorne informed Lancaster and Jessie of some troubling news: Clarke had just died in the hospital. The *Miami Daily News* headline broadcast the disturbing turn of events: "Famous Aviators Held as Bullet Ends Life of Young Miami Writer." Ernest Huston now wanted to meet with Lancaster, prompting Lancaster to ask Hawthorne if such a meeting was necessary. Hawthorne replied that Lancaster was free to do as he wished. "Isn't it your job to protect the innocent as well as prosecute the guilty?" Lancaster queried. When Hawthorne said yes, Lancaster replied that he was content to leave the investigation in Hawthorne's hands. He asked only that Clarke's syphilis be kept secret, claiming that he wanted to protect Ida Clarke's feelings and prevent her son's good name from being sullied. Hawthorne agreed.

In the afternoon Hawthorne issued a press release detailing the essentials of the case. He told reporters that Lancaster "said he was asleep and was awakened by the shot, yet his pillow showed no signs of being slept on." Lancaster explained that the ambulance driver, Ditsler, had placed his pillow under Clarke's head and then replaced it on the bed, but Ditsler denied this. Arousing further suspicion, Hawthorne noted that Dr. Deederer had found no powder burns around the bullet wound in Clarke's temple, insinuating that the gun had not been pressed against Clarke's head—and that, by extension, he hadn't pulled the trigger himself. But Dr. Deederer *had* found bruising on Clarke's head and right shoulder, suggesting a possible tussle before the shooting. Hawthorne's implication—that Lancaster had killed Clarke—was unmistakable. The state attorney admitted, however, that Lancaster "gave the impression of telling a straightforward story," according to *The New York Times*. Hawthorne also expressed his belief that Jessie didn't know how Clarke was shot.

The Miami Herald reported that the "courage which enabled [Jessie] to become a widely known aviator" was making itself manifest in her approach to these traumatic events. Though her face was "chalk-white" and her eyes "showed intense weariness," the paper wrote admiringly that "she held her head up . . . with the unconcern of a tragedy queen" as she entered the state attorney's offices on the day of Clarke's shooting, and that her demeanor in the Dade County Courthouse had appeared "as casual and nonchalant as that of any visitor." Tabloid-like, the paper noted that Jessie's "hair was slicked down and held in place by bobby-pins" and that she sported "a light tan coat, belted in the military fashion." Still, the *Herald* opined, Jessie's appearance was "in striking contrast to the carefree and debonair air she wore" back when she'd competed in the Miami air meet. In those innocent days she'd been "animation itself and was usually seen with a cigaret in her hand, gesticulating as she talked in the voice so unmistakably Australian in accent."

That evening, less than twenty-four hours after Clarke's shooting, Chubbie was released from her jail cell to attend Clarke's funeral, after which she immediately returned to the courthouse. Clarke's body was buried, without autopsy, the following morning, April 22. The newspapers all referred to Jessie as Clarke's "fiancée" and Lancaster's "flying partner," hinting at the love triangle that had preceded Clarke's death.

That same day the *Miami Daily News* reported that Clarke had contacted the paper one week earlier regarding a story published in the *Herald* about "sinister Chinamen, hidden gold, fortune tellers and smuggling planes," though no names had been mentioned. Clarke had asked if the *Daily News* would be publishing anything about the affair. When he learned that reporters were indeed investigating the story, Clarke offered up his and Lancaster's version of events, including the crucial fact that Lancaster had abandoned the project as soon as he'd learned about the smuggling operation. Clarke told the *Daily News* that he was "interested in protecting Lancaster . . . as he was convinced Lancaster had been misled by the men promoting the plane syndicate."

Now, on April 23, Hawthorne informed Jessie that his office had sifted through all the materials collected from the house and the Robin and found nothing incriminating. On the contrary: "It has been my privilege to see into the depths of a man's soul through his private diary," Hawthorne announced, "which was never intended for anyone's eyes but his own, and in all my experience—which has been broad—I have never met a more honorable man than Captain Lancaster." When asked whether the Clarke shooting would now be taken before a grand jury, Hawthorne replied, "I see no reason why the grand jury should be interested." Lancaster and Jessie were to be released immediately, after more than fifty-seven hours in custody.

While Jessie was still in Hawthorne's office she met an attorney named James "Happy" Lathero, who had been dispatched by Ida Clarke. The dark-haired, broad-shouldered Lathero, whose toothbrush mustache and trimmed black eyebrows gave him a passing resemblance to Charlie Chaplin, told Jessie that Lancaster would not be leaving the courthouse after all: Hawthorne had notified the Treasury Department about the Latin-American Airways drug-smuggling conspiracy, and Lancaster was about to be rearrested. Federal agents were hunting for Tancrel and Russell, as well.

Following this harrowing development, Lathero drove Jessie to Ida Clarke's apartment at the Everglades Hotel That night, however, the Treasury agents released Lancaster, stating they were "contented Lancaster was not part of an alleged conspiracy to smuggle drugs into the United States." After exiting the courthouse, Lancaster joined Jessie at the Everglades Hotel. The moment was fraught: Lancaster had not seen Ida Clarke since her son's death, and one day earlier Ida had announced to the press that she no longer accepted "without reservation" the theory that her son had committed suicide.

Clarke's mother had laid out several reasons for her change of heart. First, she declared, her son had possessed since boyhood "an aversion to and a fear of firearms that amounted to a complex." She and her son had recently visited family friends who possessed a vast collection of antique and modern firearms, and Clarke had refused to even touch the weapons. Dr. Deederer's findings regarding powder burns and bruising had further aroused her suspicions. Ida Clarke reported, too, that after Lancaster phoned Clarke from El Paso to say he was trying to pawn his pistol for food money, Clarke had told her, "I hope he does. I hope he doesn't bring the damn thing back here." She told the *Daily News* that she'd always been "psychic," and that a few moments after Clarke and Jessie had left her apartment on the afternoon preceding the shooting she'd had a premonition of disaster. Unsettled, she'd canceled a planned tutoring appointment and spent the evening discussing her fears with a friend. When the friend left at 1:30 a.m., Ida had lain on her couch waiting for news of the disaster she instinctively knew was going to come. Still, she said, she was making "no accusations against anyone."

Now, as Lancaster, trailed by reporters, entered Ida Clarke's apartment following his release by Treasury agents, he laid his hands on her shoulders and told her solemnly, "I swear to you that I had nothing to do with Haden's death." In front of the eager gathering of journalists, Mrs. Clarke chose to accept his statement, at least for the moment.

When Lancaster and Jessie finally returned to their house in Coral Gables, they found, to their dismay, that the Miami detectives had left chaos in their wake. Papers were strewn everywhere, as if a twister had descended inside their home. They set about cleaning up, but their mood remained grim. Hawthorne's release of Lancaster had been met with immediate public outrage, even though the State Attorney's Office had reached the maximum three days in which it could hold someone without specific charges. But Hawthorne had employed J. V. Haring, one of the world's foremost experts on forged documents, to investigate the suicide notes, and while Hawthorne continued to state his belief in Jessie's innocence, he now referred to Clarke's shooting as "murder or suicide, whichever it may turn out to be." The finger was clearly pointing at Lancaster.

Now, as he and Jessie reordered their house, the late afternoon sunlight still streaming in through the windows, Lancaster shamefacedly admitted his secret: he had forged the suicide notes. He told Jessie that, in the panic of the moment, he had been so terrified that she would think he'd shot Clarke that he had written the notes to convince her otherwise. He hadn't intended for anyone else to see them, he pleaded, which is why he had asked her to tear them up.

Immediately Jessie urged him to confess to Hawthorne. But when the two of them discussed the matter with Happy Lathero, the lawyer advised otherwise. "Say nothing whatever about it for the minute, certainly not before the inquest," he warned. "Otherwise Hawthorne will be bound to hold you." Lancaster and Jessie were taken aback, but they briefly followed his counsel. Their silence didn't last long, however, with Jessie remaining insistent that Lancaster unburden himself to the state attorney. Soon the two of them went to Hawthorne's office to acknowledge the truth.

"When I was awakened by the shooting, my first thought was to protect myself and Chubbie," Lancaster confessed to Hawthorne. "So I wrote the notes and then tried to revive Clarke to get him to sign them. When it was clear that he couldn't, I signed them myself."

In his official statement at Hawthorne's office, Lancaster took care to point out that his forging of the notes was an isolated event: "The incidents connected with the writing of the two notes are the only incidents which I feel were unworthy, foolish, and cowardly of any part I may have played in the investigation," he declared. "The fact weighed heavily on my mind from the start." He attempted to absolve himself by explaining that he had told Lathero, his lawyer, the true story, but Lathero had advised him to keep the matter to himself. In Lancaster's telling, he'd explicitly informed Lathero that he would "not leave Miami without telling Mr. Hawthorne the entire truth." Lathero, he claimed, would verify this.

Lancaster outlined for Hawthorne what exactly had occurred on the night of Clarke's shooting. "When I switched on the light and found Haden Clarke had shot himself, I suppose I was a little panicky," he said. "I had been awakened out of a deep sleep and may have been befuddled. I spoke to Haden, I shook him, and the only noise that came from him was a sort of gurgling noise. His body was twitching violently and his legs moved. When the full seriousness of the situation sank in, my first thought was: Chubbie will think I am responsible. I did not know how seriously Haden was injured. I thought he might be dying. I sat down at the typewriter and typed the two notes. I typed them as I honestly thought Haden would type such notes. I used expressions he had used to me that night in a talk we had earlier in the evening. I picked up a pencil which was by the side of the typewriter, and I went back to the bed where Haden Clarke was lying. I spoke to him. I begged him to sign the two notes I had written."

Lancaster claimed he shouted for Jessie but received no reply. "The doors of the sun porch were open. Her door was shut. . . . Uppermost in my mind was the thought of what Chubbie would think. At that time it never occurred to me what other people would think. I then took the pencil and scribbled 'Haden' on one note and the letter 'H' on the other."

Once Lancaster had woken Jessie and rang for a doctor, he realized that the notes "would weigh heavily against me were I suspected," he said. "I can only say I wrote them in the first place with honesty of purpose, as, had Clarke recovered sufficiently to sign them, it would have had the effect of setting Chubbie's mind at ease concerning the wound." The notes had been intended for Jessie's eyes only, Lancaster professed, but through "events over which I had no control, the contents of those notes became common property."

Lancaster proclaimed himself "pleased" to "have been able to make this statement, as it is the only thing I have done that is not strictly honorable in connection with the death of Haden Clarke. I did not kill him. In no way have I willingly been a reason for his death." In a bit of possibly wishful thinking, Lancaster said he trusted that his statement would convince the State Attorney's Office of his innocence.

But an undeterred Hawthorne pressed on after Lancaster finished speaking, inquiring in detail about the potentially incriminating elements surrounding the affair, including the gun Lancaster had purchased in St. Louis and his bald awareness that Clarke had betrayed his trust. Lancaster ardently denied that he'd possessed "malice in his heart" toward Clarke, declaring, "If I had come to Miami and found that Haden Clarke had behaved toward Chubbie in a manner that was dastardly, I would have borne malice, but when I arrived at Miami . . . I found nothing to indicate this."

Hawthorne acted as if he believed Lancaster's account, but this was likely just for show. Appearing almost regretful, Hawthorne informed Lancaster that, given the circumstances, he was charging him with murder.

The State Attorney's Office immediately made public the fact that Lancaster had admitted to forging the suicide notes. Hawthorne's statement noted: "We took every precaution to make certain [the notes were forged] before charging Captain Lancaster with the murder of Haden Clarke, for the evidence was at first entirely circumstantial." Hawthorne's office, the statement went on, had initially developed five potential theories: that Clarke committed suicide; that he was murdered by Lancaster; that he was murdered by Jessie; that he was murdered by Lancaster and Jessie together; that he was murdered by someone else. Given the lack of incriminating evidence, Hawthorne said, he had employed the world-renowned handwriting expert J. V. Haring, who had determined that the notes were "palpable forgeries." This was when Lancaster had admitted his wrongdoing.

Lancaster followed up with his own statement: "It comes as a great shock to me the fact that a technical charge of murder has been made against me. I am absolutely innocent, and I know that the outcomes will prove this. I have been treated with utmost fairness by State's Attorney Hawthorne, but there is a certain amount of circumstantial evidence against me. At the right and proper time an explanation will be made. . . ."

Late that afternoon, Jessie emerged from the Dade County Courthouse following her own hours-long interrogation. She was just walking down the steps when she heard street hawkers bellowing the news of Lancaster's arrest for murder. That night she released a statement: "I am absolutely confident everything will come out all right. I know the truth will be learnt and Captain Lancaster will be cleared. He is innocent and I know it. My faith in him remains unshaken. It has never wavered in the past, or now, and it never will."

In a metaphorical sense, Jessie and Lancaster were back in the *Red Rose* on their scrappy journey from England to Australia five years earlier, when it was the two of them against the world, and the only thing that mattered was their survival. Regardless of the intervening years, the intensely unique bond that they had forged during those earlier brushes with mortality had now powerfully reasserted itself, and even Jessie's shock over Clarke's death was, it appeared, subsumed by her instinctive desire to protect Lancaster at any cost.

16

THE SCARLET WOMAN

Jessie may have insisted on Lancaster's innocence, but the details released by Hawthorne's office painted a convincing portrait of Lancaster's seeming guilt. The forging of Clarke's suicide notes was the obvious clincher, but the bruising on Clarke's body and the account of Lancaster's untouched pillow proved damning, too. (These latter points were later revealed to be inaccurate.) But if the public judged Lancaster a guilty man, many also felt that his actions were perfectly justified, given how fully Clarke had betrayed him.

Speaking with reporters from his jail cell, Lancaster cast aside any notion that he might plead guilty, insisting: "I know I can convince twelve reasonable men, if I am indicted, that I am innocent of the boy's death." He cabled his father in England for money to aid his defense.

For Happy Lathero, Lancaster's lawyer, proving Lancaster's innocence required building a convincing portrait of Clarke as suicidal. Why, a grand jury would ask, would a talented young man like Clarke want to take his own life? After close consultation with Jessie, Lathero wrote up a list of reasons why Clarke might have committed suicide. Lathero's list, which Jessie signed as if she had written it herself, looked like this:

Reasons why Haden Clarke killed himself

1. Remorse at the situation he had created, after his promise to Bill Lancaster.
2. Doubt of himself and me. Fear that the past five years would prove too strong a bond and I would return to Bill.
3. Financial worries.
4. Doubt of his ability to write the book and make money with his writing. He talked constantly of this; his writings were all returned.
5. Intense sexual life over many years, suddenly discontinuing.
6. The fact that he was very young and I had placed too much burden and responsibility on him.
7. Physical condition.
8. The fact that he was very temperamental and emotional; that he rose to the heights of joy, and sank to the depths of despair.

Jessie hand-delivered the list to the State Attorney's Office in the hopes that it would influence the Dade County Grand Jury, which was meeting the following week, to refuse Lancaster's indictment. Neither Jessie nor Hawthorne released the document to the press because they were still hiding from Clarke's mother the fact of her son's syphilis.

But with all evidence pointing to Lancaster, Ida Clarke announced on May 7 that she was requesting an autopsy for her son, especially because Dr. Deederer's report of bruising on Clarke's head led her to believe that he had been beaten before he'd been shot. She also claimed that she was "perfectly attuned" with the "after-life personality" of her son, and while she had "no particular reason for expecting a spirit message" from him, she would "not be surprised at a communication of that sort." Clarke himself had been a "student, not a disciple," of spiritualism, she said, and he'd believed even more strongly than she did "that spiritual communications are possible between strong personalities who are mental affinities." They had both "believed in a life after death."

Two days later, on May 9, the grand jury handed down a first-degree murder indictment for Lancaster, meaning that he would have to stand trial. If convicted, he would be sentenced to die by the electric chair. But Lancaster's cause hadn't been wholly abandoned. The *Miami Daily News* reported that Jessie was preparing to repay the "debt of gratitude" she'd incurred when Lancaster had supported her after her forced landing on Andros Island, back when she'd made her disastrous attempt to fly from Havana to Miami. "Now the little Australian aviatrix finds her partner in trouble," the *News* wrote, with more than a hint of sexism, and so she was "scurrying here and there" searching out "money, legal advice, and friends on which to lean."

Happy Lathero told Jessie that the best man to defend Lancaster was James M. Carson, one of Miami's finest and most-respected attorneys. When Jessie entered Carson's office the following day, she was greeted by a looming figure with graying black hair, bushy eyebrows, thick lips, a fleshy neck, and an enormous head. She found him, at first glance, faintly terrifying. The forty-five-year-old Carson was a native of Kissimmee in central Florida, and he possessed two decades of legal experience. In addition to his practice, he was a professor of law at the University of Miami. The accomplished Carson had never lost a criminal case, and he didn't intend to now. When Jessie asked if he would represent Lancaster, Carson peered at her through his tortoiseshell-rimmed glasses and instantly averred: "I wouldn't touch it. He's guilty as hell."

"You're wrong there," Jessie insisted, with characteristic determination. "But all I'll ask you to do is go down to the jail and see Bill and form your own opinion."

At Jessie's urging, Carson visited Lancaster in his jail cell, where Lancaster unspooled the entire five-year tale of his and Jessie's relationship, culminating with the night of Clarke's shooting. After consulting with Lathero and performing a quick investigation, Carson apparently decided that Lancaster was telling the truth. He agreed to take the case, but he also warned Jessie, in no uncertain terms, that "because of those damn notes, it's not going to be easy. He's in a very tough spot." The public already believed resolutely in Lancaster's guilt, Carson pointed out, and people's inherent xenophobia only made matters worse.

Carson's trial strategy would need to hinge on one thing to elicit the jury's compassion: "I'm afraid I'm going to have to make you the scarlet woman," he bluntly informed Jessie. The emotional and sexual details of her personal life would be splashed all over the world's front pages, with a greedy public eagerly gobbling up the particulars. No detail would be too intimate to confess. For a woman like Jessie, who placed enormous value on her privacy, this prospect was excruciating.

"Will everything have to come out?" Jessie asked.

"Everything."

"And there's no other way of saving him?"

"In my opinion, no."

That Jessie responded "yes" speaks volumes about her deep regard for Lancaster, even if she was no longer in love with him. Their connection, even in such an extreme situation, was indissoluble. Jessie knew that if Lancaster was declared guilty he would face the electric chair; sparing him from such a fate was, for her, worth any amount of humiliation. From Carson's perspective, Jessie's willing participation, despite its steep personal cost, would help sell the notion of Lancaster's innocence.

Because Carson intended to argue that Clarke committed suicide, he was granted access to the materials the State Attorney's Office had gathered, including Lancaster's diary and the letters and telegrams sent during the Latin-American Airways excursion. He asked the court for enough time to thoroughly investigate Clarke's and Lancaster's backgrounds, so that he might develop a rich portrait of each as he weighed the evidence for suicide versus murder.

Lancaster had a wealth of friends who would testify to his character, but investigating the emotional and mental background of Clarke, in order to prove his instability, was a trickier matter for Carson and Lathero. The two lawyers decided to consult a competent psychiatrist who could guide their investigation so that it focused only on those parts of Clarke's life that were material to the case. They chose Dr. Percy Dodge, a practicing physician who had decades of experience as a specialist in nervous and mental disorders.

Dr. Dodge informed Carson that most cases of suicide possessed explicit physical indications of the act. If the pistol's muzzle was held directly and tightly against the scalp, for example, there would be no outside powder burns. But because the gases generated by the explosion needed someplace to escape, the typical result was that the scalp was torn loose from the skull and ballooned, and the powder stains appeared *between* the scalp and the skull. If the pistol was held to the skull by someone else, however, there would be enough flinching, even in sleep, that some gas would escape and external powder burns would appear. Thus, Dodge concluded, if powder burns were found between the scalp and the skull, the indications of suicide were practically conclusive, simply because no other person except the one shooting could or would hold the pistol tightly enough against the scalp to produce those results. These findings directly contradicted the theories that Hawthorne's office had promoted.

After consulting with Dr. Dodge, Carson and Lathero found themselves dissatisfied with the county physician's report on Clarke's body, and with the newspaper statements of Dr. Deederer, Ida Clarke's physician. Neither doctor had performed the kind of scientific examination for which Dodge advocated. An autopsy was clearly needed—and yet, what if the autopsy indicated that Clarke had *not* shot himself? Carson and Lathero decided the best way forward was to put the proposition directly to Lancaster, telling him that an autopsy would show whether or not Clarke had committed suicide. Lancaster's response seemed that of an innocent man: he insisted his lawyers apply for an autopsy, which they did. The state attorney concurred.

Because Carson had heard that Clarke's body was not embalmed—meaning it was subject to quick disintegration—he requested the soonest possible disinterment and autopsy. The trial's appointed circuit court judge, Judge Henry F. Atkinson, promptly granted the motion. To oversee the autopsy, Judge Atkinson appointed a medical commission consisting of Dr. Dodge for the defense, Dr. Donald Gowe for the state attorney, and Dr. M. H. Tallman for the court. The autopsy was set for May 31. Carson and Lathero announced that they "eagerly" awaited the report, which would take weeks to prepare.

As the suffocatingly hot days limped by, and May turned into June, Lancaster languished in his jail cell, his world constricted to a grimy, foul-smelling eight-by-ten-foot room. He placed two pictures of Jessie, who was only allowed to visit him for sixty minutes a week, in prominent view, and he depleted countless hours pacing the perimeter of his cell in a useless attempt to stay fit. With little else to occupy his time besides reading and radio-listening, Lancaster also opted to write a private letter to Pat, his elder daughter, who was now ten years old. Because there is no record of Lancaster having seen or communicated with his young daughters since 1927, nor does he mention them in his letters or journals, the letter seems a clear attempt to establish himself, at least in his family's eyes, as a sympathetic figure, a loving father and upright gentleman, and thus someone incapable of cold-blooded murder. ("I used to ask, 'Where's my daddy? Why isn't he here?' " his daughter Nina Ann remembered decades later, when she was in her eighties. "I was a bit—I'd better choose my words carefully here—*peeved* that he'd left us. Deserted us. I thought, 'How could a father do that?' ")

Dated June 21, 1932, the letter to Pat read as follows:

My Dearest Pat,

I want you to understand a little of the thoughts and actions of "Old Bill" during the five years that have passed since you waved goodbye to a small aeroplane on the aerodrome at Croydon.

At the present time my small kingdom consists of a room ten feet by eight in a gaol. Not a nice place, in spite of it being on the twenty-second floor of the Town Hall, and commanding a view of the sea, and the beach, and the boats. The gaolers are not inhuman people, and treat me very well. Fortunately some friends still remain, and I have my food brought to me from the outside world. I have . . . a radio which I can turn on and imagine I am far away. Sometimes when certain strains of old songs or operatic music come from the loudspeakers I lean back and conjure up memories of those days that have gone before. India, Australia, New York, and England.

Of course some people will have condemned me already, and will have said that I am lost to the world, at least the world as I would have you know it. A world of brightness, of ambitions, of love. But this is not so, because they put me in gaol without real cause. They accused me of something that I did not do. And the newspapers carried stories of the circumstances as they would like them to be (to sell their papers), not as they really were.

Soon an opportunity will be given me to tell the true story, and to produce the evidence which will support the story. Then things will be much better, because I shall be released from the gaol, and everyone will say that I was treated badly. . . .

Your Mother, dear sweet person that she is, wrote a letter to the lawyer who is helping me with my case, and she told him of two ways to put forward a defence. She did not know the true story, but had just read warped reports printed in the newspapers. Still it was kind of her to obtain the opinion of some learned lawyer in England.

Your Mother, Pat, is one of the nicest mothers in the whole world a little girl to have, and I hope you will always love her very much, and be sweet to her, helping and loving her so that she too will love you so much.

You see darling, Old Bill knows. He has wandered all over the world, and met many many people. But never has he met anyone nicer than your Mother. Always think of this, and try to do things which will make your Mother happy, and glad that she has you for her little girl. When Nina Ann grows as big as you are now, you must tell her too.

Some day you may meet me again, flying an aeroplane back to the same field that I flew away from. I have tried very hard to make this possible during the last five years, but somehow the days, months, and years have come and gone, and still I have no aeroplane in which to fly back. I wonder if you would be very excited and joyful if this did happen.

I think of you often, and wonder how tall you have grown, and what you are doing, and if you are becoming a clever girl. London, where you are, is the nicest town in all the world. America is not really a nice place to live in. American people are so insincere and crude. Of course not all of them. I have some American friends who are just as nice as anyone in England.

. . . Perhaps I had better tell you a little of the true story which will be told in a little while for all the world to know. You see they said I shot a man and killed him. But this man shot himself, because he did not want to live any more. He was not a nice man at all. He had no money, and he was a failure. He drank to excess, and he used a dope which had undermined his constitution. Well, he went from bad to worse, and finally he decided he had nothing more to live for, so he took his own life.

Now he was my friend, so I did not want everyone to know what kind of a man he was. But now I am afraid everything will come out, as there are other people who knew all about this, and they insist on telling, as they think they should do this for my sake.

Then the doctors had to confer over the case, and exhume this man, so as to be able to express an opinion as to what caused his

> death. They were very clever doctors, and I had to pay a lot of money for their services. But they talked and talked, and examined everything, and finally agreed (all of them), that this man took his own life.
>
> All this is not a very nice thing to talk about, and you will have to ask your Mother to explain it all to you. She has probably been very worried about it all. For remember darling, if you ever do wrong, or are accused publicly of doing wrong, it hurts people who are your relations, or friends, as in my case now. But when the truth is made known, and it is shown that you really did not do wrong, in a measure things are put right.
>
> When you write, address your letter to the Army & Navy Club, New York City. Kiss Nina Ann and Mother for me. And remember my thoughts are of you darling. By the grace of God, and the love of your Mother, you will grow up to be like her and never be in a situation such as I now find myself in.
>
> Goodbye darling until my next letter.
>
> Bill

Despite the slight against Americans, the letter effectively presents the image that Lancaster wanted to cultivate: that of a decent, caring man who has been victimized by circumstances and railroaded by the press. He certainly spoke the truth in regards to Kiki's character, whatever she may have meant to him. But his assessment of the medical evidence in the case, following Clarke's autopsy, was excessively rosy, whether by ignorance or design. He may have been trying to comfort his daughter—or himself—or Carson may have somewhat misled him. Regardless, the medical commission could not declare conclusively that Clarke had committed suicide.

Three weeks later, on July 14, Lancaster wrote a private letter to Kiki in which he again portrayed himself as an innocent, hapless victim, and again railed against America:

> Your letter of July 4th reached me this afternoon. It is one of the few things that are worth while that have come to me for such an age.
>
> When Haden Clarke shot himself he placed me in a ghastly

position, which I made even worse by trying to get him to sign notes which I had typed—self-preservation instincts caused me to do this. I did no wrong in the matter.

Trial is now set for August 2nd. The authorities have been unfair, but NOT as unfair as have the Miami newspapers. It is going to be an ordeal, but I am fortified by the knowledge that I am innocent of the charge.

Unless there is unfairness, which is not unlikely, the courts here are rotten, I shall be cleared in an honourable way. James Carson, my chief lawyer, is a learned man, a "gentleman."

I have been terribly handicapped by a lack of money. In America "justice" is a matter of dollars and cents. Have been 3 months in gaol the *whole* time in a cell 10 feet by 8 feet. They are setting the court in the typical American manner (for a gloating public), wired so that everything can immediately be given out. The various newspaper syndicates sending special representatives etc. etc.

You can depend on my keeping the chin up! No white feathers around. Just annoyance. I suffer greatly at the thought of such harm as may be done to you and the babes through all this.

Will write again before the trial. Appreciated photos sent by Pat. Kiss the babes for me.

B

Two weeks remained before the world's attention focused on Miami and the sensational trial just getting under way. On July 31, Lancaster issued a statement: "I am very glad that the time has come for me to be given a trial. I have been in custody for three months, but during this time I have been fortified with the knowledge that I did not kill Haden Clarke." He pronounced himself satisfied with the jail's conditions, and with the "kind consideration" shown to him by the jail's officials. After praising Carson and Lathero's unstinting efforts to gather the facts of the case, Lancaster declared, "I am anticipating an honorable acquittal when all these facts are presented."

Shortly before the trial, Jessie gave her own interview to the press. "My love for Captain Lancaster was worn out before I met Haden," she said, "though I consider Lancaster the finest human being. Haden and I suddenly loved with the maddest rapture, hysterically. He came and helped me with my autobiography. We hardly worked; we loved madly and insanely. Both of us were broke. Haden always said, 'God will provide.' I usually did. We were delighted in each other and hated separation. I could scarcely buy food, and the lights were often out. When downtown for a few hours, Haden would spend a precious nickel and ask if I still loved him. He adored my voice, and I read aloud every day, mainly from Oscar Wilde's 'The Ballad of Reading Gaol,' which was like a symbol of our love. In great sorrow, I am realizing the great wrong Haden did me. I planned to marry him. Captain Lancaster, whom I loved without being in love after years of companionship in flying adventures, was upset but only wanted my happiness. On that dreadful night I heard Captain Lancaster and Haden talking and laughing. Haden's voice and laugh were the last I remember of him."

PART III FLIGHT TO NOWHERE

17

THOSE DIM DAYS OF THE PAST THAT ARE DEAD

At 9:30 a.m. on August 2, 1932, the first day of Bill Lancaster's trial, State Attorney N. Vernon Hawthorne took his seat at the prosecutor's table, next to his assistant state attorney, Henry Jones, and a special assistant prosecutor. In an unannounced move, Haden Clarke's brother, Dr. Beverley Clarke, head of the New York Telephone Company's chemical research laboratory, strode into the courtroom and took a chair between Hawthorne and Jones. He would, it transpired, be consulting for the prosecution. The crowd in the swarming, overheated courtroom was vocal in its surprise.

Another shock presented itself shortly: Carson, Lancaster's attorney, abruptly moved to postpone the trial. One of the defense team's key witnesses, Dr. Dodge, the psychiatric expert, was experiencing heart trouble, and so he would not be available until the following month. Carson explained to Judge Henry Atkinson that Dr. Dodge had dealt with numerous suicides during his long career. This intimate knowledge, Carson argued, gave Dodge's assertion that Haden Clarke had committed suicide the weight of fact. (In Dodge's wording, Clarke's mental makeup, along with the powder burns on his head, made suicide "eminently probable.") Carson also planned to argue that Clarke was addicted to marijuana; Dr. Dodge, as it happened, was a rare expert on the effects of the drug's use. Dodge's testimony was therefore singular, Carson argued, and crucial to the defense's case. Lancaster listened tensely but without any outward show of emotion as Carson made his case.

Judge Atkinson, a genial, white-haired man of seventy-one, quickly denied Carson's motion. Because Dodge had chaired the medical commission in charge of Clarke's autopsy, Atkinson said, his essential testimony was present in the commission's report, which the court possessed. Lancaster accepted the court's unfavorable ruling without change of expression.

Hawthorne and Carson then began to question prospective jurors. Both sides emphasized that Lancaster was a British citizen, and sought in their questioning to determine whether this would influence people's judgments. Carson also focused on the concept of "moral laxity," the fact that Lancaster had spent years living with a woman who was not his wife. He asked pointedly whether this would prejudice prospective jurors. By 2 p.m., when the court reconvened after a lunch break, twelve final candidates had been chosen. The trial arguments began.

Hawthorne launched into his indictment by characterizing the story of Clarke's shooting as "containing practically all the elements of human interest," including "drama, tragedy, adventure, love, hate, and financial reverse, riding one day on the crest and the next day in the gutter." Behind it all, he said, was "the undying love of Bill Lancaster for Chubbie, which was exploded when he received the news that his beloved half had been taken by the best friend of his life." Before heading off on the Latin-American Airways venture, Hawthorne said, Lancaster "became so 'sold' on Haden Clarke that he regarded him as the one individual he could trust to keep Chubbie for him during that absence."

Once Lancaster was out west, Hawthorne continued, "he began to hear rumors and reports that Chubbie was falling in love with Clarke and that they were having wild drinking parties," and he recorded his fears, "his very heart throbs," in his diary. When Lancaster received confirmation that Jessie and Clarke were having an affair, he "paced the floor saying 'I'll get rid of him,'" adding later that he would "kill that son of a bitch." One week later, Hawthorne said, Lancaster repeated this latter phrase "in the presence of associates, adding that he 'had seen hundreds of dead men, and one more won't matter.'"

Hawthorne described how Lancaster had arrived in St. Louis and read the letters from Jessie and Clarke. "It was then that he bought a pistol and a box of cartridges," Hawthorne intoned. "On the last night out from Miami, in Nashville, Tennessee, he broke open the box of cartridges in a hotel room, and loaded the pistol." Hawthorne took the jury through Lancaster's return to Miami, the tension at dinner with Clarke, and the way Lancaster "threatened" to leave and return to St. Louis, until he was "prevailed upon to remain." At three o'clock that morning, Hawthorne said, Ernest Huston received a call that Clarke had shot himself.

When the ambulance arrived at the house, the driver discovered that Clarke was still alive and that Jessie was "more or less hysterical," Hawthorne reported, but Lancaster, while agitated, was "holding his own." Lancaster's primary concern, Hawthorne said, was whether Clarke would be able to talk again.

In his conclusion, Hawthorne noted that Lancaster had admitted to forging Clarke's "suicide" notes; that the pistol used to shoot Clarke was the one Lancaster had bought in St. Louis; that Lancaster had asked Ernest Huston to claim ownership of the pistol; and that the pistol had been wiped clean of fingerprints. The facts spoke for themselves, Hawthorne argued: not only was Clarke's murder premeditated, but Lancaster had attempted to mislead the subsequent investigation into his shooting.

After Hawthorne took his seat, Carson began his opening statement by saying that, while parts of Hawthorne's statement were "absolutely untrue," the defense agreed that the case contained "almost every possible element of human and dramatic and emotional interest." He cast Lancaster as a "war hero," one of "the great and famous fliers of the world," who now sat in a courtroom in a strange country, four thousand miles from his home in England, on trial for murder.

Carson acknowledged, too, that the case contained circumstances that were "sufficient to arouse the greatest suspicion." There would be, he admitted, "no denial that the so-called 'suicide notes' were forged by Captain Lancaster." But the defense would prove, Carson said, that the notes "were written after Haden Clarke had destroyed his own life by shooting himself in the head with a pistol; that they were written under the stress of great excitement; that they were written perhaps with a view in the Captain's mind of preventing the ghost of this dead man coming between him and

Chubbie, whose devotion Mr. Hawthorne has told you that he so ardently desired."

Carson framed his subsequent remarks by saying that in cases of circumstantial evidence, "the circumstances depend almost entirely for their efficacy upon the point of view" from which one examines them. If one starts with the belief or presumption that Lancaster is innocent—a presumption, Carson reminded the jury, that the law requires—then the circumstances are consistent with the theory of innocence. But if one starts out from the viewpoint of the prosecution—that a man is guilty—then every circumstance merely confirms that belief.

Carson traced the history of Lancaster and Jessie's relationship, their record-setting flight, their journey to the United States in "those dim days of the past that are dead, [when] all the money in the world was supposed to be in America," their move to Miami, and their subsequent struggles for money. He described the arrival of Haden Clarke, "a young man evidently of brilliant mind, of charming personality, of interesting imagination." But, he cautioned the jury, while Clarke was undoubtedly brilliant, charming, and interesting, the evidence would show that "emotionally he was unstable, almost unbalanced, probably neurotic and certainly erotic in his disposition."

Carson detailed the intense financial difficulties the trio faced in Miami, the times when the lights in their house were cut off, when they had to steal chickens in order to eat, when their only stove was a homemade fire in the backyard. After Lancaster headed out west with Latin-American Airways, Carson said, he received almost daily messages telling him how broke Jessie and Clarke were in Miami, even as he realized his own venture was a washout. The stress on Lancaster intensified, made all the worse by the whispers that Jessie and Clarke were having an affair.

On the night Lancaster returned to Miami, Carson said, there "was tension unquestionably on the way to the house," as Lancaster learned for the first time that, about two weeks into his journey out west, Clarke and Jessie had gotten drunk and "begun having sexual intercourse with each other," and that the intercourse "had continued with excessive violence for about two weeks." Until, that is, a shocking discovery had been made: Clarke "was suffering from one of those vile diseases that people who spend their lives in certain ways may expect." (Carson avoided the word "syphilis.") This discovery had not only halted Jessie and Clarke's lovemaking, it had forced them to stop drinking.

And yet, Carson said, that night at the dinner table Lancaster and Clarke had not quarreled exactly, nor had there been any violence, only "a passage at arms with words." Despite some obvious tension between the three, Lancaster, Jessie, and Clarke had gone to bed on good terms. But when Lancaster was woken by the sound of the pistol shot, and saw Clarke in his "death struggle" on the bed, he panicked at the thought of how Jessie might perceive the situation. He then made the "colossally foolish" mistake of forging the notes. "Except for those two notes," Carson argued, "there would be no indictment here."

Carson then listed the subsequent events that looked "terribly suspicious" when viewed through the lens of Lancaster's innocence: the doctor who examined Clarke's body at the house was Ida Clarke's personal physician, Dr. Deederer; Lancaster and Jessie were jailed for a day or two but then released; Ida Clarke had spoken in signed stories of her son's suicide; and Clarke was buried without a coroner's inquest or autopsy. Carson pointed out that Lancaster had voluntarily admitted, against his lawyer's wishes, that he had forged the suicide notes, and he had immediately agreed to the idea of exhuming Clarke's body for an autopsy. "All the defendant had to do if he had been guilty," Carson said, "was to let the body stay where it was."

The defense would also show that in January of that year Clarke had been in New Orleans, drinking heavily and, Carson said, "taking drugs in the form of torpedoes or cigarettes, a drug which is known as marijuana, which is a derivative of one of the drugs of the hasheesh family," and which had "a very upsetting and nerve-racking effect on his nervous system." While in New Orleans Clarke had talked repeatedly to a friend about suicide, saying that if one wanted to kill oneself, there was "no use fooling with poison" and "no use jumping in the river"; the only way to do it was "by shooting yourself in the head with a pistol." In addition, Carson asserted, two or three weeks before Lancaster's return to Miami, Clarke had sat in the living room of 2321 S.W. 21st Terrace and discussed suicide with two friends, bragging, "I know where is the safest place to shoot yourself, and that is the only safe way to commit suicide, and the safest place is just above and slightly behind your right ear"—not far from where the bullet hole in Clarke's head was later found.

"We ask you, in listening to the evidence," Carson concluded, "not only to see whether it fits the picture of guilt, but in measuring any circumstance, to decide for yourself whether the circumstance is consistent with that presumption of innocence which the law affords the defendant."

It was now late in the afternoon; participants and spectators alike were weary from spending so many hours in the steaming, humid confines of the courtroom. Judge Atkinson recessed the court until 9:30 the following morning.

Hawthorne kicked off the next day's proceedings by calling Ernest Huston, the attorney, to the witness stand. Huston described how he'd been summoned to the Coral Gables house on the morning of April 21. Jessie had greeted him with a relieved "thank God you're here," and the two of them had rushed upstairs, where Lancaster, on the stair landing, said grimly, "It's terrible, isn't it?" Huston entered the sun porch and saw Clarke moaning in his bed. Even outside the house, Huston had been able to hear Clarke's tortured breathing through the open sun-porch windows.

After Lancaster showed him the suicide notes, Huston continued, the two men headed downstairs to the living room. When Jessie fretted that the notes would cause a scandal if made public, Lancaster suggested ripping them up, but Huston, in his role as attorney, warned against it.

"Was anything said about the gun to you by Lancaster?" Hawthorne asked Huston.

"On the way to the Everglades Hotel I asked Lancaster if it was my gun and he said no."

"Did he make any suggestion about the gun involved in the shooting?"

Before responding, Huston turned to ask Judge Atkinson a question of his own: "I presume that any questions between myself and Lancaster as my client have been waived?"

Carson jumped at this opportunity to prove the defense's transparency. "We waive nothing," he told the judge.

Huston said Lancaster had asked if he could claim that the gun belonged to Huston, or, failing that, to Latin-American Airways. To the courtroom, Lancaster's questions sounded dubious. But Huston added that when he'd first loaned Lancaster his gun, "I told him that the gun had belonged to a friend of mine and I cared a great deal about it. He answered that he would take the best of care of it and if anything happened he would replace it." Huston's answer made Lancaster's purchase of a pistol in St. Louis seem less suspicious than the prosecution contended.

Carson began his cross-examination of Huston by displaying a picture taken of Lancaster's bed a few hours after the shooting. "Is that a fair picture?" he asked Huston.

"No," the attorney responded. "When I first saw the pillow it was mussed." Here the defense was implying an essential detail: that the police had smoothed out Lancaster's pillow, which explained why later on it appeared to have been unslept on.

Carson then raised another vital point for the defense: "Did Lancaster say he wished Clarke could speak *so he could tell why he did it*?" he asked Huston. This latter half of the question was the kicker.

"He did," Huston answered.

Hawthorne's next witness was the ambulance driver, Charles Ditsler, who described the scene in Lancaster's bedroom, and how Jessie had vigorously objected to the removal of Clarke's body.

"Did Haden Clarke's body strike the walls or banisters while being carried to the ambulance?" Hawthorne asked.

"I'm not sure."

Ditsler's answer appeared to catch Hawthorne off-guard. By acknowledging that the bruise on Clarke's body might have resulted from the body hitting the walls or banisters, Ditsler loaned credence to the defense's claim that Clarke and Lancaster hadn't scuffled before the shooting. The assistant manager of the funeral home, who was next on the stand, confirmed Ditsler's account.

The following witness, Earl Hudson—the policeman with whom Clarke had been friends—told of meeting Lancaster and Jessie at Jackson Memorial Hospital on the night of Clarke's shooting. He said Lancaster had asked repeatedly whether Clarke would be able to talk again. Carson returned to this issue during his cross-examination, asking, "Did Lancaster say he hoped Clarke would talk so he could tell how it happened?"

"Yes," Hudson replied.

By again emphasizing the latter part of Lancaster's question, the defense had scored another point. Moving on, Carson asked whether Lancaster had offered any reasons as to why Clarke might have wanted to commit suicide.

"Yes," Hudson said. "He said Clarke had contracted a disease which preyed heavily on his mind."

The front page of that morning's *Miami Daily News* featured a story headlined "Love Affairs with Lancaster, Clarke Bared by Keith-Miller." An editor's note below the headline informed readers that the "following unusual document is the signed statement of a world-famous woman who is willing to sacrifice her own reputation to save the life of a man she admires." The article had been Carson's brainchild, part of his strategy for raising much-needed money to fly important witnesses to Miami for the trial. Though a reluctant participant, Jessie had agreed to grant an interview to the International News Service, which then used the interview to craft a supposed first-person account of events. The article was blatantly trashy, more suited to a dime-store pulp magazine than to a respectable newspaper—it featured phrases like "our love had found most violent expression for about two weeks," referring to lovemaking. But Carson argued that not only was the money essential, but the article painted Lancaster in a flattering light. So it was that on Wednesday, August 3, mere hours before Jessie began her testimony, the most intimate details of her love life were broadcast to an eagerly waiting international audience. Jessie read the article in her new room at the Everglades Hotel, having been forced from her Coral Gables house by endless sightseers traipsing on the lawn and looking through the windows.

To Jessie the Miami courtroom, as she had observed it thus far, seemed chaotic, the proceedings almost ludicrous. "Everybody was excessively friendly," she later recalled, "the prosecution and the defense laughing and joking together. It seemed to me more like a stage comedy than a trial where a man's life was at stake." The constant waving of fans by onlookers made the stultifyingly hot room appear as if it was in perpetual motion.

Now, as she approached the witness stand, following the morning's testimony by Huston, Ditsler, and Hudson, Jessie was so nervous that she was physically shaking. She was terrified that she would say the wrong thing and somehow imperil Lancaster even further. Hawthorne began his examination by leading her through the basics of her relationships with Lancaster and Clarke, including Lancaster's growing realization, during the Latin-American Airways trip, that Clarke had stolen her affections.

"Did you anticipate trouble when Lancaster received the letters [in St. Louis]?" Hawthorne asked.

"Not trouble, but I knew he would be upset."

"Did he intimate that he was upset by telephone or letter?"

"Yes," Jessie responded.

Hawthorne was laying the groundwork for his argument that Clarke's shooting was premeditated, and he continued to question Jessie closely about the tensions that had marked Lancaster's return to Miami. Jessie was so nervous that her lips trembled and her voice dropped to a whisper; Hawthorne repeatedly had to ask her to speak up. But his questioning only gained so much ground. When Hawthorne asked Jessie if she knew who killed Clarke, she responded, as she had all along, "I am convinced he killed himself."

As Hawthorne pressed Jessie for reasons why Clarke might have committed suicide, she spoke of his heavy drinking, and added, "He had a nervous, violent temper. I have frequently seen him in a rage of temper with his mother." Jessie attributed this anger to the fact that Clarke's mother "nagged him. She was always talking about what she had done for him, what he had cost her, and what an ungrateful son he was."

Jessie also testified that Clarke had frequently talked of suicide, an assertion that Hawthorne planned to dispute via subsequent witnesses. But Jessie deepened her claim by saying that, on the night of Lancaster's return to Miami, "I was frightfully wretched over what I had done to Bill, and I told Haden that I wished we could end it and both go out together." Clarke, she said, had agreed with her.

Hawthorne shifted his questioning to Jessie's testimony in his office following Clarke's shooting, when she had declared that Clarke rarely drank, and that his demeanor was always gentle except on the few occasions when he had imbibed.

"I certainly did not say that Haden seldom got drunk," Jessie protested. "If I did, I was trying to shield his memory."

At this, Hawthorne leaped. "Are you not equally anxious to protect Lancaster?" he asked. "In trying to save Lancaster, did you not say that you would issue a statement to the newspapers that you killed Clarke yourself if

Lancaster was held?" This was the crux of Hawthorne's examination: Jessie had freely admitted that she was willing to lie for the men she loved.

Jessie, despite her nervousness, didn't take the bait. "It sounds dramatic, but I did say that," she admitted.

When Carson took the floor for cross-examination, he immediately guided Jessie to the document she had provided Hawthorne's office outlining the reasons why Clarke might have committed suicide. Carson wanted to show that Jessie had been truthful in describing the pressures bearing upon Clarke, and in saying that Clarke had exhibited regular signs of rashness and instability. Slowly, Carson led Jessie through the document, working to build in the jury's mind a portrait of Clarke as a convincingly suicidal individual.

Jessie's manner on the stand, as in life, was forthright, a quality Carson felt would impress the jury. He thus asked her directly about her myriad efforts over the past three months to help Lancaster's case. The jury, he thought, would interpret these efforts as evidence that Jessie believed Lancaster was innocent, not that she was trying to help him cover up a murder. After three and a half hours of close grilling, during which Lancaster appeared visibly nervous at Jessie's obviously tormented state, the court adjourned until the following morning.

Jessie seemed more composed the next day, August 4, with Lancaster, in turn, appearing more relaxed. Dressed in a light gray suit, blue shirt, and blue tie, Lancaster even joined in the laughter when Carson, in a mock down-home manner, told Jessie on the stand that what she described as a "face-washer" was called a "face rag" in his Florida hometown. As the questioning progressed, Carson took Jessie in painstaking detail through the events preceding Clarke's shooting, as well as her subsequent arrest and release. By the time Carson finished, Jessie had been on the stand for almost six and a half hours.

The day's next big witness was Jack Russell of Latin-American Airways. A key element of the case against Lancaster involved the threats he had supposedly made against Clarke's life, and for this Russell was a key informant. Under Hawthorne's questioning, Russell recounted the forming of his relationship with Lancaster, and how worried Lancaster had been about Jessie's "financial destitution and his failure to hear from her." Hawthorne then introduced one of the letters Russell had received when he and Lancaster were out west, in which his wife had described Jessie and Clarke's burgeoning relationship. Hawthorne wanted to show that this letter had helped set Lancaster on his murderous path. "I told him that he had lost out with her," Russell testified, "and that . . . Clarke had the inside path. Bill asked if I thought Haden had double-crossed him. I said I thought he had. Bill turned on his heel and muttered, 'I'll get rid of him.'" The letter itself was so damaged and unreadable that the next day Carson questioned its authenticity.

Carson's cross-examination of Russell, which took place on the morning of August 5, relied on a simple strategy: painting Russell as a liar and a thief. That task was made easier when Carson forced Russell to admit that he was currently serving a six-month jail sentence for drug-and-illegal-alien smuggling, the latest in a long string of such sentences.

Russell didn't help his cause by acting both antagonistic and comically vague on the stand. At one point Carson questioned him about a letter Russell had written to Lancaster identifying the spot in Arizona where Lancaster was to drop the drug-carrying Chinese nationals smuggled over from Mexico. "Is that it?" Carson asked Russell, handing him the letter for verification. Russell examined the letter in silence for such a long time that the court grew restless.

"I only asked if you wrote it," Carson finally said.

"I can't tell unless I read it," Russell responded. At this the courtroom exploded in laughter, which continued until the bailiffs called for order.

Humor aside, Carson's grilling of Russell was sharp. "When Lancaster left you standing on the ground at the Burbank Airport, did you think it was a dirty trick if there were federal men waiting at the other airport?" he asked.

"I hold no feelings against Lancaster," Russell said. "There was no federal officer waiting at the other airport."

"They found you, didn't they?"

"No."

"They didn't?"

"No," Russell lied. "I gave myself up at El Paso." Carson didn't pursue the point.

After Russell left the stand, Hawthorne introduced into evidence Lancaster's personal diary from the Latin-American Airways trip, along with the letters Lancaster, Jessie, and Clarke had exchanged during this period. His point, Hawthorne explained to the jury, was to link Russell's testimony to Lancaster's diary entries. Hawthorne then read out loud the entirety of Lancaster's diary, and though the process took hours, the fascinated audience appeared to hang on every word. (The text was repeated faithfully in the following day's Miami newspapers.) An embarrassed Lancaster stared sheepishly at the ground as Hawthorne began his narration, but as the reading progressed, an unexpected shift—one that surely played against Hawthorne's intentions—occurred in the room. Because Lancaster came across in his diary as a sympathetic, deeply human figure, the faces of the jurors and the spectators began showing signs of heretofore-unseen sympathy.

Russell wasn't Hawthorne's only witness to claim Lancaster had made threats against Clarke. On Saturday, August 6, Mark Tancrel, Russell's former Latin-American Airways partner, took the stand to level a similar accusation. Tancrel had another thing in common with Russell: both were currently occupying prison cells in the Dade County Courthouse. The so-called Captain Tancrel confessed that he'd been indicted for impersonating a United States Navy officer. But he still claimed to be a captain, saying he was "a master mariner of the United States Merchant Marine."

Under Hawthorne's questioning, Tancrel outlined the founding of Latin-American Airways, and accused Lancaster of failing to meet his promise to contribute two planes to the venture. Lancaster only provided "half a plane," Tancrel said, explaining that the aircraft was in such bad condition that it required a wholesale mechanical overhaul in Texas. But Hawthorne didn't linger on the issue; he was guiding Tancrel to a more damning charge.

"Lancaster and myself were at the Houston Hotel," Tancrel said, in response to a follow-up question. "Going to our room I found Lancaster there with a stranger, who was introduced to me as Ince. I then went to bed and was reading while Lancaster discussed Mrs. Keith-Miller and Clarke with Ince. He said, 'I don't think Haden Clarke has double-crossed me, but if he has, well, I've seen a lot of dead men and one more won't make any difference.' "

Hawthorne then asked whether Tancrel had seen Lancaster after the latter had abandoned Russell in California.

"Yes," Tancrel responded, "he came to the hotel [in Nogales]. . . . He said, 'I'm tendering my resignation. You fellows can paddle your own canoe.' I said, 'All right, if that is the way you feel about it.' Lancaster asked me if Russell had shown me a letter he had received from [his wife] stating that there was no need for Lancaster to come back, as Mrs. Keith-Miller and Clarke were in love. Lancaster said, 'I'll go back east and get rid of that son of a bitch.' "

"Who was he talking about?" Hawthorne asked.

"He was talking about Clarke."

Carson's primary goal in his cross-examination was to show that Tancrel was not just a criminal but a habitual liar, someone for whom telling untruths came as naturally as breathing, and who was deeply spiteful toward Lancaster to boot. The defense would be introducing evidence to underscore this second point.

"How close to your cell is Russell?" Carson asked.

"They put me in the same cell with him yesterday."

"Have you talked to Russell about the case?"

"We can't express ourselves; there are too many in there hanging around."

"Did Russell tell you what he testified about?"

"No."

"Did you tell him what you would testify about?" Carson's tone made it clear that he thought Tancrel and Russell had concocted false testimony together.

"No, that's my private business."

"It's rather public now, isn't it?" Then Carson asked whether Tancrel had discussed Lancaster with his jail escort.

"Yes, I said that I didn't want to be placed in the same cell with Lancaster."

Carson seized upon the statement: "Did you tell your escort after your arrest on May 22nd that, 'If you put me in a cell with Lancaster I'll kill him. I'm back here now and I'm going to do everything possible to see that Lancaster burns'?" Tancrel denied the accusation, but Carson's words hung in the juror's minds.

Tancrel's testimony also provided the courtroom with some much-needed comic relief after Carson inquired whether Tancrel was a member of the Wallpaper Hangers' Union.

"I am not," Tancrel replied.

"Did you make some mention of the wallpaper in the lobby of the El Paso Hotel and show Lancaster a copy of what you claimed to be a card from the paper hangers' union?"

"No. If I had such a card it would be in my briefcase. I would like to have the briefcase here."

"You would need it to answer the question about you being a member of the paper hangers' union?" Carson mocked. "Now, didn't you tell Lancaster in El Paso that you had hung thousands of square miles of wallpaper?"

"Yes, I have," Tancrel replied. "In my home I have hung thousands of miles of wallpaper."

"Then you are a paper hanger?"

"No, I'm not a member of the paper hangers' union."

"Yet you've hung thousands of miles of wallpaper?" Carson asked.

"Oh, not that many. No paper hanger in his lifetime could hang that much wallpaper."

Spectators and jurors alike were clearly enjoying watching Carson toy with Tancrel, who was coming across as a ridiculous figure, but Judge Atkinson put an end to the display by declaring the questioning irrelevant.

After Tancrel stepped down, Hawthorne moved to the issue of the pistol used in Clarke's shooting. He and Carson offered, via their questioning of a series of witnesses, competing theories as to why no blood or fingerprints had been on the pistol when it was handed over to the Miami Police Department's identification bureau. After these witnesses, Hawthorne called the embalmer for the W. H. Combs Funeral Home, who testified that he'd found no powder burns on the side of Clarke's head. This contradicted the defense's claim. Carson used his cross-examination to cast doubt on the embalmer's credentials.

The final witness that Saturday was the policeman Earl Hudson, making a return appearance. He verified that Lancaster, Jessie, and possibly Ernest Huston had all been in the room when he found the gun. When Hawthorne asked whether any blood had been on the pistol, Hudson said yes.

"How did you take the gun from the bed?" Hawthorne asked.

"I dropped my handkerchief over it and slipped the pistol into its box, which I found on the table at the foot of Clarke's bed. Later I gave the gun to [the] fingerprint man at police headquarters."

Carson wanted to prove that Hudson was both an incompetent police officer and a highly compromised witness. He began his cross-examination by emphasizing that Hudson's sister-in-law, Peggy Brown, had been Clarke's girlfriend. He also hinted that Hudson himself had provided the illegal alcohol at Jessie and Clarke's parties by using stocks the police had confiscated during police raids, which Hudson vehemently denied.

Next Carson directed Hudson's attention to the pistol used in the shooting. "You say you didn't put that gun in your pocket?"

"Yes, I did, after placing it in its box," Hudson replied.

"Then you shoved the box in your pocket?"

"Yes."

The box sat on display before the jury. Its hefty size, much too large to fit in someone's pocket, showed Hudson's claim to be laughably false. Carson didn't bother pointing this out; it was obvious to the jury. Hudson was dismissed, and the courtroom adjourned until Monday morning.

On Sunday, the newspapers delivered a surprise: Jessie was to be recalled by Hawthorne the following morning. As usual, the papers referred to her size, calling her the "diminutive aviator" and emphasizing that she weighed less than a hundred pounds, but a condescending admiration shone through. "Although her intimate life has been shorn of its glamour and held up to the world as a sordid love triangle," *The Miami Herald* breathlessly wrote, and "although moments of ardent love-making . . . have been exposed to the cold and critical light of a courtroom trial to become the sensation of suburban housewives the world over," with her home becoming a "love nest" and a "death house," Jessie was "showing the fortitude she displayed during her aviation career."

The trial was already being trumpeted by the *Herald* as "the most sensational triangle ever aired in Florida courts," and the previous week's media coverage had only increased the public's already-intense fascination. Now the news that Jessie would face off again with Hawthorne brought unprecedented numbers of voyeuristic onlookers to the courthouse on Monday morning. By 6 a.m. a vast crowd had started to gather in the sixth-floor hallway, eager to witness the proceedings. Though the courtroom was bursting with people by the time Judge Atkinson entered, hundreds more were left standing outside, unable to gain a coveted seat.

Hawthorne had planned carefully for his second pass at Jessie, intending to expose her as a hypocrite who would do and say anything to save Lancaster's skin. He began by taking Jessie again through the story of the night of Clarke's shooting. Jessie repeated how she had been reading a detective story in bed when she heard Clarke go to the bathroom and laugh. (Clarke had been laughing at Lancaster's story of Tancrel's wallpaper hanging exploits.)

"What was your belief when you were shown the alleged suicide notes?" Hawthorne asked.

"I had no belief."

"Didn't you tell me in my office that you were positive that Bill didn't write them?"

Jessie was unruffled: "I don't remember saying that."

"Didn't I say to you in my office, 'Are you as sure about the notes as you are that Lancaster didn't kill Haden Clarke?' "

"You didn't ask me that," Jessie protested.

"Then you knew Lancaster wrote the notes?"

"No."

"Were you shown fourteen discrepancies existing in the notes?"

"Yes."

"Did you not say that Lancaster didn't and couldn't have written them?" Hawthorne's pace was unrelenting. "Did you say the language made you know Lancaster didn't type those notes?"

"Yes," Jessie answered.

"Didn't you assert that Lancaster's code of honor wouldn't have permitted him to write those notes?"

"I did state that."

"Then the first time you knew of the forgery was when you asked Captain Lancaster directly at the house after your release [from jail]?"

"Yes."

"If you had asked him if he had killed Haden Clarke and had received the answer yes, would that have surprised you more than the admission of forgery?"

"Most decidedly," Jessie replied.

Hawthorne had reached the culmination of this line of pursuit: "Although you had stated to me previously that you were as positive that Lancaster had not written the notes as you were that he had not killed Haden

Clarke?" Confident that he'd made his point to the jury, Hawthorne assumed a gentler tone.

"Do you still love Haden Clarke?" he asked.

"No."

"Do you love Lancaster?"

"No."

"When did your affection die for Lancaster?"

"About two years ago."

"Did it die a natural death?"

"Yes. I am still intensely fond of him."

"Was there anything Lancaster did to cause a natural death of your love for him?"

"No."

Abruptly Hawthorne's tone changed to one of indignant accusation: "Then why did you deliberately betray him in every letter, telegram, and telephone message to him? Weren't you a traitor to him during all that time when he was sending you even single-dollar bills in his letters?"

"Objection!" Carson shouted.

Hawthorne tried again: "Weren't you a deliberate traitor to Lancaster in all those letters, in all those telegrams, all those times you said 'all my love to you'?"

Jessie's response was steely but seemingly heartfelt. "Mr. Hawthorne, you don't understand the feeling that exists between Captain Lancaster and myself," she said. "We have been through hardship and misfortunes. We were pals, not ordinary friends. We trusted each other."

Hawthorne moved on. "So you no longer love the memory of Haden Clarke?" he asked.

"No," Jessie said firmly. "I have been completely disillusioned."

"By what?"

"Proofs."

"Are you referring to his illness?"

"Among other things."

When Hawthorne pressed her to explain, Jessie said, "I believed in, trusted, Haden Clarke, and he lied to me."

"Did he lie about his love for you?"

"No, I don't think so. . . . He lied to me about his age, his university degree, he told me he had never had that malady before, he lied about things he had done."

"Then the principal thing that killed your love for Haden Clarke was because he was a liar?"

Jessie said it was.

Now Hawthorne was positioned to make his larger point: that Lancaster was no more truthful than Clarke. "Do you know [Lancaster] pleaded guilty of a crime for which he was not guilty to save you?" he asked.

"He always tried to save me, to help me." To Jessie, this was a sign of Lancaster's honor, not of dishonesty.

"You don't love him even though you have said you would die for him?"

"No."

"You'd lie for him?"

Hawthorne intended, with his question, to put Jessie on the defensive, but this time she was ahead of him. "No," she countered, "because you would know."

At Jessie's answer, the courtroom erupted in noise, the spectators buzzing about her verbal parry. Judge Atkinson pounded his gavel to silence the crowd. Hawthorne, undeterred, plunged forward.

"One of the principal things you admire in Lancaster is his code of honor?" he asked.

"Yes. He is one of the finest men I ever knew."

"He'd steal for you, wouldn't he?"

Hawthorne's approach was crafty, but it was met by Jessie's ire: "He doesn't steal," she icily replied.

"Didn't he steal a chicken for you?"

Abruptly the interrogation veered into comedy: "No," Jessie said. "It was a duck."

At this the courtroom convulsed with laughter, which, despite the bailiffs' concerted efforts, continued uproariously for several moments. His momentum lost, Hawthorne approached Jessie from another angle.

"Do you know Lancaster has a wife?" he asked. Before Jessie could answer, Hawthorne continued: "From whom he is not divorced?"

"Yes, but—" Jessie managed, before Hawthorne interrupted: "And two little girls?"

"Yes," Jessie admitted.

Carson shouted his objection. But Hawthorne's point had been made: Lancaster was a man who had abandoned his helpless family, a far cry from the upstanding individual that Jessie had made him out to be.

Hawthorne wasn't finished. Referring to an earlier incident in Miami, he said, "If Lancaster committed perjury to save you from the penalties of a fine for driving after you'd been drinking, did that increase your admiration for him?"

"Objection!" Carson said.

"You said earlier that you intended to marry Lancaster, that you believed it was inevitable?" Hawthorne asked.

"Yes, I always felt that when Bill was free from his wife in England I would marry him."

"But you weren't in love with him?" Hawthorne pressed.

"Being in love and just loving a person are two different things," Jessie answered, returning to her earlier point. "I was not thrilled or infatuated with Lancaster, just terribly fond of him."

"Were you infatuated with Clarke?"

"Yes."

"Now you do not even love his memory?"

Jessie, who had been fighting all morning to keep her emotions in check, finally lost her composure. "No," she said, starting to cry. "Unfortunately, no." Turning away, Hawthorne pronounced his questioning complete. As Jessie left the stand her tears turned into sobs, and she bawled to a friend at the door that she was being "crucified." She was taken into a nearby room until her weeping subsided.

The other significant moment that afternoon came when Carson recalled the attorney Ernest Huston to the stand. Seeking to prove that Lancaster hadn't wiped any fingerprints from the pistol, Carson had Huston describe how he'd watched Earl Hudson, the policeman, wrap the gun in a handkerchief and slip it into his pocket. Contrary to the policeman's testimony, Huston said Hudson had not put the pistol into its box.

"Was there blood on the gun?" Carson asked.

"It was running with blood," Huston replied.

At 2:50 p.m. Hawthorne rested the state's case. He had been unable to locate his intended final witness, Fitzhugh Lee, the driver of the police emergency vehicle that had responded to the emergency call from 2321 S.W. 21st Terrace on the morning of the shooting.

After the jury was excused from the courtroom, Carson moved that all exhibits except the pistol, the bullets, and the photographs of Clarke be withdrawn, and that all testimony except that of Dr. Carleton Deederer and the undertaker be stricken from the record. He argued that all of the evidence advanced by the state except in "isolated instances" was circumstantial. Carson did not, however, move for a directed verdict in favor of his client.

"The fact that the defendant made a statement that he would 'get rid' of the deceased is certainly not circumstantial," Hawthorne countered, before listing other examples of non-circumstantial testimony. Judge Atkinson quickly rejected Carson's motion, and the jury returned to the courtroom.

For the first time in the trial, Lancaster, his voice sore and, in the words of the press, "heavily British-accented," was called to the stand.

18

A TISSUE OF LIES

The months Lancaster had spent in jail awaiting trial were evident in the pronounced pallor of his skin, highlighted by the midafternoon light, as he took the witness stand. His eyes were bright and clear against the paleness of his flesh, and they darted over the room as he responded to Carson's questions. Lancaster answered Carson slowly, invariably hesitating before he spoke, but his manner was clear and direct. Frequently he paused to wipe the sweat from his chin; the August heat was suffocating for witnesses and spectators alike.

Carson's interrogation kicked off at a leisurely pace as he focused on giving the jury a complete picture of Lancaster the man, not Lancaster the disgraced aviator. Carson began with Lancaster's birth in 1898 and proceeded through his family life as a child; his schoolboy days; his service with the Royal Air Force before and after the war; his relationship with his wife, Kiki; his first encounter with Jessie at a London party; and their meeting the following day at the Authors' Club in Whitehall. The story quickened as Lancaster described his and Jessie's record-setting flight to Australia and their sudden celebrity. Carson made sure Lancaster emphasized that he and Jessie had shared one-third of their profits with Kiki. This information,

Carson hoped, would make Lancaster's abandonment of his family seem less harsh.

Nods of recognition began to appear in the courtroom as Lancaster told of his arrival in America with the crew of the *Southern Cross* and his subsequent travails, including his crash in Trinidad. These events had been covered in the newspapers and were familiar to many in the room; they brought back the days when Lancaster's reputation, unsullied, had been that of a heroic aviator.

At 5 p.m. Judge Atkinson recessed the court. Lancaster had been on the stand for two hours, narrating his life up to the point of his initial association with Latin-American Airways and his departure with Russell and Tancrel for Arizona.

Media reports that evening were critical of Carson for proceeding so painstakingly through Lancaster's life, and for building such a complete portrait of events unrelated to Clarke's shooting. Carson's goal had been to humanize Lancaster, to present him as a sympathetic, fully rounded individual, and indeed, many in the courtroom appeared to find Lancaster an appealing figure on the stand. But to jaded newsmen—not to mention Hawthorne—Carson's presentation had been ponderous and unnecessary.

The next day, August 9, four hundred people crowded into the courtroom in the morning, while two hundred others lined up in the corridor in hopes of gaining entry. Perhaps stung by the media's criticism of his performance, Carson began his questioning by addressing the crucial issue: "Captain Lancaster," he asked, "did you kill Haden Clarke?"

"No, I did not," Lancaster answered calmly, without obvious emotion. His unruffled manner had the effect, perhaps counterintuitively, of making his answer seem more believable.

A satisfied Carson, in his trademark white suit, resumed his exploration of Lancaster's history. "When did you first find yourself in love with Mrs. Keith-Miller?"

"Mrs. Keith-Miller and I suffered many dangerous trials on the trip to Australia," Lancaster said. "I grew to admire her character. We suffered many things together. I am sure I was intensely in love with her on our arrival." The previous day Lancaster had spoken of how Jessie's courage and cheerfulness in the face of adversity had endeared her to him. He admitted that by the time they reached Persia their level of intimacy had exceeded friendship.

"Was it physical passion or unselfish love?" Carson asked.

"Both."

"In Australia, on how many occasions did you have intimate relations with Mrs. Keith-Miller?"

"I can't remember, although I am sure it was not many." Given their newfound celebrity, Lancaster explained, he and Jessie had found few opportunities to be alone.

"And your love for Mrs. Keith-Miller increased or decreased during the years?"

"Increased."

"When did you first meet Haden Clarke?"

Lancaster consulted his diary, which he had brought to the stand. "February 9, 1932," he replied. "We had met in New York before, he told me, but I didn't remember him."

"You roomed together from the first day?"

"Yes."

"Did any other person share a room with Clarke except yourself?"

"Yes, women."

"How many times?"

"On at least three occasions."

"After Clarke moved in, did he do any writing?"

"He started to."

"How much did he do?"

"Very little," Lancaster answered, before qualifying his reply. "I blame myself for that, somewhat, because he always wanted to accompany me on walks, when I took the ship up, and whatever else I did, and I let him." To the courtroom, Lancaster's acceptance of partial blame seemed the answer of a decent man.

"Would Clarke fly into rages?"

"Yes."

"What would he do?"

"Oh, just shout a bit." Lancaster's English reticence, and his seeming reluctance to denounce Clarke, again played well with the room.

"Do you recall some of the occasions?"

"Well, once, when [a creditor] took the tires off his car and put them on his own. He [also] got into a temper one day in Huston's office."

"Was there drinking at the house?"

"Yes."

"By whom?"

"Oh, all of us, and any guests we might have." Lancaster didn't mention how much greater Clarke's and Jessie's alcohol intake had been than his own.

Guided by Carson, Lancaster described how he and Clarke had grown close. Leaning forward in the witness chair, he said, "A day before I left for the West on the trip I hoped would recoup my financial fortunes, I told Haden Clarke the story of my love for Chubbie, of our intimacy over a five-year period, and asked him to protect her and watch over her while I was gone. I asked him not to let her drink and I asked him not to drink. His reply to me was, 'Bill, I will care for her in such a way as to make you remember my friendship forever.'" At this, Lancaster's lips twisted into a sardonic smile and he settled back in the witness chair.

Carson then questioned Lancaster about his initial meetings with Tancrel and Russell. "Was the contract with Tancrel signed before you met Clarke?"

Lancaster consulted his diary. "Yes, the day before." He mentioned his initial suspicions of Tancrel, and his inability to locate navy records that would confirm Tancrel's service. "I was still doubtful," Lancaster said, "but as I had accepted money—over two hundred dollars—I felt I should go through with the deal. If I had had two hundred dollars at the time I would have returned his money."

"Did you have any suspicions of Russell?"

"None, except that Tancrel said he didn't trust Russell."

"He didn't have a uniform," Carson said, grinning.

Lancaster didn't acknowledge the joke. "Russell never posed as anything," he replied. "At one time he showed me his honorable discharge from the army. He was a private." Again, Lancaster's apparent unwillingness to deprecate his enemies impressed the court.

Carson opened a new line of inquiry. "Captain Lancaster, who saw you off on the start of your Australian trip?"

"Many people, my wife among them."

"What is your wife's religion?"

Hawthorne immediately objected to the question, calling it irrelevant. Judge Atkinson sustained the objection. But Carson argued that Kiki Lancaster had been brought into the testimony by the state and that he should be allowed to question Lancaster about her. Judge Atkinson then reversed his ruling and allowed Lancaster to respond.

"She is Roman Catholic," Lancaster said.

Carson's question had not been as random as it appeared. He was underscoring the fact that Kiki had refused, on religious grounds, to grant Lancaster a divorce. By this Carson hoped to shine a gentler light on Lancaster's abandonment of his wife and children by implying that Lancaster had been forced to live illicitly with Jessie not because he was morally corrupt but because Kiki had acted unreasonably.

Carson's effort to present Lancaster as an upstanding individual continued as Carson questioned him more closely about his trip out west with Latin-American Airways.

"When and where did you discover the true purposes of the expedition?"

"I doubted Tancrel's story of the expedition's purpose from the start," Lancaster answered, "but I wanted to make sure. This I couldn't do without going. At El Paso, Tancrel said Russell had talked to him about Chinamen. . . . [I]n El Paso [Tancrel] suggested that the company could ford Chinamen across the border."

"And what did you say?"

"I told him I would have nothing to do with anything illegal."

"When was dope first mentioned?"

"While in El Paso." Lancaster said he had again informed Tancrel and Russell that he would not engage in any illegal activities, and that when they'd repeated their proposal later on he had told them, in disgust, that he was returning to Miami.

Thus the theme of Carson's questioning continued: though surrounded by crooks, physically starving, and desperate for money, Lancaster had behaved morally. He was an honest man, no matter how dire the circumstances.

To emphasize the point, Carson rolled out an impressive roster of character witnesses: five famous aviators, all friends of Lancaster, who had traveled to the trial of their own volition—and on their own dimes—from as far away as France to testify on his behalf. The papers had trumpeted the news, calling it "Aviation Day" at the trial, and increasing the already swollen crowd that had swarmed the courthouse that morning, making the day's attendance the largest yet. Now, Captain Frank Upton, a Congressional Medal of Honor winner; Lieutenant A. Irving Boyer, a British war flying hero; Rex Gilmartin, a World War I ace and past commander of the American Legion's Aviators Post; Clyde Pangborn, a round-the-world and transpacific flier; and Keith Bon, another World War I hero, each took the stand to sing Lancaster's praises. For twenty minutes they spoke of Lancaster's sterling reputation among the world's top aviators, calling him "generous," "calm," "peaceful," "honorable." When their testimony was complete, the court recessed briefly, and the five fliers chatted with Lancaster at the defense table.

When Lancaster resumed his place on the witness stand in the late afternoon, his spirits seemed considerably buoyed by the visit from his friends. Carson took him through the sequence of events that had led to his departure from Latin-American Airways and his arrival in St. Louis, where he had read the letters from Jessie and Clarke informing him of their intention to marry. Lancaster said he'd been deeply depressed by the news and "acted like a schoolboy." After spending time in the city, he had borrowed a hundred dollars from Gentry Shelton's father and bought a gun to replace the one Huston had loaned him. Heading east, Lancaster spent the first night out in Nashville, where he loaded the gun. The following day he flew to Miami and was met at Viking Airport by Jessie and Clarke. Lancaster testified that he kissed Jessie in greeting and was cordial to Clarke.

At this the courtroom clock ticked 5 p.m., and court was recessed for the day.

On Wednesday, August 10, Lancaster resumed his place on the stand. Carson began by asking whether he and Clarke had ever foraged for food.

"Yes," Lancaster responded. "Haden and I went to a place he knew of and took some rabbits and chickens."

"What did you do with them?"

"Ate them."

As Carson intended, Lancaster's forthright admission of wrongdoing—another mark for his apparent honesty—impressed the courtroom.

"Did you ever tell Tancrel and Russell you were going back to Miami and get that lousy bastard?"

"No." Lancaster's tone was resolute. "The entire testimony of both Tancrel and Russell was a tissue of lies."

"Yesterday, you testified you loaded the gun at Nashville," Carson said. "Why?"

"I don't know why exactly. Mr. Huston's gun was loaded when he gave it to me and I wanted to return it in the same manner." This answer, like Lancaster's previous ones, appeared guileless. Surely a liar, the implication went, would have spun a more elaborate tale.

Carson questioned Lancaster about the night of his return to Miami, his argument with Clarke at the dinner table, and how he had at one point left the house to buy cigarettes. When he returned, Lancaster said, Jessie and Clarke were reclining on the chaise longue. He had talked with them briefly and then headed upstairs, where he'd sat on his bed in the sun porch and sorted through his mail. Eventually Clarke had joined him.

"And then what did you talk about?" Carson asked.

Lancaster paused a moment before responding. "I refrained from telling Mr. Hawthorne much of our conversation when I was first arrested," he said. "I did this to protect Clarke's name and to keep his mother from knowing about the malady from which he suffered. I do not want to tell of that conversation now and I will not unless it is absolutely necessary."

"On my shoulders rests responsibility for the conduct of your defense," Carson said. "Please answer my questions."

With seeming reluctance, Lancaster said, "Haden talked of his illness. He was almost in tears. He expressed great remorse and regret over what had happened between him and Chubbie. Previously we had discussed the beginning of their intimacy."

"Was there any discussion then regarding the permanence of Clarke's and Chubbie's love for each other?"

"Yes, he was very frank. He said, 'I have had many affairs in my life, but this time I am absolutely in love. I shall do everything in my power to make her happy. Now I have something to work for.' I was impressed with his sincerity."

"Was the question of his age discussed?"

"Yes. He said, 'I'm sorry, but I'm not thirty-one.' He said he was either twenty-six or twenty-seven, I can't remember which, and he asked if I thought it would make any difference to Chubbie."

"Did you discuss any of his other false claims?"

"Only about the book. He said he didn't know whether he would be able to put it over. I remember the phrase he used. He said he didn't know if he could 'make the grade.' He also told me he didn't have his degree."

"Did he say anything about his writings being accepted?"

"Yes. He said the Depression had started everybody writing. He remarked how terribly hard it was to get money, and he showed me the telegram from his wife, remarking it would cost him from fifty to one hundred dollars to get a divorce in Miami and that he didn't know how to raise the money."

"Was anything said of the month's delay?"

"Yes, I told him to talk to Chubbie in the morning, that he must tell her what he had told me tonight, and that if she loved him she would overlook his misstatements."

"Was any other subject discussed?"

"Yes. I remember switching the subject. He appeared so frank and honest and so very sorry at what had happened that I tried to get his mind off it by telling him of the trip. I remember telling one incident at which he laughed, about Tancrel's statement in El Paso. I said, 'Can you imagine a United States Navy captain carrying a paper hanger's union card and claiming to have hung thousands of square miles of wallpaper?' "

"Was Clarke's mother discussed?"

"Yes. He acted rather as if he treated me as a father-confessor. He talked of how he might have done more for her than he had and how sorry he was. He said, 'Mother is having a tough time. The University of Miami is not paying her salary.' "

"Had you previously discussed Mrs. Clarke, that is, before you left on the western trip?"

"He explained that it was difficult for him to work with her around. In that confidential conversation the day before I left, I . . . asked him why he didn't have his mother come to the house. He said they were the best of friends apart but couldn't get along together. Both were temperamental and got on one another's nerves. He wouldn't have it."

"Was there anything else said?"

"I was lying back on my bed yawning, half asleep, and I said, 'Let's talk it over in the morning with Chubbie.' I can remember his last words: 'You're the whitest man I ever met.' Then I turned off the lights. It was brilliant moonlight that night."

"Were you tired?"

"Darned tired."

"How was the trip?"

"Bad trip."

"What happened next?"

"I was awakened by a noise. . . . A 'bang.' When I first came to I was under the impression a window had fallen. I called out, 'What's that, Haden?' "

"And what did you hear then?"

"A gurgling sound came from Haden's bed. I turned on the light and looked at Haden's bed. I could see something had happened. It was blood running over his face."

"Did you see the pistol?"

"No. I said to him, 'What have you done?' His right arm was bent upward at the elbow, with the hand turned in toward the body. Then I saw the pistol half under his body."

"When and where did you last see the gun?"

"On the table between our beds. Haden had picked it up and I told him to be careful, it was loaded. We had talked about my buying the gun to replace Huston's, earlier in the evening."

"Where did you first see blood on Clarke?" Carson asked.

Lancaster pointed to his own lower right jaw and under his neck.

"What did you do?"

"I asked him a second time to speak to me. He just moaned. I looked around for a note indicating what had happened."

"When did you first see the wound on Clarke?"

"Before typing the notes."

"When did you type the notes?"

"After trying to get him to speak to me the second time, I sat down at the typewriter. It took me about five minutes. I then took a pencil and the notes and went to the bed and asked Haden to speak to me again. I asked him to try to sign the notes. Then I shouted 'Chubbie' and got no reply. Then I did something I should not have done. I scribbled 'Haden' on one note and wrote 'H' on the other."

Lancaster then related for Carson the rest of that night's events, including his comments to Officer Hudson that he wished Clarke would talk so he could explain his actions. He seconded Ernest Huston's claim that Hudson had picked up the pistol from the center of Clarke's bed, wrapped it in his handkerchief, and slipped it into his pocket without its box.

By the time Carson concluded his questioning, Lancaster had been on the stand for a total of nine hours and ten minutes over a three-day period. But Carson's friendly inquisition had been merely a warm-up. No sooner had Carson resumed his seat than Hawthorne began the state's cross-examination.

19

AMERICAN JUSTICE IS ALL WET

The courtroom steamed in the afternoon heat. The trifling breeze through the windows did little to ease the wilting discomfort of the jurors, the jammed-in spectators, or the pale, exhausted Englishman on the witness stand. But Hawthorne, despite his sweat-soaked suit, was all bustling energy as he kicked off his interrogation.

"Captain Lancaster," Hawthorne began, "the first question asked you this morning was, 'Did you kill Haden Clarke?' Your answer was in the negative. Who did kill him?"

Lancaster appeared unruffled: "Haden Clarke committed suicide."

"In your presence?"

"I didn't see him."

"Was it in your presence?"

"I must have been in the room with him."

Hawthorne picked up one of the forged suicide notes and read it aloud. "This note on Latin-American Airways stationery. Did you write that note?"

"Yes."

"Positive?"

"Yes."

Hawthorne picked up the second note. "This note addressed to Chubbie. Is that your work?"

"It is," Lancaster replied uncomfortably.

"Positive?"

"Yes."

"Are you as positive as you were on April 23 that it wasn't yours?"

"Yes."

"Did anyone ask you in my office on that date if you wrote these notes?"

"No."

"Didn't Jones?"

"No."

"Did you afterwards send word to Jones that you were sorry you didn't tell him the truth about the notes when he asked you?"

"I didn't mean that. I meant I was sorry I acted a lie."

"When you were shown these notes in my office and the discrepancies between the typing of Clarke and the typing of the notes, and the similarity between them and your own, what did you say?"

"I believe I said, 'Isn't that a coincidence?' "

"What else did you say?"

"I can't recall."

"When you were being examined in my office were you being subjected to abuse or discourtesy by anyone in the office?"

"No."

"Were you more excited in my office than when you wrote these notes beside Clarke's body?"

"I was less excited."

"What else did you say about these notes?"

"I suggested getting outside experts to look at them."

"What was your purpose in suggesting that?"

"To put you off the scent."

Hawthorne then returned to the matter of the pistol. Lancaster confirmed that he had bought it for thirty dollars at a sporting goods store and registered the gun's number with the local sheriff.

"Did you give a check to Gentry Shelton, Sr.?" Hawthorne asked.

"Yes, for a hundred dollars."

"On what bank was that check drawn?"

"On my bank," Lancaster said. "I gave him that check with the understanding it was not to be presented."

"Then he, too, betrayed your trust, Captain Lancaster, by presenting that check?"

"No, he didn't present the check."

"Would you recognize that check?" Hawthorne asked.

"I certainly would."

Hawthorne handed Lancaster a paper slip. "Examine this and see if you can identify it."

"That looks like—it is a photostatic copy of my check."

"And on the back is Mr. Gentry Shelton, Sr.'s endorsement. On the front is marked, 'Returned. First National Bank. Account closed.'"

Lancaster appeared genuinely baffled. "Until this moment I didn't know that check had been presented."

"Then he has betrayed your trust?"

"Yes, he has. Very much so."

Hawthorne was attempting to portray Lancaster as a liar, but the jurors' faces indicated that they thought Lancaster was telling the truth. Still Hawthorne pressed ahead.

"Why did you give him the check? Why not a memorandum—an I.O.U.?"

"His son asked me to."

"So you gave him a check on a bank where you had no account?"

"The account was closed since I have been in this jail. I didn't close it."

Hawthorne's tone was sarcastic: "Then, Captain Lancaster, the bank has betrayed you too?"

"To my knowledge, the account is not closed. But all my checks and statements are in the state's possession." Lancaster's serene response made Hawthorne's manner appear overbearing. His line of questioning appeared to be backfiring.

Hawthorne denied that he possessed Lancaster's financial records. "I have also been charged with having letters Haden Clarke wrote to you in St. Louis," he added, "but I have never seen them."

Carson stood up. "May it please the court," he noted wryly, "we have never accused Mr. Hawthorne of having these letters, but if he wishes to plead guilty we will accept his plea."

At this, the spectators burst into cheers, stomping their feet and clapping their hands in approval, proving just how thoroughly Hawthorne had lost the room. "This is not a vaudeville show," Judge Atkinson bellowed, the sound of his gavel barely audible above the crowd's continued applause. The bailiffs shouted for calm, and Judge Atkinson threatened to clear the court, but the noise continued. When at last the spectators quieted, Judge Atkinson angrily declared that further interruptions would not be tolerated. The next time, he said, all spectators would be removed.

Hawthorne acted unfazed by the disruption. "Isn't it true," he continued, "that the manner of closing an account is to take all your money out of the bank?"

"Yes," Lancaster answered, "unless they write that they no longer want your account and enclose a check for the balance."

"Did they write to you?"

"As far as I know, no. I just have a two or three dollar balance there."

"Didn't you make an affidavit in this court that you were totally without funds?" Hawthorne was again trying to catch Lancaster in a lie.

"Yes."

"Are you?"

"To the best of my ability I can say I am without funds. Gentry Shelton was indebted to me."

"What amount?"

"One hundred and twenty dollars."

"Have you tried to collect that?"

"Yes. Gentry Shelton told Mr. Lathero in a phone conversation that he would send five hundred dollars to pay off that debt and to assist me here."

"Did he send it?"

"No."

"Does Latin-American Airways owe you any money?"

"Yes. Two or three hundred dollars."

"Did you mention that in your affidavit?"

"No. I had no hope of getting it."

The spectators emitted murmurs of understanding, which Judge Atkinson promptly hushed.

Hawthorne returned to the pistol. "Didn't you say you didn't know why you loaded the gun at Nashville?"

"Yes."

"Didn't you tell me the reason you loaded it was because you wanted to return it to Huston as he gave it to you?"

"Yes."

"Nashville was the last stop out of Miami, wasn't it?"

"Yes."

"Did you load the gun at night or morning?"

"Night."

"The next night you were in Miami, weren't you?"

"Yes."

"Your diary shows there was dire need of funds at home." Hawthorne was implying that it was suspicious for Lancaster to spend thirty dollars on a gun instead of sending the money to Jessie, who was broke. "Wasn't Chubbie, and Haden Clarke, uppermost in your mind?"

"No, I was afraid she might have been harmed."

"By whom?"

"Haden."

"In what way?"

"Well, drinking," Lancaster admitted.

"The reason you were so worried about Chubbie was because you loved her better than anything in the world, wasn't it?"

"Yes."

"Would you lie for her?" Hawthorne asked.

"I have," Lancaster said.

"Would you steal for her?"

"I *have* stolen for her."

"WOULD YOU KILL FOR HER?" Hawthorne shouted.

"I WOULD," Lancaster boomed back.

"*Did* you?" Hawthorne pushed.

"I did not," Lancaster said wearily.

The tone of Lancaster's response, which seemed genuine as opposed to practiced, played well with the room. Hawthorne shifted course, detouring into questions about Lancaster's family life, seeking to highlight Lancaster's abandonment of his wife and daughters. "Have you any children?" he asked.

"Mr. Hawthorne, I'd like to keep my wife and children out of this," Lancaster replied.

An objection by Carson was sustained; Hawthorne, stymied, again changed course.

"You said you acted like a schoolboy after receiving the letters of Chubbie and Clarke in St. Louis. What were your actions?"

"I wouldn't eat my dinner."

"Did you go to a nightclub that night?"

"Yes."

"Did you act like a schoolboy?"

"Yes. There were girls there and I wouldn't dance with them. I was blue and sat at the table, thinking about Chubbie."

Next Hawthorne brought up Russell's testimony that Lancaster had pledged to "get rid of" Clarke. Lancaster, echoing his response to Carson's earlier inquiries, dismissed Russell's claims as "absolute lies."

"You found out before you got home, and from the lips of Clarke, that he had a serious malady?" Hawthorne asked.

"You're quite right."

"Did the love affair of Clarke and Chubbie still appear quite beautiful to you?"

"Yes."

"The knowledge of the malady didn't affect you?"

"No. They were very much in love and I saw only that."

"Then you learned later of the intimacies between them, while you were away, and it still appeared beautiful to you?"

"There was a beautiful side to it which I wanted to consider. That was the better side of Clarke's character."

"He proved that in the end by committing suicide, didn't he?" Hawthorne's tone was edged with sarcasm.

"Not in the manner in which he did, but the fact that he did showed he had good intentions."

"Do you still feel that way?"

"I would like to."

"I'm asking you."

"Yes."

"Did you feel relieved when you dropped off to sleep that night?"

"Yes. In my heart I knew that Clarke would never marry Chubbie."

"Why? Because he would commit suicide before morning?"

"No, because he had promised to tell Chubbie in the morning all of the misstatements he had admitted to me that night, and if he didn't I would."

Hawthorne pounced: "But you were going back to St. Louis."

"No, that was earlier in the evening when I planned that," Lancaster countered, in keeping with his and Jessie's earlier testimony.

Hawthorne asked why Lancaster had entrusted Jessie to Clarke's care in the first place: "You left Chubbie with Clarke, a drinker, and she was a drinker?"

"Yes, but his reputation was quite good."

"According to your standards, Captain Lancaster? Hadn't he used your home as a home of prostitution?"

"No."

"Hadn't he stayed there three nights with a woman to whom he was not married?"

"Yes. That was not prostitution as I understand it."

Hawthorne and Carson tussled briefly over the definition of the word "prostitution."

"But he had used your home as a house of debauchery, hadn't he?" Hawthorne asked.

"Haden spent some nights drinking there with girls."

"Had anybody else?"

"No."

"But Clarke had—with your knowledge, consent, and approval."

"I didn't consent, but I didn't hold it against him."

Hawthorne's sarcasm was immediate: "It was beautiful to you."

"No."

"Who was head of that household?"

"Mrs. Keith-Miller's name was on the lease."

"Didn't you live with her?"

"I didn't live at her apartment with her in New York."

"But you lived under the same roof in Miami."

"Yes."

"So it became beautiful in Miami."

"I never described the relationship as beautiful."

To his probable frustration, Hawthorne's attempt to paint Lancaster as debauched appeared to be gaining little traction in the room. Sensing this,

Hawthorne switched to what he surely thought would be a damaging point. "Did you write an entry in your diary for January 7?"

When Lancaster said yes, Hawthorne asked him to read the entry out loud.

"Fined fifty dollars with a suspended license on a complaint filed by driver of Buick," Lancaster began. "American justice is all wet. The evidence given was insufficient to convict me but, like all matters in American courts, they are subject to the inefficiency of the court officials and police."

"What did you mean when you wrote: 'American justice is all wet'?" Hawthorne asked.

"I had been found guilty of something I hadn't done. I now realize that I should not have written it. I'm sorry you don't like it."

Hawthorne gave a snort. "Being an American," he pronounced imperiously, "I don't like any of it." But again Hawthorne had misjudged his audience, which appeared to find Lancaster's response appropriately contrite. Carson leaped up to object. Hawthorne withdrew his comment.

"Did you ever utter threats about Clarke in front of Tancrel and Russell?" he asked.

"No."

"Did you ever tell Gentry Shelton that you had seen hundreds die under machine-gun fire and you wouldn't mind seeing another dead man?"

"No."

"Shelton isn't here, is he?"

"He promised he'd come down."

"He promised *me* he would, too," Hawthorne said meaningfully, implying that there was something dubious about Shelton's absence from the trial.

"If Russell testified that he showed you in Los Angeles letters from his wife," Hawthorne continued, "was that true?"

"Yes, true."

"If he told you he would meet you at the Burbank Airport, was that true?"

"Yes, true."

"Then your statement that Russell's testimony was a tissue of lies relates only to what he testified you told him about Haden Clarke?"

"No."

"What, then? You previously said it was all a tissue of lies."

"You produced letters which Russell said he showed me, untrue. He said I made threats against Haden Clarke, untrue. He said he had been for gasoline for the flight to Los Angeles, untrue. If you will have the reporter read Russell's testimony I can point out other lies." Lancaster's rapid-fire answer played well in the already sympathetic courtroom.

"Just state what you remember, Captain," Hawthorne said.

"The only thing I told him about Haden Clarke in Los Angeles was, 'Oh, don't worry about that, I trust Chubbie.' "

"Did you tell Gentry Shelton you would see Haden Clarke dead before he would marry Chubbie?"

"I did not. That night I drank the pint of Scotch I might have uttered threats. . . . I said, 'If Haden Clarke hurts Chubbie, he'll have to answer to me.' "

"Would you consider his behavior as harming her?"

"I would, but when I arrived here I overlooked it."

"You went to bed with an entirely different picture as a result of that confidential talk with Haden Clarke, didn't you?"

"Yes."

"And Haden Clarke went to bed laughing?"

Lancaster ignored Hawthorne's exaggeration. "Yes, he laughed at the story of Tancrel's paper-hanging exploits."

"And his last words were?" Hawthorne appeared to be fishing for inconsistencies in Lancaster's various testimonies.

" 'Bill, you're the whitest man I know.' "

"And he also said, 'Bill, you can have Chubbie'?"

"I have never said that."

"But did he say that?"

"No."

"And in the stress and strain you wrote the notes before calling for a doctor?"

"Yes."

"You saw many persons die in the war?"

"Yes, quite a few."

"Did you ever remember a person living with a similar wound in the head? Live or talk again?"

"Yes, I have."

"How long did it take you to type the notes?"

"Five minutes."

"How long was it from the time the shot was fired until you had completed the notes and called Mrs. Keith-Miller?"

"No more than eight minutes."

Though Hawthorne thought Lancaster had shot Clarke, he also wanted to emphasize Lancaster's negligence in waiting so long to call for help. Now he tried to prove that Lancaster was underestimating, deliberately or not, how long it had taken to ring for medical assistance.

"Would you mind rewriting the notes on the typewriter now?" Hawthorne asked.

"Certainly not."

Clarke's typewriter, which had been introduced in evidence, was placed on the court reporter's table, and Lancaster was handed paper and the two "suicide" notes. The court clerk, the attorneys, and several spectators took out their watches, but Lancaster didn't notice because he was adjusting the paper in the typewriter. He began typing, but paused after a few words. "I haven't the exact wording here," he said.

"Go on, Captain," Hawthorne replied.

Lancaster noticed the watches. "Am I being timed?" he asked. "Is it a contest?"

"This is not a contest, Captain Lancaster," Hawthorne said with exasperation. "It is just an exhibition."

"Then you want it to be a fair exhibition?"

"Yes, I do."

Lancaster started over again; as he worked, the click of the typewriter, along with the occasional cough, were the only sounds in the room. The spectators leaned forward as he finished typing the second note.

"Two minutes and a half," the court clerk announced. Hawthorne, it seemed, had misjudged; Lancaster had shown that eight minutes might in fact have been a *lengthy* estimate.

Lancaster was handed the "death pencil," as the newspapers had dubbed it, and he signed the two notes.

"You told Mr. Carson this morning that Clarke had said he was 'not making the grade,'" Hawthorne said. "Were you trying to use those words or did they come to you spontaneously?"

"I must have been. I came to the typewriter, thought for a second, and then typed the notes."

"You wrote the notes in the same manner and touch as you wrote them here?"

"Not much difference. I've been in jail three months and I am under a strain here, but I was probably under a greater strain then."

Lancaster's demonstration complete, Judge Atkinson recessed the court until the following day.

20

THE MAN FROM AUBURN

On Thursday, August 11, Judge Atkinson began the proceedings by ordering that the jury be taken from the courtroom. He then stood up on the bench and announced to the hundreds of spectators that any outbursts like those of the previous day, when audience members had stamped their feet and clapped their hands, would force him to "drastic action." Those sorts of demonstrations were against the law, Atkinson noted sternly, because they were inclined to influence jurors, and the whole point of keeping the jury segregated during a murder trial was to keep the members' minds from outside influence.

His speech concluded, Atkinson asked the attorneys if they wished to supplement his remarks. Hawthorne declined, but Carson, for the defense, asked the crowd to refrain from further demonstrations so as not to prejudice Lancaster's chances for a fair trial. Then, in a surprise move, perhaps inspired by his missteps the previous day, Hawthorne announced that he would not further cross-examine Lancaster.

Carson, after briefly questioning Lancaster about his finances, called J. P. Moe, a deputy U.S. marshal, to the stand. Moe had admitted Tancrel to the courthouse jail after Tancrel had been transferred from California to Miami for the trial.

"What did Tancrel say on the way to the cells?" Carson asked.

"I asked him how he'd like to be put in the same cell with Lancaster, and he said, 'Don't do that, I'd have to kill him.' "

"Anything else?"

"Yes," Moe replied. "He said, 'I'll do all I can to see that Lancaster burns.' "

Coming from a U.S. marshal, Moe's testimony, despite its lack of witnesses, had a noted effect on the jurors, as it called into question Tancrel's—and, by extension, Russell's—entire testimony.

Carson then moved to deepen his previous portrayal of Haden Clarke as an unstable, even suicidal, individual. He called to the stand a young man named Dick Lavender, Clarke's former roommate from New Orleans. Lavender had met Clarke in a speakeasy where both men were drinking.

"Did you and Clarke have any habits in common?" Carson asked.

"Just drinking."

"Did he have any in which you did not share?"

"He smoked marijuana torpedoes," Lavender said, explaining that torpedoes were slightly larger than cigarettes. (The day's newspapers reported that marijuana was "commonly called hasheesh.")

Lavender testified that Clarke's physical condition—his syphilis—was "not good," that "he took no means of protecting others" (that is, wearing condoms), and that he'd once said, "Somebody gave it to me, I don't care if I give it to somebody else."

Clarke told Lavender that he worked for the *Times-Picayune*, but after three visits to the newspaper plant, he had ditched the job. In its place Clarke set off on a hitchhiking and train-riding journey to Miami from New Orleans in order to generate material for a magazine article. Lavender tagged along. The two men began their excursion with a two-day stop in Pensacola, where they did nothing but drink, followed by a day and a half in Tallahassee, where the drinking continued. In Jacksonville, Lavender picked up two checks from the Veterans' Bureau, which, he informed Carson, Clarke had stolen to buy alcohol in Daytona Beach.

As Lavender told it, Clarke had thought Lavender was suicidal, and so one night, as they drank in a speakeasy, Clarke had advised him that the best way to commit suicide was to shoot oneself in the head, because this led to instant death.

Hawthorne, in his cross-examination, sought to prove that Lavender was a drunken and unreliable witness. "Who was present when the suicidal thesis was delivered by Haden?" he asked.

"No one was present," Lavender responded. "I didn't pay much attention to him. I thought it was just liquor talk."

"Did he say *he* would ever commit suicide?"

"He said if he ever got in a jam he would."

"Was he very drunk at the time?"

"No, just normally so."

Lavender said Clarke had been generally cheerful, but that the last time he saw him, at 2321 S.W. 21st Terrace, Clarke had been depressed because one of his stories had been returned.

"Did he have a cowardly nature?" Hawthorne asked.

"Apparently not," Lavender replied, indicating, to Hawthorne's likely consternation, that he thought Clarke had committed suicide.

Carson wasn't finished with his parade of damning witnesses. The owner of a restaurant Clarke had frequented took to the stand to describe the young writer as chronically depressed. Then Carson brought up Dick Richardson, a playwright friend of Clarke, who reported that Clarke had indeed been a heavy drinker.

"Did you ever hear him discuss suicide?" Carson asked.

"Yes, at the home of Mrs. Keith-Miller, three weeks before his suicide." Chubbie had also been in the room, Richardson said.

"How did the conversation start?"

"I had written a play, *Rasputin*, and remarked how difficult it was to kill [the main character]."

"Did Clarke explain an easy and sure method?"

"Yes," Richardson answered. "He said the best way was to shoot oneself above and a little behind the right ear."

After Richardson stepped down, Carson turned his attention to the medical evidence for Clarke's suicide, for which the key document was the autopsy report generated by the court-appointed medical commission. But the report itself was mute on the issue of suicide; none of the commission's three doctors were criminologists, and they did not feel qualified to rule on the issue. Dr. Dodge, the commission member with the most relevant experience, was ill and unable to attend the trial, and so Carson was deprived of one of his most valued witnesses. In Dodge's absence Carson called to the stand Dr. M. H. Tallman, the commission's court-appointed representative. Tallman possessed twenty-one years of experience in five different states, and he was now chief surgeon at Victoria Hospital. Though Tallman would not offer an opinion regarding suicide, he provided the trial's most shocking moment to date.

"Do you have an exhibit?" Carson asked him.

"Yes," Tallman replied. From a box on his lap he withdrew a round, blackened object. A collective gasp escaped from the audience as they realized that the object was Haden Clarke's skull. A female onlooker leaped up and ran from the room. But Lancaster, at the defense table, appeared fascinated, leaning forward in his seat to gain a closer look.

Dr. Tallman produced a slide of tissue that had been taken from within an inch of the bullet wound. Though the tissue appeared to contain powder grains, Tallman said, this would have to be determined by a chemist. After entering the skull as a defense exhibit and marking the slide for identification, Carson excused Tallman from the stand.

Because Tallman's testimony could not fully replace that of Dr. Dodge, Carson called to the stand another expert witness, Dr. Albert H. Hamilton. Of all the individuals who appeared in the courtroom that summer, Hamilton had perhaps the most outsized reputation; over the preceding decades, he had been celebrated and vilified in equal measure. Taking the stand with his usual haughty confidence, Hamilton announced that he had forty-seven years of experience as a ballistic and criminological expert. His work had taken him, he said, from the eastern states to Arizona, and from the Dakotas to Florida and Texas. The Lancaster case, he declared, was the 296th homicide he had investigated.

In truth, Dr. Albert Hamilton was not really a doctor. A native of upstate New York, he had started his career, in the late nineteenth century, as a maker of patent medicines. But Hamilton, a canny observer of human nature, had sensed, as forensic expert Colin Evans writes, "the public's growing awe of all things scientific." Realizing "that a title might be a useful marketing tool," Hamilton had "encouraged his clients to refer to him as 'Doctor,' and the moniker stuck." Hamilton's eye for opportunity remained robust as the twentieth century dawned. With science playing an ever-larger role in criminal trials, Hamilton set himself up as a "Micro-Chemical Investigator," charging clients the exorbitant fee of fifty dollars a day plus expenses for his trial testimony. Hamilton purchased a microscope and a camera so he would appear more "professional."

To promote himself more broadly, Hamilton published a booklet called *The Man from Auburn*. The booklet, like Hamilton himself, was an exercise in grandiosity. "When Dr. A. Conan Doyle conceived his world famous character Sherlock Holmes," *The Man from Auburn* declared, "he probably little thought that there was a man in this State who was destined to be an almost exact materialization of the famous detective, both as to the method and to a great extent as to personal appearance."

In the booklet Hamilton claimed to be a qualified expert witness in "chemistry, microscopy, handwriting, ink analysis, typewriting, photography, finger prints, toxicology, gun shot wounds, revolvers, guns, cartridges, bullet deflection, gunpowders, nitroglycerine, dynamite, explosives, blood and other stains, human and so forth, cause of death, suicide as against homicide, embalming in fluids, determination of distance revolver was held when discharged, when a gun bullet was fired from a gun or revolver, and several other subjects." When questioned about those claims during a 1913 trial in New York City, Hamilton bragged that he had been "permitted to qualify on those subjects by Supreme Court justices."

The fraudulence of Hamilton's ballistics "expertise" was first exposed in the 1915 trial of Charles Stielow, a German farm laborer in West Shelby, New York, who was accused of murdering both his employer and the farm's housekeeper. Stielow possessed the intelligence of a small child, and, while innocent, he was easily railroaded into confessing. Hamilton's deceitful testimony on the stand helped to seal Stielow's fate. Stielow was already in Sing Sing Prison, sentenced to die by the electric chair, when an optics expert from the Bausch and Lomb Company in Rochester at last stepped in to prove Hamilton's errors. In 1918 Stielow walked out of Sing Sing a free man.

Yet the case did little to harm Hamilton's reputation; at the time, local trial coverage was rarely reported in other states. In 1921 Hamilton received the biggest break of his career, when he testified for the defense in the notorious Sacco and Vanzetti case. On the stand Hamilton argued vigorously that the two Italian-American anarchists were innocent of murdering a guard and a paymaster during an armed robbery in South Braintree, Massachusetts. Hamilton performed an in-court demonstration involving three different revolvers, but at the last minute the judge caught him illegally attempting to switch out parts of Sacco's pistol in order to bolster his testimony that Sacco's gun had not been used in the robbery.

Despite this public embarrassment, Hamilton remained in demand for high-profile trials, including one for the murder of notorious gambler Arnold Rothstein. And so it was that on August 12, 1932, James Carson called Hamilton to the witness stand to testify on Bill Lancaster's behalf. Hamilton had contacted Carson after reading an AP article about Clarke's death; in typically high-handed fashion, Hamilton claimed the article had given him "certain information that told him considerably about the case which the local authorities might . . . have missed." The Miami newspapers described "Dr. Hamilton" admiringly as a "ballistics expert and nationally known criminologist," showing how robust his reputation remained.

Upon taking the stand, Hamilton told Carson, in his usual overblown manner, that the autopsy report on Clarke was the best he'd ever seen.

"And did you make a conclusion, Dr. Hamilton?" Carson asked.

"Yes, I did. There was but one conclusion, and only one conclusion that could be arrived at from this examination, and that was that this shot was a self-inflicted, close, hard-contact shot at the instant the gun was hard against head and head hard against gun."

"Was it suicide or homicide?"

"Absolutely suicide. There is not a scintilla of evidence to support a theory of homicide or murder."

Hamilton said he based his conclusion of suicide on the fact that no powder burns had been found on the wound's exterior, and that subcutaneous ballooning had occurred. This, Hamilton claimed, pointed to "sealed contact," meaning that the gun was pressed so tightly against the head that explosive gases were prevented from escaping. This happened only in cases of suicide, he said.

Hamilton testified further that bloody residue and tissue, along with human hair, were visible through a microscope at the front sight of the "death pistol." At the bullet's exit point Hamilton said he had found at least fifty microscopic pieces of lead. These had been thrown off, he claimed, as the bullet rotated rapidly through the skull, indicating the gun had been fired at extremely close range. Hamilton said the bullet had traveled from right to left across the head and slightly backwards. To explain his point, he brought out rough diagrams he had made of the bullet's course. As he talked,

Clarke's skull was passed among the jurors, causing a ripple in the courtroom.

When the time for cross-examination arrived, Hawthorne challenged Hamilton on his qualifications as an expert. Because Hamilton's contention of a "sealed contact" wound was backed up by the medical commission's report, Hawthorne focused on proving that Hamilton's claim of suicide was an opinion, not a fact.

"If you were asleep," Hawthorne asked, "and subconsciously felt a gun barrel against your head, would you try to push your head out against the gun?"

"I'd say it was impossible."

"If a man is struck or touched while lying in bed, isn't his tendency to rise?"

"No, dodge away."

Hawthorne appeared incredulous: "You claim it would be impossible to hold the head of a man lying down asleep and kill him by shooting him with a pistol and produce similar exhibits as at this trial?"

"Impossible."

Hoping to rattle Hamilton's confidence, Hawthorne tried a different approach: "How did you acquire the title of doctor?"

"Lawyers started that," Hamilton replied dismissively. "I am not a doctor."

Before Hawthorne could press the point, the court recessed for the day. As the long line of spectators filed from the courtroom, the jurymen, along with Lancaster, were taken to 2321 S.W. 21st Terrace to examine firsthand the location of Clarke's shooting.

The next morning, Saturday, August 13, the *Miami Daily News* featured a front-page photograph, taken years earlier, of Jessie with her hair and makeup done and wearing a fancy dress. "Here's 'Chubbie' All Dressed Up!" the headline exclaimed, illustrating how far the trial coverage had blurred the lines between tragedy and entertainment.

Judge Atkinson allowed Lancaster to begin the day's proceedings with a special statement. "The position of Haden Clarke's bed at the house yesterday," Lancaster said, "was not the same as on the night of the tragedy. I remember distinctly that the window-winder came through the rails of the head of the bed so that the windows might be closed by the person in bed. Yesterday the bed was a considerable distance from the wall." The beds had been much closer together on the night of the shooting, as well.

Following Lancaster's statement, the first experts called to the stand were the remaining two members of the court-appointed medical commission, Drs. Gowe and Jones, neither of whom could state with certainty whether Clarke's wound had been self-inflicted. But their caution was offset by the return appearance of Albert Hamilton. When "The Man from Auburn" took the witness seat, Hawthorne attacked him from all angles, attempting to expose his testimony as a sham. He mocked Hamilton's supposed credentials, and questioned his analysis of the autopsy report. But Hamilton proved unflappable, doubling down on his claims: "I found nothing to support anything but suicide," he said with his usual bluster. "I say this not as an opinion, but actual knowledge." Hamilton's confidence, however unfounded, clearly impressed the jury, who watched admiringly as he left the stand. But the prosecution didn't give up: Hawthorne moved that the whole of Hamilton's testimony be expunged from the record. Judge Atkinson overruled him, and the court recessed for the Sunday break.

Monday's session began with a last-minute witness: Joseph Ince, an old friend of Lancaster's from the Royal Air Force. Ince's flight to the trial had been paid for by the *Detroit Times*, which had notified him he was wanted as a witness. Ince and Lancaster had fought in the same squadron during the war, and had shared a hotel room in El Paso during Lancaster's Latin-American Airways expedition. Under Carson's questioning, Ince, wearing a gray suit and sporting a tiny brown mustache, reported a conversation in El Paso during which Lancaster, speaking with Tancrel, had seemed reassured that Haden Clarke was taking care of Jessie in Miami. Lancaster had been worried financially, Ince said, but he had exhibited no resentment toward or doubt of Clarke.

Hawthorne's cross-examination focused on Ince's status as a war buddy and longtime friend of Lancaster. The inference was that Ince's testimony was unreliable—any old comrade would want to help his close friend out of a jam. After Ince was dismissed, Hawthorne turned to the matter of

Haden Clarke's temperament, which Carson had portrayed as morose and unsteady and subject to wild swings. Hawthorne called to the stand an old bridge-playing companion of Clarke's, Latimer Virrick, who had been at the party at 2321 S.W. 21st Terrace during which Lancaster had phoned from California, and who said he had never seen Clarke depressed. Virrick testified that Clarke had seemed troubled after hanging up, saying, "I think there'll be trouble, damn it. He's coming."

Another party attendee, Paul Prufert, told much the same story, claiming that Clarke had said, "There'll be trouble—that son of a bitch is coming back here." Prufert also testified that he had never seen Clarke act moody or glum. Hawthorne then called four more friends of Clarke, all of whom reported the same thing: they had never seen Clarke "depressed or downhearted." Two friends described him as "happy-go-lucky," with one saying that Clarke "never thought of yesterday or tomorrow." To round out his argument, Hawthorne brought to the stand a mechanic from Viking Airport who had witnessed Lancaster's return to Miami on April 20. The mechanic reported that Lancaster had acted coldly toward Clarke, neglecting to shake his hand.

Lastly, Hawthorne called on three medical experts who challenged Albert H. Hamilton's analysis of the evidence found on the death pistol's barrel. What Hamilton had identified as human hairs were in fact, the three experts testified, cotton fibers.

After the final expert stepped down, Hawthorne declared that the state had completed the witness phase of its case.

21

THE VERDICT

Shortly before noon on August 15, Assistant State Attorney Henry Jones began closing arguments. "You men are reasonable men," he told the jurors. "Will you be guided by self-serving professions of innocence or by facts presented to you?" Lancaster would say or do anything to save himself from the electric chair, Jones said, while Jessie was a fallen woman, "a poor thing, weaker by far morally than physically." Looking mournful, Jones added, "When a woman loses her virtue, she loses all. She also, it seems, loses the power to tell the truth."

The truth, Jones said, was that the supposed reasons for Clarke's suicide didn't hold up under scrutiny. "If every man who drank to excess, who ran after a woman, was short of money, or had a violent temper committed suicide," he exclaimed, "we'd have a list that would reach around the world." Instead, as in every murder case, one had to look at motive—and who possessed a greater motive than Lancaster? "Sex, if you please, was the motive," Jones said. "You have but to scratch the veneer of civilization to get down to the animal that is in all of us. The greater a man's love for a woman, the greater his motive for killing a rival." Every word of Lancaster's diary proved how all-consuming was his love for Jessie. "When Haden lay sleeping that night this man like a coward sent a bullet through his head," Jones charged, pointing at Lancaster. "It was the most dastardly and ignominious murder ever committed."

After Clarke was shot, Lancaster "didn't call a doctor, he didn't call the woman in the house," Jones scoffed. "Was there anything more cold-blooded and calculated than that? What would you do if you were awakened in the middle of the night to find your roommate shot and dying? Sit down and forge his name to some notes you wrote, or would you call a doctor?" Lancaster may have seemed honest and amiable on the stand, but that was only because he was "a supreme actor, shrewd beyond degree."

The key physical clue to Lancaster's guilt came, Jones said, from the angle at which the bullet had torn through Clarke's skull. Despite Hamilton's testimony, "When you get out there in the jury room, lie down on the floor and see if you can shoot yourself through the head where this man did." As forensics expert Colin Evans notes, "A .38 Colt revolver is a long-barreled, heavy weapon, with a trigger pull of eight to fourteen pounds." Given the bullet trajectory found in his skull—the bullet entered the front temple from right to left and exited above the left ear—Clarke "would have had to lie down and balance the gun against his temple; then, unless he was extraordinarily flexible, he would have had to depress the trigger with his thumb." This was an "implausible and unlikely" scenario. However, the bullet trajectory was "exactly what one might expect had the shot been fired by someone standing between the two beds."

During the lunch break that followed Jones's statement, Haden Clarke's mother, Ida, entered the courtroom for the first time. Although she had been subpoenaed as a witness, she was not called to the stand. Instead, she sat at the prosecution table next to her son, Dr. Beverley Clarke. She followed the afternoon's proceedings closely but kept her expression neutral.

Jessie, who had previously appeared only when she was required to give testimony, also slipped into the packed room, where she remained for the rest of the day. She stood inside the rail that separated the attorneys from the spectators. Like Ida Clarke, Jessie followed the arguments intently but with no outward signs of emotion.

At 4:28 p.m., Carson started his closing argument, which would continue into the following day. Despite his folksy courtroom manner, Carson adopted a tone of high rhetoric to make his final pitch.

"When I was a boy attending Osceola High School in my hometown of Kissimmee, I learned a declamation," Carson began, "concerning . . . General Robert E. Lee. I wish now to quote to you the sentence that I have never forgotten: 'Just as the oak stripped of its foliage by the wintry blast, then and then only stands forth in solemn and mighty grandeur against the wintry sky, so Robert Lee, stripped of every rank that man could give him, towered above the earth and those around him in the pure sublimity and strength of that character which we can only fitfully contemplate when we lift our eyes from earth to see it dimmed against the Heavens.'

"If you will permit the paraphrase," Carson continued, "William Newton Lancaster, four thousand miles from his home, facing an American jury upon a charge of murder in the first degree; having gone through periods of financial distress, deprivation, and almost starvation; and having for many months paced the narrow confines of his lonely cell, deserted by many, but not by all of his friends, stands forth above those who have surrounded him in such pure sweetness, strength, unselfishness, and sheer nobility of character, so that we can only begin to appreciate it when we see it shine like a brilliant diamond, against the muck and dirt and filth which form the sordid background of this trial."

The next morning the number of courtroom spectators was the largest yet. So intense was the demand from local attorneys for viewing space that Judge Atkinson ordered the entire area within the rail that divided the spectators' benches from the remainder of the courtroom to be cleared, thus making room for the additional lawyers. On previous days of the trial about seventy-five spectators, nearly all of them women, and most of them friends and relatives of court attachés and county officials, had filled this space. Now these spectators were forced to leave. A number of the women grew angry and argued with the bailiffs, but Judge Atkinson's order was enforced.

Among the remaining onlookers was Jessie, who again betrayed no emotion at the surrounding events. "I am interested only in freeing old Bill," she told reporters. "Nothing else matters to me."

As he had done in his opening statement, Carson attempted to prove Lancaster's innocence by freely admitting his wrongdoing: "There are certain circumstances in this case . . . that standing alone and unexplained are suspicious. I think you will bear me out that there has been no attempt upon the part of the defendant, nor of the defense, to deny the existence of those circumstances which were true." The prosecution's case, Carson said, rested on five circumstances: Lancaster's tremendous love for Jessie; the "so-called" threats made to Tancrel and Russell; Lancaster's purchase of a pistol in St. Louis; the forgery of the suicide notes; and Lancaster asking whether Clarke would speak again. But the defense had rebutted each of those circumstances one by one, leaving the prosecution at a loss. "Where is the State's case?" Carson asked. "They have utterly and completely failed."

In fact, Carson argued, Assistant State Attorney Jones's theory of the shooting was completely backwards. The reason for the bullet's right-to-left trajectory through Clarke's skull was that Clarke wanted to kill himself without endangering Lancaster. Clarke had lain flat on his back and turned his head "so that the bullet would not hit the whitest man he had ever met."

Much of the drama in the case, Carson argued, stemmed from its subject matter. "We all know, and we all regret, that there have been many sickening and unusual and sordid details concerning sex (more than we like) brought into this case," he said, "but it is your duty to deal with it." Carson unloaded the blame for the case's squalidness directly onto Jessie's shoulders, reinforcing her role as the trial's scapegoat. "There are women, all doctors know it and the books show it," Carson said, "who, due to some pathological condition, are utterly unable to live up to the standards of virtue and chastity which you and I have been taught to believe constitutes the crowning virtue of the sex to which our mothers belong." Jessie's bravery and courage as an aviator had made her an admired figure, but because of "some peculiar physical or mental . . . defect" she possessed, her deepest secrets had now been broadcast "to be read, to be condemned, to be gloated over by those of sordid minds in the far corners of the world."

Carson claimed that the case had become intensely personal to him, so great was his responsibility, given Lancaster's heroic background and worldwide reputation, to restore his client's good name. In emphasizing this point, Carson drew easily on the vicious racism that marked his time and place, so much so that his comments went utterly unremarked upon by the newspapers. "I may have gone further than my ordinary duty in an ordinary nigger murder case," Carson admitted. "There was a story told . . . about one nigger coming into the courtroom, after another one had been convicted. The one entering the courtroom was, of course, nervous and tremulous; the one who had just been convicted had had mercy recommended for him. That was all he wanted, and as he went out and this other nervous nigger was coming in, he said, 'Well, boy, how you coming along?' and the nigger who had been convicted said, with a grin all over his face, 'Fine, but I got to go to jail,' and the other nigger asked, 'For how long?' 'Oh,' he said, 'just from now on.'" But in Lancaster's case, Carson stressed, "acquittal alone would not be performing my duty to this client."

Lancaster had proved his strength of character on the witness stand by acting "cool, calm, courteous, and collected." He was, Carson noted, "scrupulously fair to the State Attorney . . . and to all others who had questioned him. He also was scrupulously fair to the memory of Haden Clarke." Lancaster had even resisted the urge to fully condemn Tancrel and Russell.

"Weigh the character of the witnesses on the one side and on the other," Carson instructed the jury, before ramping up for a grand conclusion. "Compare the jail-birds of the State with the war-birds for the defense, and have your verdict find the defendant 'Not Guilty,' and send word back to old England from whence we get our Common Law, that in American courts justice is administered in the high, fair, and solemn fashion that our ancestors won on that soil by their blood."

Carson's speech, with its soaring calls for justice and its celebration of Lancaster as a brave and humble war hero and record-breaking aviator, captivated the crowd, which day by day had viewed Lancaster with increasing sympathy and admiration. Now Hawthorne, in the prosecution's final argument, sought to bring the case back down to earth. Clarke hadn't been some meek, pathetic figure living in Lancaster's shadow, Hawthorne said. He had become, in Lancaster's absence, the "cock of the walk" at the Coral Gables house.

"Haden Clarke most certainly was not depressed or had suicidal tendencies," Hawthorne told the jury. "To the victor belongs the spoils—and Haden Clarke was at the top that night, Haden Clarke was in the driver's seat that night at the Keith-Miller home. Haden Clarke had told Chubbie not to speak alone to Lancaster, and she obeyed. Haden Clarke in a fit of rage at the dinner table showed he was not a coward—and only cowards commit suicide—told Lancaster he was the head man at the house that night. Lancaster, realizing this, said he would leave the house, go to a hotel, and start back to St. Louis in the morning. Lancaster foresaw trouble; Haden Clarke expected it.

"At the airport Lancaster meets the man who alienated the affections of the woman he loved more than anything in the world and he doesn't speak to him. He doesn't even shake hands. The meeting was not friendly." At the house Jessie had told Lancaster, in no uncertain terms, that she loved Clarke. When Clarke angrily forbade her from speaking with Lancaster alone, she obeyed. When Clarke told her to lock her bedroom door, she obeyed. "Don't you see where the poisoned arrow points?" Hawthorne exclaimed.

"The gun goes off and he thinks, he says, a window slammed." Hawthorne's tone was dismissive. "I submit that the report of a .38 caliber pistol, held less than three feet away from your head, would burst your eardrums.

"There is not a single fact or circumstance when the rule of common reason is applied that does not point to the guilt of this defendant. Every page in his diary points to his guilt. His own testimony that he bought a gun while Chubbie was hungry and that he loaded the gun the night before he arrived in Miami points to his guilt. A guilty conscience needs no accuser, and the fact that he wrote those notes when Clarke was dying doesn't sound so good. Lancaster asked Huston if he could say the death gun was his. Over and over again he asked if Clarke would be able to speak again. These things point to his guilt."

Haden Clarke's head had been lying on his pillow when the fatal shot was fired. But to create a "sealed contact" wound the pressure between gun and head had to be intense. "Why lie down and then rear up to meet the gun?" Hawthorne asked. "But if someone else should suddenly, while the victim is asleep, bury a gun in his head, his subconscious mind would make him come up, not dive through the pillow.

"Finally, let me say this, before this case is put away: you are a trial jury, not a pardon board. Do not let sympathy or emotions play a part. Decide simply if Haden Clarke committed suicide or if William Newton Lancaster killed him."

At 11:30 a.m. on Wednesday, August 17, 1932, Hawthorne concluded the state's case.

After a brief recess, Judge Atkinson summarized the case for the jurors. He elucidated points of law and outlined the jurymen's specific duties. And while he did not analyze the evidence, Judge Atkinson made his own feelings abundantly clear: "It has been my privilege to see into the depths of a man's soul through his private diary, which was never intended for anyone's eyes but his own," he stated. "In all my experience, which has been broad, I have never met a more honorable man than Captain Lancaster."

For four hours and fifty-nine minutes the jurors debated the case. While their sympathies lay with Lancaster, the myriad incriminating circumstances—especially the forging of the suicide notes—were simply too egregious for the jurors to dismiss. They attempted an early ballot, but the effort went nowhere. As the hours ticked by, the jurymen's arguments eventually centered on a single issue: Were their suspicions weighty enough to offset a reasonable degree of doubt? They reached out to Judge Atkinson for clarification. The jurors also requested another viewing of the exhibits, but Carson, sensing victory in the wings, and employing a legal privilege, anonymously denied their request.

Though the jurors strenuously debated the forged notes, another suspicious element of the case escaped their attention. The defense claimed that the right-to-left trajectory of the fatal shot was the result of Clarke's attempt to aim the bullet away from Lancaster. But there were two other beds on the opposite side of the sun porch, well away from where Lancaster lay sleeping. If Clarke were truly concerned about Lancaster's safety, wouldn't it have made more sense for him to lie on these? Or, at the very least, sit up straight in his bed before pulling the trigger? For that matter, why not go to a different room entirely to perform the deed?

A few minutes before 5 p.m., the jurors reentered the courtroom. The buzz of anticipation was palpable. The jury foreman handed a note to E. B. Leatherman, the circuit court clerk. In a booming voice, Leatherman announced the verdict:

"Not guilty."

An ecstatic wave of cheers, screaming, clapping, and foot-stomping swept over the courtroom. Fashionably gowned women broke down in tears, shrieking their delight, while others gasped in gleeful astonishment, scarcely able to catch their breath. The courtroom presented a carnival-like scene, with bailiffs, deputies, sheriffs, and police officers vainly striving to contain the crowd as people surged forward in a desperate effort to shake Lancaster's hand. Lancaster himself nervously clasped and unclasped his fingers, eventually stepping forward before the jurors, who remained in their box.

When the noise in the room finally began to subside, Lancaster shook hands with his lawyers and gamely posed for photographs. "I have been convinced all along that my innocence would be established," he announced to the reporters. "My trial has been eminently fair and I have been treated cordially and courteously at all times."

Turning to the jury, Lancaster said, "Gentlemen, you have been very patient with your time. I want to give you my heartfelt thanks for exonerating me." He clicked his heels, gave the jurors a brisk bow, and tried to return to his chair at the defense table, but the crush of well-wishers prevented this. "I am delighted at my acquittal," he called to reporters.

Hawthorne, presenting a brave face, uttered a brief statement: "The performance of my duty to the best of my ability is sufficient compensation. The jury, the only agency provided by law to determine the issue, has rendered its verdict, and I accept it without regret."

But the newsmen's attention was all on Lancaster. "Do your present plans include Mrs. Keith-Miller?"

"Please don't ask me to answer that," Lancaster wearily responded. "I don't now know what my answer would be."

Jessie herself had been in an office adjoining the courtroom when the verdict was announced. The earsplitting cheering and clapping had told her all she needed to know. As she walked out into the hallway, hoping to slip out of the building, a lone reporter blocked her path. How did she feel? he asked. "I am delighted," she responded. "I knew old Bill would come through."

22

A TRAGIC FIGURE

"I must start life all over again," Jessie told *The New York Times* before she departed from America. Lancaster's trial had ended nine weeks earlier, but reporters were still pestering her with questions about whether she and Lancaster would now wed. Lancaster's parents clearly wished otherwise, telling the press they hoped Lancaster and Kiki would be reconciled. But Jessie hinted that reports about her and Lancaster getting married at some future date might not be off base.

On October 14, 1932, Jessie boarded the American Merchant liner *American Banker* in New York for the voyage back to England. Although the assistant immigration commissioner announced that Jessie was leaving of her own free will, officials at American Merchant said she was being deported. According to *The Baltimore Sun*, the Department of Labor had agreed to drop deportation warrants against Jessie and Lancaster in return for an agreement that both would leave the country within a week. Deportation measures had been pending against the two since the conclusion of Lancaster's trial.

Lancaster went to the docks to see Jessie off, but by mistake he initially boarded the wrong boat. After he realized his error, he accidentally left behind a rug he was carrying for Jessie in his haste to find the correct ship.

A swarm of reporters followed him as he searched for the *American Banker.* To the gathered journalists, Jessie expressed considerable relief at getting out of the country, and a great deal of bitterness toward the American press, which she said had not treated her fairly. She also expressed fear that the stigma of Lancaster's trial would follow her always, and admitted that she was nervous about what the public's reaction to her and Lancaster in England would be. "I have been hiding out around New York for a month, not seeing anybody except a few friends," Jessie said sadly. "Do you think I'll ever live this thing down? Will people and the press forget it? Can I do anything—fly the Atlantic, or anything like that, which will make them put a new tag on me?"

Several hours later, Lancaster himself sailed for England on the Cunard liner *Scythia*. An immigration officer accompanied him to the ship.

When she arrived in London, Jessie found an immediate opportunity to make money by selling her story to the *Daily Express*, which ran a series of installments, in late October and early November, featuring her version of Haden Clarke's death and her subsequent ordeal with the police. Jessie used the money to move into a one-room apartment in Oxford Terrace.

Lancaster disembarked in Liverpool on October 24. "I have not yet decided when I shall make my next flight," he announced to reporters, "and I shall have no other pilot than [Jessie]." He stated that he had received the fairest possible trial and been accorded the most generous and sympathetic treatment by the American people.

Despite his positive outlook, Lancaster, as the autumn progressed, proved unable to find work. The scandal attached to his name made employment difficult enough, but this difficulty was compounded by the Depression's continued effect on the world of aviation. His only happiness came from his frequent calls on Jessie in Oxford Terrace.

"I didn't have the same feelings for him at all, but I would have done anything to help him," Jessie recalled later. "There was no question of partnering up then, though. He would still have liked to, but I was through. There was no future for us. I was very fond of him but the romance had gone." But at least one person did not believe this to be true. One winter night Lancaster arrived to take her to a dance, for which they were both dressed in evening clothes. As she stepped outside her door, Jessie was slapped hard in the face by someone who darted out of the shadows and then dashed quickly away. Lancaster sprinted after the assailant in pursuit. When he returned panting a few minutes later, he shamefacedly told Jessie that the attacker had been Kiki.

By January or February 1933 Lancaster had come to accept that his employment opportunities were nonexistent, and that the taint of his murder trial would not wash easily away. He could think of only one way to transform his fortunes: by setting another world's record for flying. As he cast around for options, he focused on the record recently set by Amy Mollison, who in November had flown from London to South Africa in four days, six hours, and fifty-four minutes. This was ten hours faster than the previous record setter: Mollison's own husband, Jim.

Lancaster's father, now seventy-three years old and frail, and his invalid mother agreed to finance Lancaster's journey, even though paying for his costly defense in Miami had depleted most of their savings. Lancaster chose as his aircraft an Avro Avian that his old acquaintance renowned Australian flier Charles Kingsford Smith had recently used for an aborted journey from Australia to England. Named the *Southern Cross Minor*, the plane, for which Lancaster paid seven hundred pounds, differed from the *Red Rose* in that it was a single-seater with a powerful Gipsy II four-cylinder in-line engine. The 120-horsepower Gipsy II, with its 1,600-mile range, was one of the most popular engine models of the interwar period. The *Southern Cross Minor*'s only downside was its ninety-five-mile-per-hour cruising speed, which was twenty miles slower than Amy Mollison's Puss Moth aircraft. This difference in speed added to the pressure on Lancaster: to beat Mollison's record, he would have to go almost entirely without sleep on his journey.

Jessie helped Lancaster map the route, but her collaboration ended there. Years later, she remembered that, during this period, Lancaster looked "absolutely haggard. I saw him standing there with hollow eyes and cheeks. He looked like a death head. He looked exhausted before he started and I remember thinking, 'He's not going to make it.'" The last time she saw Lancaster was when he came to visit her one night just before his journey. Lancaster asked if he could take her watch along as a memento, but Jessie declined on the grounds that the watch face was far too small for him to read while he was flying. He needed a much larger watch, she told him. Resignedly, Lancaster agreed. He waved farewell and walked back out into the night.

Lancaster, on his own, gathered the *Southern Cross Minor* from the Cheshire Airfields, acquired the necessary permits, and gave a hundred pounds to the Trans-Saharienne Company to help fund the search costs if he went missing during his trip. Lancaster's father took out insurance on the plane.

In the first week of April, with only days until his flight, Lancaster took Kiki and his daughters, Pat and Nina Ann, out to eat. He also had his lawyer draw up a will naming Jessie as the sole beneficiary of his meager £170 estate—with the excuse that Jessie, like his parents, had spent much of her own money paying for his trial defense. Lancaster's only asset was the insurance policy on his life. On April 8, he hopped a train from London to Manchester, where he had stored the *Southern Cross Minor.* The next day Lancaster flew to Lympne, Kent, where the civil airfield was a popular destination for attempted record-breaking flights. His parents met him at the nearby Grand Hotel.

On Monday, April 9, 1933, Lancaster held a press conference at the Grand Hotel in which he announced his goal of breaking Amy Mollison's record. "I am going 'all out' on this flight," he declared. Despite predictions of inclement weather along his intended route, he had faith in the *Southern Cross Minor*'s capabilities. "I can't wait for the months that must elapse before conditions are good," Lancaster told reporters. He also gave heartfelt thanks for his parents' faith and financial investment in him, saying that his mother and father believed, as he did, that he would "be able to make the world forget" the murder trial in Miami. There was thus no attempt to downplay his motivation for the journey.

The next morning, April 10, Lancaster arrived at the airfield before dawn. He wore a windbreaker over flying overalls and a thick bright scarf around his neck. By way of luggage he carried his flying goggles, a light hat to protect his head from the subtropical South African sun, and the maps on which he'd marked his path. Airfield workers had filled the *Southern Cross Minor* with one hundred gallons of fuel, enough for about eighteen hours of travel. The plane also carried, in accordance with French regulations, a two-gallon drum of water.

Lancaster planned to spend his first day flying from Lympne to the city of Oran in northwest Algeria, a 1,125-mile journey over France, the Spanish coast, and the Mediterranean. But from the Lympne control tower that morning he learned that twenty-mile-per-hour headwinds would dog him the whole way, severely slowing his speed and raising the possibility that he would need to refuel along the way. Given the disadvantages he already faced in outdoing Mollison's travel time, the situation warranted serious consideration. But Lancaster refused to be deterred.

Along with weather and speed, the journey was fraught with more personal complications. As Ralph Barker points out, Lancaster "had done no flying at all for almost exactly twelve months, and for three of those months he had been confined to a cell eight feet by ten." Lancaster also knew the pain, both emotional and financial, he had caused his parents, and he was desperate to prove their faith in him justified. His stress and desperation were compounded by the relentless pace he would have to keep: to beat Mollison's record, Lancaster would need to squeeze seventy-two hours of flight time into four and a half days, with almost all of his ground time allocated for servicing and refueling his plane. Even the healthiest, most mentally stable individual might break under that regimen, and Lancaster was already a near-wreck. But he was betting his entire future on this journey, and he accepted the inherent risks. He had already announced that this would be his final attempt to rehabilitate his flying career. On the other side lay permanent failure and disgrace.

Only Lancaster's mother and father, an old RAF compatriot named K. K. Brown, and a few airfield officials gathered to see him off at Lympne in the heavy morning mist. To the officials, Lancaster seemed like a gaunt, anxious shadow of the hale, good-humored pilot they had once known. "I owe this chance to come back to my father and mother," he told the small group, "and for the old folks' sake alone I hope to win through." Still, he added, "I want to make it clear that I am attempting this flight at my own risk. I don't expect any efforts to be made to find me if I'm reported missing." But he knew this latter statement carried no weight. He also knew that, in the event of a forced landing, pilots believed in sticking close to their downed aircraft.

Lancaster's mother made a brief speech before he departed. "I have every confidence in my boy," she said. "My prayers are for him to win through. I want the world to forget the Miami tragedy and to remember that my boy joined up during the war at the age of seventeen and was a wartime airman.

That is why his father and I have bought this plane and we know he will win through."

For sustenance Lancaster carried a little beef extract and a thermos each of coffee and water, along with a pack of chicken sandwiches his mother had prepared. Just before he stepped up into the cockpit, his mother gave him a kiss goodbye and handed him a bar of chocolate. At 5:38 a.m., with the morning light still dim, Lancaster taxied the *Southern Cross Minor* down the runway, quickly achieving liftoff. Before long the plane was swallowed by the murky sky.

Lancaster touched down briefly at Le Havre in France and then headed for the eastern Pyrenees, but the driving headwinds were draining his fuel faster than expected. Recognizing he would now need to refuel before crossing the Mediterranean, Lancaster aimed for Barcelona instead, though this change in plans would cost valuable time he could little afford to spare. A British pilot who encountered him at the Barcelona airfield observed how stressed and harried he seemed. When Lancaster finally reached Algeria at 9 p.m., he was running four and a half hours behind Mollison's record. At Oran he encountered further headaches involving servicing, refueling, and insurance issues, such that he wasn't able to depart until 3 a.m. Now he was six and a half hours behind schedule. The date was Wednesday, April 12.

Lancaster flew across the Atlas Mountains in pitch darkness, lighting matches along the way to check his route. When the sun rose he could see the Trans-Saharan Motor Track beneath him. Following the motor track south, Lancaster spotted, shortly before 8:30 a.m., the airfield at Adrar, Algeria. Though he had initially planned to refuel at the town of Reggane, one hundred miles to the south, Lancaster again changed plans, and filled his tanks at Adrar. By 9:15 a.m. he was back in the air, with his next stop planned for Gao, Mali, a commercial center on the Niger River, eight hundred miles away. He would continue following the motor track's pyramid-shaped beacons along the way.

This latter plan was soon rendered moot by a punishing sandstorm that swirled over the region. As Lancaster struggled to locate the narrow line of the motor track below, he mistakenly veered off course toward the south-central Algerian town of Aoulef. Though he spent a fleeting ten minutes on the ground there, the wasted flying time meant that he would have to soon stop for additional fuel. At 1 p.m. the *Southern Cross Minor* touched down in

Reggane, where Lancaster was greeted by a man named Borel, head of the town's Trans-Saharienne Company outpost.

Borel could see the profound weariness etched into Lancaster's face and sense the worry and aggravation that lay like an almost physical weight on his body. Concerned about Lancaster's ability to fly in such a state, Borel convinced him to sleep while his plane was being refueled. Perhaps by the time Lancaster woke up the sandstorm would have subsided. Lancaster reluctantly agreed, but he instructed Borel to rouse him in three hours. Borel offered food, but Lancaster declined it.

When Borel woke Lancaster in the late afternoon, the sandstorm was still blowing at full strength. Lancaster could not pilot in these conditions, Borel argued; his visibility would be nil. A dismayed Lancaster duly waited for the storm to die down, but as the minutes turned into hours, his already frayed patience appeared to snap. He must have known the jig was nearly up: he was already ten hours behind schedule, making it almost impossible for him to top Amy Mollison's record. But from Lancaster's perspective, any risk must have been worth taking. If he didn't succeed, he would be broke, his future prospects nonexistent. All hope of ending up with Jessie would be dashed. Perhaps, in this reckless state, death seemed a better option than failure.

The sandstorm had just started to abate when Lancaster informed Borel that he was leaving for Gao. This provoked another argument. Unless Lancaster waited for the moon to rise, Borel protested, the motor track, which ran to Gao, would be invisible in the evening darkness. But Lancaster would not be dissuaded.

Borel handed Lancaster a flashlight and matches. "We'll give you twenty-four hours," he told the exhausted aviator. "If we don't hear anything of you from Gao by tomorrow evening we'll send a convoy along the track. If you can burn something to light a beacon they'll see you."

At 6:30 p.m., the *Southern Cross Minor* again took flight. To those on the ground, the takeoff appeared markedly wobbly, as if Lancaster was too fatigued to keep the plane on a steady course. He also headed off in the wrong direction at first, before realizing his error and turning the plane around. Soon the Avro Avian vanished into the twilight. It was the last anybody ever saw of Captain William Lancaster.

Lancaster had planned to follow the narrow Trans-Saharan Motor Track heading due south, but within an hour the pitch-black night had swallowed his vision. He remained calm, thinking that his compass would guide him accurately even if he could not actually see the road below. An hour later he hit the five-hundred-mile-long expanse of desert called the "Land of Thirst," which even local nomads feared to cross.

Fifteen minutes later the *Southern Cross Minor*'s engine gave a strange hiccup, then spluttered and died out. Helpless in the dark, Lancaster tried to guide the plane down gently, but it crashed hard into the desert sand and flipped on its back. When Lancaster regained consciousness, he was suspended upside-down in the cockpit. He had no idea how long he had been out. He had deep cuts on his forehead and nose, and his eyes were filled with dried blood. Eventually he was able to force them open. Checking his rations, he figured he had a week's supply of water at most.

At 6 a.m. the next morning the French authorities at Gao reported that Lancaster was three and a half hours overdue. Delays were common for fliers—Lancaster might have stopped to rest or to wait until daylight for greater visibility—but as the day continued, the wireless chatter between the French military stations on the Niger River increased, until at 6 p.m. Borel dispatched the first search truck from Reggane. The vehicle would trace the motor track southward; in the morning another truck would be sent down the route from Gao.

Jessie received word that Lancaster had gone missing from her contacts at the *Daily Express* that same afternoon. She'd been following Lancaster's journey with apprehension, uncomfortably aware that his record-setting plans were likely to fail. The unplanned stop at Barcelona alone seemed to Jessie to render Lancaster's hopes moot. Now she waited anxiously for news that Lancaster had been found alive, his plane forced down somewhere not far off from his expected route.

After two full days had passed, Jessie could wait impotently no more. She headed to Fleet Street to meet with the editor of the *Sunday Express*, who agreed to help spread the word that Jessie required financial and material assistance to mount a rescue flight, which she would pilot herself. Most importantly, she needed a capable long-range aircraft. But as she consulted with other pilots, no one could think of any workable planes in the country capable of flying the necessary distances that were not currently in use. Jessie was racked with worry. "I had a dreadful dream last night that he was lying in the desert and crying for food and water," she told a reporter. "I live with hopes that he is safe with natives in some village. I cannot bear to think that he is out there alone."

Frantic but stymied, Jessie returned to London to seek out other options. But even as she did so, the newspapers published an interview with Lancaster's father: "It is not our wish that anyone who doesn't know the terrible flying conditions of the Sahara Desert should go out there to try to find our son," Edward Lancaster declared. "It would be a futile attempt and very much against our wishes. Everything that can possibly be done is being done." Lancaster Sr. was in regular contact with the Trans-Saharienne Company, who had informed him that an airplane would soon be joining in the hunt for his son.

For several days French vehicles and airplanes traversed the region, but no signs of Lancaster or his aircraft were found. By April 23, the authorities were ready to call off their efforts. One of the French pilots who had led the search issued a statement: "When Captain Lancaster was ready to resume his flight there was no moon and a strong northwest wind was blowing. M. Borel, the head of the Trans-Saharienne Company at Reggane, told him it was madness to take off when he would not be able to see the day beacons on the motor-track, and when he had no lighting on his instrument board for steering a compass course. Captain Lancaster made a very bad take-off, and that was the last seen of him." Perhaps, the pilot suggested, Lancaster, flying low, had unwittingly crashed into a sand dune.

"Captain Lancaster's father is now a tragic figure," *The New York Times* reported the next day, "haunting Fleet Street offices for news of his son, although the French air authorities have practically lost hope, believing he crashed in a sandstorm." But Lancaster's parents harbored no false expectations. "I did not want him to go on this last flight," Maud Lancaster told reporters, "but he was promised a job if he succeeded. That is why I let him go. I could not bear to see him unhappy because he could not get work." At an event the following month honoring Lancaster's memory, his mother, a robust believer in the afterlife, announced that she had been communicating with his spirit. Her husband concurred. "I do not now believe that my son is alive," Edward Lancaster said. "Indeed, I know he is not. Messages have come to us from the other side. He did not suffer; that is a great relief to his mother and to me. Sooner or later we shall know everything. He and his machine will be discovered. . . . I have been assured that he will be found."

Edward Lancaster's prediction would come true, but not for another twenty-nine years.

23

THIS PERIOD OF AGONY

On February 11, 1962, three large trucks belonging to a French Camel Corps platoon, the "White Squadron," wound their way across the desolate plains of the Sahara Desert in southern Algeria. Off to the east the Hoggar Mountains marked the edges of a vast plateau, while far to the west a vast, arid expanse of sandstone deposits angled progressively downward. This was the notorious Tanezrouft region, the Sahara's barren core, a landscape devoid of water, vegetation, and landmarks.

The White Squadron had embarked on its journey two days earlier and three hundred miles to the north. The platoon conducted regular reconnaissance missions through the Tanezrouft, though uncovering anything of note in the desiccated expanses of the region proved an elusive goal. After veering off the Trans-Saharan Motor Track at Bordj Pérez for the uncharted territory of the so-called Land of Thirst, they encountered little more than the occasional ancient tomb and a particular type of chalky soil that even their reinforced army vehicles found treacherous to cross.

The White Squadron drove for seventy miles to the north, and then headed due east for another sixty-five miles. Lulled by the punishing heat and endless horizon, they might have been excused for failing to notice a tiny black rectangle that appeared in the far distance.

But notice it they did, and Warrant Officer Titus Polidori became intrigued by what he could only identify as an "indeterminate carcass." The platoon veered off to the right to go examine the mystery object. But even as they moved closer, the black rectangle remained hazy in the shimmery midday heat.

As the platoon drew to within a mile of the object, Warrant Officer Polidori finally identified it as "the cabin of a small plane from an old model." When he reached the wreck he saw that it was a single-engine biplane, warped and misshapen from the crash, the propeller blades shattered. The plane lay awkwardly upside down, its fabric casing rotted away. As Polidori scanned the ground beneath the wings, his eyes fastened in amazement on a single object: a human skull.

Angling his head, Polidori saw that the long-dead pilot's skeletal body lay twisted on its side, partially buried in the sand. Mummified by the decades, the areas of the pilot's skin that lay uncovered in the dry Sahara air were crinkled like stiff, translucent paper; his right arm was crooked, the fingers frozen in a half-fist. A deep scar, no doubt the result of the plane crash, angled over his right eyebrow. Tattered but identifiable clothing hung in strips off his body. Even some of his hair could still be seen.

On the biplane's starboard wing, jutting diagonally above him, the pilot had tied his passport, wallet, and a large waterproof envelope that held his aircraft logbook, which he had turned into a diary. Though Polidori didn't realize it at first, these belongings contained the answer to a mystery that had remained unsolved for twenty-nine years.

A glance at the passport revealed the pilot's identity: Captain William Newton Lancaster. Tucked into Lancaster's wallet was a photo of a slim, grinning young woman in a bomber jacket, sporting a flying helmet and goggles on her head. "Now my water will give out today," one of the final entries in Lancaster's diary read. "It is then just a matter of a few hours and please God a *quick* end."

Warrant Officer Polidori quickly informed his superiors in Adrar of the platoon's find. The White Squadron transported Lancaster's remains to the hospital morgue at the French military base in Reggane, after which the bones were placed in a casket and buried in a palm grove a few hundred meters north of the nearest buildings. Because he was a former RAF officer, Lancaster was awarded full military honors.

After his crash, as Lancaster lay wounded in the desert with little to do but ponder his fate, he had filled his diary with thoughts of Jessie and his family, taking full responsibility for the jagged path that had led him to his present situation. The crinkled pages made for brutally riveting reading. During the day the desert sand was so hot that, even in the shade, it nearly burned Lancaster's bare skin. At night the temperatures dropped so precipitously that he had to throw on, he wrote, his "[v]est, shirt, sweater, coat, flying jacket, muffler of wool, trousers, flying trousers over them, socks and underpants," although he still remained cold.

In the early morning hours immediately following his crash, Lancaster's first thought was of water: Had it run out? "No, thank God," he wrote. "Two precious gallons of it. I can live for a few days. I am naturally feeling shaky but must keep my head at all costs. I hope the French will search for me, but it is going to be difficult to find me as I am away from the track. I thought of walking to the track and prepared to set out, but Chubbie's and my talk about this came to my mind. No: I must stick to the ship.

"I am going to ration my water. A week at most I suppose. I wonder where everyone thinks I am. I think mostly of my mother and Chubbie. I love them both. Chubbie is my own sweetheart, but mother is such a darling. They both were proud of me before I set out. Alas I have truly bitten the dust of disappointment."

By 11 a.m. that day, the desperate reality of Lancaster's situation had taken hold. "The first day is passing like a year," he wrote. "Find it difficult to fight against taking a drink *but I must.* My very life depends on strict rationing. Hope I don't go blind—the blood is clotting around my eyes. Weird ideas one gets when minutes seem hours. Watching the vulture fly [above me] made me wish I could catch him and tame him and leap astride and fly to a pool of water. I would not mind how dirty it was. . . .

"I can now quite realize this period of agony in the Sahara desert is going to be as long to the mind as my whole life-time. Truly am I atoning for any wrong done on this earth. I do not want to die. I want desperately to live. I have the love of a good mother and father and a sweetheart whom I adore.

If anything happens to me Chubbie go back to your mother and think of some of the good things about me. There must be some because you have so often told me all you think of me."

At 6 a.m. the following morning Lancaster noted that he had passed a quiet night. "My flares were a success, at least they showed a brilliant light for 60 seconds," he wrote, before scrawling with frustration, "I burnt one every fifteen minutes to half an hour. No one saw them!!!" He drew the obvious conclusion: "It is evident to me that I may be further off course than I anticipated otherwise the car would have seen me in the night. I certainly saw no lights at all. Oh! Please send out your aeroplanes now. I am not strong as I have had no real food since I left England."

Four hours later Lancaster wrote, "Have just tried to inspect extent of injuries. The main worry is the cut between the eyes and more over the left eye than the right. I am terribly afraid of blood poisoning settling in. I removed the bandage after some painful work of pulling it away from where it had stuck. Now what to do I don't quite know, whether to cover up or leave to dry up. Lots of sand got into the cuts last night."

His thirst was a constant torment: "What a temptation it is to go to the water bottle. What absolute nectar does it contain. It is my only desire for the moment, water, water, water. Mother, what would you think if I were to dash into your bathroom while you were bathing and plunge my head into the water, clean or dirty, and drink and drink and drink?

"Just saw a white butterfly and a dragon-fly (no, not dreaming, actually), this gives me hopes I am near an oasis. . . . Come on planes! It was strange, I was just as thirsty at night as during the day."

That night, overcome with exhaustion, Lancaster slept a great deal. "I must now conserve every bit of energy to keep alive for about three or four days in the hope that I will be rescued," he wrote on Saturday, April 15. "If the planes start searching today I hope for relief. My water will hold three or four days longer—unless I go mad and consume it before. You see, my wounds have made it hard for me as I lost a lot of blood and they trouble me terribly in the day when the sun is up. Mind you I do not unduly complain of my plight. After all I brought it on myself and must call it the luck of the game and play it out to the end."

By this, his third day, Lancaster had learned the desert's rhythms. "The hours from 11 a.m. to 4:30 p.m. are the dreaded ones," he wrote. "The heat of the sun is appalling. That I shall be ill after this even if found is inevitable. But I don't mind as long as I can get water. That is my constant craving. WATER."

By the next day, Lancaster was losing hope. "Now I know I am to the right of my proper course, this fact makes me anxious as they may not suspect this," he noted grimly. "The days when the sun comes up are indescribable. I just lie it seems for years on my back under the shelter of the wing thinking all sorts of mad thoughts. . . . I feel weak, so weak, in the body. It is shriveling up around my stomach and ribs.

"Chubbie my sweetheart, and mother my best friend, and father my pal, do not grieve, I have only myself to blame for everything. That foolish, headstrong self of me.

"Life after all is only just a very short span in the scheme of things. I wish I had done more good in my time that's all.

"Come to me Chubbie but take care in the coming, believe me I shall *never fly over a desert again*. I suppose I can last two or three more days. Then it will be a few hours—madness—and death at last."

The next day's hell was much the same: "Am suffering mental torment again. I am positive I saw that light last night and the person who fired it must have seen mine, yet nothing has come. . . . No machines in the sky etc. I wish I had not drunk that extra flask of water last night. I have cut my chance by a day. Things seem very bad to me. . . . Heat is going to be ghastly today. Am thinking of you mother and Chub.

"Not a breath of air. I am resigned to the end if it has to be. . . . Oh for water, water."

Lancaster began his sixth day with a prayer, even as he acknowledged that the possibility of rescue was now "almost unbelievable." As he braced himself for the day's "five hours of hell," the sense of suffocation was overwhelming. "Not a breath of air," he wrote. "Flies bad today. After my poor cut head."

On the seventh day after his wreck Lancaster knew his time was almost up. Thinking it would be his final entry, he wrote advice to his loved ones: "Chubbie *give up flying* (you won't make any money at it now). . . . Darling Mother whom I have neglected far too much in my life—I want you darling to see Chubbie and talk everything out with her. . . . To my Father—you and I just need a handshake in thought form. We understand. Mother, see little Pat and Nina Ann for me, kiss them for me and explain what is in my heart. See Kiki, tell her she can now really forget." His state of mind was surprisingly philosophical given the circumstances. He noted with pride how long he had held out after his crash, and said that the accident itself was just luck of the draw. "No one to blame, the engine missed, I landed upside-down in the pitch-dark and there you are," he opined. "*Mother and Chub.* If there is another world, if there be something hereafter (and I feel there is), I shall just be waiting."

Against his expectations, Lancaster woke to another morning, Thursday, April 20, 1933—one year exactly from the night of Clarke's death. "So the beginning of the eighth day has dawned," he wrote. "It is still cool. I have no water. I am waiting patiently. Come soon please. Fever wracked me last night. Hope you get my full log. Bill."

In all likelihood Lancaster died later same that day, parched in the Sahara's agonizing heat.

EPILOGUE THE PAST REACHES OUT

On May 16, 1936, in Epsom, England, Jessie married Flight Lieutenant John Barnard Walter Pugh, a well-known British pilot, who one year earlier had been rescued from the English Channel after his plane was forced down by engine trouble. From that point on, Jessie was known as Mrs. Jessie Pugh. She and her husband had met in 1935, when Jessie worked for him as manager of the Commercial Air Hire Company's office at Heston Aerodrome, just west of London. After they announced their engagement, Jessie told the press there would be "no more flying stunts for me. . . . My wild days are over. I've had my fun. I'm just going to sit back and let John do the piloting for both of us now."

Now, after lengthy stints in both Singapore and Spain—they had been living in the former when the Japanese invaded during World War II—the happy couple resided in a cozy apartment in Berkshire. They had been married for a quarter century when, on the morning of February 19, 1962, the phone rang in their downstairs hallway. When John Pugh answered, he was greeted by the voice of their next-door neighbor telling him that Jessie was in the newspaper.

John walked out to the mailbox to get that morning's *Daily Express.* As he settled back in the dining room to peruse it, Jessie heard him exclaim, "My god!" The startling discovery of the wreck of the *Southern Cross Minor*, along with Lancaster's sun-bleached skeleton and the diary he had so assiduously kept during his ordeal in the Sahara, had just been reported. It was a "most appalling shock," Jessie remembered later. "I didn't know what to think. What can one think? It was the most colossal shock that anyone can imagine."

Though Jessie no longer wore the bomber jackets or flying helmets that she sported in her twenties, she retained the vigor and trim, dark looks of her youth, mixed with an air of contentment that stemmed from decades of agreeable partnership with her husband. Now, as she read the news of the French Camel Corps' discovery, a wave of acute grief swept over her as she thought of Lancaster perishing in the desert. But in the weeks to come, as the media swarmed over the story, this pathos was replaced by apprehension, as Jessie worried that the diary might contain scandalous information about her past—a past she had worked for decades to put behind her.

In April 1962 Jessie picked up the diary from her lawyer. She could scarcely believe what she held in her hands. Though she had been warned by French officials that the document was almost unbearably poignant, she was ill-prepared for the emotions that roiled her as she read through the pages. Her husband, seeing her turmoil, asked her what was wrong. Jessie had planned on putting forward a brave face, but she couldn't help herself: she began reading the diary out loud. When she had finished, John Pugh declared that Lancaster's story had to be told. "Anyone who has the guts to die like that deserves to be heard," he said. Six months later, in October 1962, the *Daily Express* presented the whole of the diary's contents, with an added foreword by Jessie.

"I had never forgotten Bill Lancaster," Jessie wrote in her foreword. "The world we had known together, the roaring 'twenties, the death-or-glory record flights in tiny biplanes, the Depression, when there wasn't much in the way of picking for pilots like us, then drama, headlines, and Bill's tragic exit from it all; it was half a lifetime away.

"The passing years had taken the sharp edges off the memories. Sometimes it seemed like a different world. But it hadn't been another world. The headlines that said his body had been found told me that. I have been happily married for 26 years. Then suddenly the past reaches out and takes hold of the present."

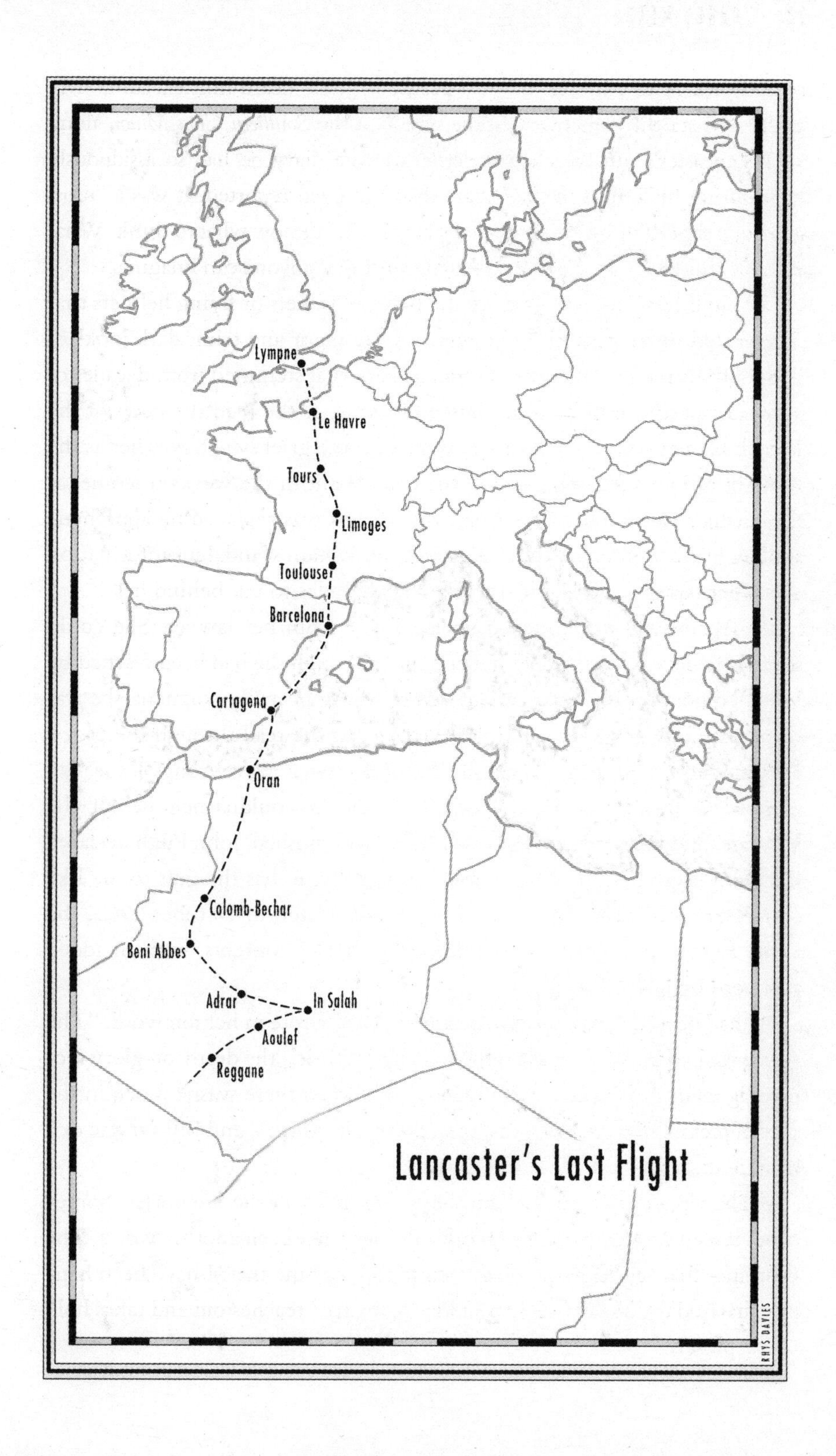

Lympne
Le Havre
Tours
Limoges
Toulouse
Barcelona
Cartagena
Oran
Colomb-Bechar
Beni Abbes
Adrar
In Salah
Aoulef
Reggane
Lancaster's Last Flight
RHYS DAVIES

ACKNOWLEDGMENTS AND SOURCES

I wish to express my deep appreciation and gratitude to Andrew Lancaster (Bill Lancaster's great-nephew) and Noni Couell for their willingness to share their archive of materials on the Lancaster-Miller case, including items privately held by the family. Andrew's moving 2014 documentary, *The Lost Aviator: The True Story of Bill Lancaster*, which Noni produced, is a finely wrought, highly personal piece of work, and essential viewing for anyone interested in the story of Bill Lancaster and Jessie Miller. Among the research items I credit to Andrew Lancaster/*The Lost Aviator* are:

- "The Lancaster Case," by James Carson, Bill Lancaster's lawyer, a 118-page account of the trial in Miami, prepared privately for the Lancaster family in 1935.
- Bill Lancaster's diary, letters, and telegrams from his trip to Nogales on behalf of Latin-American Airways.
- An extensive collection of media coverage, both local and international, of Bill Lancaster's trial.
- Lancaster's and Jessie's trial testimony.

In addition to the above materials, Ralph Barker's superbly written and researched *Verdict on a Lost Flyer*, published in 1969, was immensely valuable, as he was the sole individual to interview Jessie in detail about her life and her relationship with Lancaster. Grateful acknowledgment is made to Pen & Sword Aviation for permission to quote from the 2015 reprint of Barker's book.

The Australian scholar Chrystopher J. Spicer was also immeasurably helpful and generous with his time. I offer him my heartfelt thanks for his penetrating insights into the nature of Jessie and Lancaster's relationship. Chrystopher's 2017 biography, *The Flying Adventures of Jessie Keith "Chubbie" Miller*, is *the* definitive work on Jessie, and does a brilliant job of documenting and recovering the too-little known legacy of this pioneer aviatrix.

Colin Dickerman and James Melia are the finest editors I've ever worked with, and I can't thank them enough for their relentless enthusiasm and their brilliantly incisive feedback. They pushed me at every step to make this a fuller, more engaging work, and in so doing, they showed me, frankly, how to be a writer. I am deeply in their debt. Hearty thanks, as well, to the rest of the stellar team at Flatiron, and to Georgina Morley, my editor at Macmillan UK.

I am also profoundly grateful to my agent, Andrew Wylie, and to Kristina Moore, for so ably and professionally steering the ship.

AS and WM.

To Laura, Caleb, Mom, Dad, Ken, and the rest of my family: I love you.

BOOKS

Barker, Ralph. 1969. *Verdict on a Lost Flyer.* London: Harrap. (Reprinted in 2015 as *Bill Lancaster—The Final Verdict: The Life and Death of an Aviation Pioneer.* London: Pen & Sword Aviation.)

Butler, Susan. 2009. *East to the Dawn: The Life of Amelia Earhart*. Boston: Da Capo Press.

Evans, Colin. 2002. *A Question of Evidence: The Casebook of Great Forensic Controversies*. Hoboken: Wiley.

Gibson, Karen Bush. 2013. *Women Aviators*. Chicago: Chicago Review Press.

Grant, R. G. 2007. *Flight: The Complete History*. London: DK Publishing.

Jennings, Peter, and Todd Brewster. 1998. *The Century*. New York: Doubleday.

Jessen, Gene Nora. 2002. *The Powder Puff Derby of 1929: The True Story of the First Women's Cross-Country Air Race*. Naperville, IL: Sourcebooks.

Kessner, Thomas. 2010. *The Flight of the Century: Charles Lindbergh and the Rise of American Aviation*. Oxford: Oxford University Press.

Lebow, Eileen. 2002. *Before Amelia: Women Pilots in the Early Days of Aviation*. Washington, DC: Brassey's.

Levell, Mary. 2009. *The Sound of Wings: The Life of Amelia Earhart*. New York: St. Martin's Griffin.

McIver, Stuart. 2015: *Murder in the Tropics: The Florida Chronicles*, vol. II. Sarasota, FL: Pineapple Press.

Spicer, Chrystopher J. 2012. *Great Australian World Firsts*. Sydney: Allen & Unwin.

———. 2017. *The Flying Adventures of Jessie Keith "Chubbie" Miller: The Southern Hemisphere's First International Aviatrix*. Jefferson, NC: McFarland & Company.

Taylor, D. J. 2010. *Bright Young People: The Lost Generation of London's Jazz Age*. New York: Farrar, Straus and Giroux.

NEWSPAPERS AND MAGAZINES

Advocate (Australia)
The Baltimore Sun
Daily Express (UK)
Daily Mirror (UK)
Empire
Flight
The Manchester Guardian (UK)
The Mercury (Australia)
Miami Daily News
The Miami Herald
The Morning Bulletin (Australia)
The New York Times

Pittsburgh Post-Gazette
Reality (Australia)
The Register (Australia)
Wisconsin State Journal
Yorkshire Post (UK)

SELECTED CHAPTER SOURCES

PROLOGUE

Miami Daily News, Aug. 2, 1932.

CHAPTER 1

Ralph Barker, *Verdict on a Lost Flyer.*
Chrystopher J. Spicer, *The Flying Adventures of Jessie Keith "Chubbie" Miller.*
Andrew Lancaster, *The Lost Aviator.*

CHAPTER 2

Ralph Barker, *Verdict on a Lost Flyer.*
Chrystopher J. Spicer, *The Flying Adventures of Jessie Keith "Chubbie" Miller.*
Andrew Lancaster, *The Lost Aviator.*

CHAPTER 3

Keith-Miller, Jessie. 1928. "Tracing North Africa." *The Mercury*, April 19.
———. 1928. "From Egypt to Baghdad." *The Mercury*, April 20.
———. 1928. "Only One Frock for Half a World's Journey." *Morning Bulletin*, April 21.
———. 1928. "Kaleidoscope of Mesopotamia." *The Mercury*, April 24.
———. 1928. "Red Rose in Africa." *Morning Bulletin*, May 19.
———. 1928. "Over Desert Wastes." *Morning Bulletin*, May 20.
———. 1928. "Two Weeks at Basra." *Morning Bulletin*, May 21.
———. 1928. "Down the Persian Gulf." *Morning Bulletin*, May 23.

CHAPTER 4

Keith-Miller, Jessie. 1928. "Flirting with Death: Risks on the Red Rose." *The Register*, April 24.

———. 1928. "Snake as Passenger in Cockpit: New Use for Joystick." *The Mercury*, April 30.

———. 1928. "Darwin at Last. Red Rose in the Rain." *The Register*, April 30.

———. 1928. "Another Lap of Flight: Thrills on the Journey." *Morning Bulletin*, May 25.

———. 1928. "An Unofficial Passenger." *Morning Bulletin*, May 29.

———. 1928. "Crash at Muntok." *Morning Bulletin*, May 30.

———. 1928. "Crossing the Timor Sea." *Morning Bulletin*, June 2.

CHAPTER 5

Ralph Barker, *Verdict on a Lost Flyer.*

Chrystopher J. Spicer, *The Flying Adventures of Jessie Keith "Chubbie" Miller.*

Andrew Lancaster, *The Lost Aviator.*

CHAPTER 6

Ralph Barker, *Verdict on a Lost Flyer.*

Chrystopher J. Spicer, *The Flying Adventures of Jessie Keith "Chubbie" Miller.*

Andrew Lancaster, *The Lost Aviator.*

CHAPTER 7

Ralph Barker, *Verdict on a Lost Flyer.*

Chrystopher J. Spicer, *The Flying Adventures of Jessie Keith "Chubbie" Miller.*

Andrew Lancaster, *The Lost Aviator.*

CHAPTER 8

Lancaster's personal diary was reprinted in full in the *Miami Daily News*, August 5, 1932, the source for all his quotes (and related information) in this chapter.

Ralph Barker, *Verdict on a Lost Flyer.*

Chrystopher J. Spicer, *The Flying Adventures of Jessie Keith "Chubbie" Miller.*

Andrew Lancaster, *The Lost Aviator.*

CHAPTER 9

Lancaster's personal diary was reprinted in full in the *Miami Daily News*, August 5, 1932, the source for all his quotes (and related information) in this chapter.

Ralph Barker, *Verdict on a Lost Flyer.*
Chrystopher J. Spicer, *The Flying Adventures of Jessie Keith "Chubbie" Miller.*
Andrew Lancaster, *The Lost Aviator.*

CHAPTER 10

Lancaster's personal diary was reprinted in full in the *Miami Daily News*, August 5, 1932, the source for all quotes from it (and related information) in this chapter.
Lancaster's letters and telegrams were reprinted in the *Miami Daily News* and *The Miami Herald*, August 1932, the sources for all quotes from them in this chapter.
Ralph Barker, *Verdict on a Lost Flyer.*
Chrystopher J. Spicer, *The Flying Adventures of Jessie Keith "Chubbie" Miller.*
Andrew Lancaster, *The Lost Aviator.*

CHAPTER 11

Lancaster's and Jessie's letters and telegrams were reprinted in the *Miami Daily News* and *The Miami Herald*, August 1932, the sources for all quotes in this chapter, unless otherwise noted.
Ralph Barker, *Verdict on a Lost Flyer.*
Chrystopher J. Spicer, *The Flying Adventures of Jessie Keith "Chubbie" Miller.*
Andrew Lancaster, *The Lost Aviator.*

CHAPTER 12

Lancaster's personal diary was reprinted in full in the *Miami Daily News*, August 5, 1932, the source for all quotes from it (and related information) in this chapter.
Lancaster's letters and telegrams were reprinted in the *Miami Daily News* and *The Miami Herald*, August 1932, the sources for all quotes from them in this chapter.
Ralph Barker, *Verdict on a Lost Flyer.*
Chrystopher J. Spicer, *The Flying Adventures of Jessie Keith "Chubbie" Miller.*
Andrew Lancaster, *The Lost Aviator.*

CHAPTER 13

Lancaster's personal diary was reprinted in full in the *Miami Daily News*, August 5, 1932, the source for all quotes from it (and related information) in this chapter.

Jessie's letters and telegrams were reprinted in the *Miami Daily News* and *The Miami Herald*, August 1932, the sources for all quotes from them in this chapter.

Ralph Barker, *Verdict on a Lost Flyer.*

Chrystopher J. Spicer, *The Flying Adventures of Jessie Keith "Chubbie" Miller.*

Andrew Lancaster, *The Lost Aviator.*

CHAPTER 14

Unless otherwise noted, all quotes in this chapter are from the *Miami Daily News* and *The Miami Herald*, August 2–18, 1932.

Ralph Barker, *Verdict on a Lost Flyer.*

Chrystopher J. Spicer, *The Flying Adventures of Jessie Keith "Chubbie" Miller.*

Andrew Lancaster, *The Lost Aviator.*

CHAPTER 15

Unless otherwise noted, all quotes in this chapter are from the *Miami Daily News* and *The Miami Herald*, April 23–May 10 and August 2–18, 1932.

Ralph Barker, *Verdict on a Lost Flyer.*

Chrystopher J. Spicer, *The Flying Adventures of Jessie Keith "Chubbie" Miller.*

Andrew Lancaster, *The Lost Aviator.*

CHAPTER 16

Unless otherwise noted, all quotes in this chapter are from the *Miami Daily News* and *The Miami Herald*, April 23–May 10 and August 2–18, 1932.

Ralph Barker, *Verdict on a Lost Flyer.*

Chrystopher J. Spicer, *The Flying Adventures of Jessie Keith "Chubbie" Miller.*

Andrew Lancaster, *The Lost Aviator.*

CHAPTER 17

Unless otherwise noted, all quotes in this chapter are from the *Miami Daily News* and *The Miami Herald*, August 2–18, 1932.

Andrew Lancaster, *The Lost Aviator.*
James Carson, "The Lancaster Case."

CHAPTER 18

All quotes in this chapter are from the *Miami Daily News* and *The Miami Herald*, August 2–18, 1932.

CHAPTER 19

All quotes in this chapter are from the *Miami Daily News* and *The Miami Herald*, August 1932.

CHAPTER 20

Unless otherwise noted, all quotes in this chapter are from the *Miami Daily News* and *The Miami Herald*, August 2–18, 1932.
Colin Evans, *A Question of Evidence.*
Jim Fisher, "Firearms Identification in the Sacco-Vanzetti Case," http://jimfisher.edinboro.edu/forensics/sacco1_1.html

CHAPTER 21

Unless otherwise noted, all quotes in this chapter are from the *Miami Daily News* and *The Miami Herald*, August 1932.
James Carson, "The Lancaster Case."

CHAPTER 22

"Mrs. Keith-Miller Sails for England." 1932. *The Baltimore Sun*, October 15.
"Captain Lancaster Plans Long-Distance Flight." 1932. *The Baltimore Sun*, October 25.
"Three Long-Distance Flights." 1933. *The Manchester Guardian*, April 11.
"Captain Lancaster in Cape Flight Bid." 1933. *Daily Mirror*, April 12.
"Airwoman to Hunt for Lost Friend." 1933. *Daily Express*, April 17.
"The Diary of Bill Lancaster: An Incredible Story of Courage." 1962. *Daily Express*, October 22.
Ralph Barker, *Verdict on a Lost Flyer.*
Chrystopher J. Spicer, *The Flying Adventures of Jessie Keith "Chubbie" Miller.*

CHAPTER 23

"The Diary of Bill Lancaster: An Incredible Story of Courage." 1962. *Daily Express*, October 22.

Alain Brochard and Michel Fernez, "A Butterfly in the Desert; Or the Tragic History of William Newton Lancaster," April 2009, http://www.3emegroupedetransport.com/Unpapillondansledesert.htm.

Ralph Barker, *Verdict on a Lost Flyer.*

Chrystopher J. Spicer, *The Flying Adventures of Jessie Keith "Chubbie" Miller.*

Andrew Lancaster, *The Lost Aviator.*

EPILOGUE

"The Diary of Bill Lancaster: An Incredible Story of Courage." 1962. *Daily Express*, October 22.

Ralph Barker, *Verdict on a Lost Flyer.*

Chrystopher J. Spicer, *The Flying Adventures of Jessie Keith "Chubbie" Miller.*

NOTES

PROLOGUE: A TIME LIKE THIS

1 The Dade County Courthouse: National Register of Historic Places, Continuation Sheet 8:1: The Dade County Courthouse (United States Department of the Interior).

1 The date was August 2, 1932: All trial information in this prologue is from the *Miami Daily News*, August 2, 1932.

1 At a quarter past nine: "Lancaster Jury Nears Completion at Recess." 1932. *Miami Daily News*, August 2.

2 "It's hard to smile": Ibid.

1 BRIGHT YOUNG THINGS

7 They were the Bright Young Things: Taylor 2010.

8 "This is Flying Captain": Barker 1969, 14.

8 "[Before Lindbergh's flight] people seemed": Jennings and Brewster 1998, 420.

9 "Colonel Lindbergh has displaced": Kessner 2010, 127.

9 "It is impossible today": Kessner, Thomas. 2012. "Charles Lindbergh, a new hero." *OUPblog*, May 20. https://blog.oup.com/2012/05/charles-lindbergh-a-new-hero/.

9 After his record-setting flight: Kessner 2010.

10 "Come and have tea": Barker 1969, 14.

10 She was born Jessie: All background information on Jessie in this section is from Spicer 2017.

11 "We were quite maladjusted": Spicer 2017, 13.

11 "the right to live": Ibid.

12 As one of her customers: Ibid., 14.

2 A NIMBLE LIFTOFF

13 History surrounded Bill Lancaster: The Authors' Club, http://www.authorsclub.co.uk/.

14 "You said the plane": Barker 1969, 24.

14 "In the first place": Ibid.

15 "I don't know whether": Spicer 2017, 19.

15 "Look, Bill, you've been talking": Barker 1969, 24.

16 Situated in a charmingly: Stanfords, http://www.stanfords.co.uk/.

16 Bill Lancaster's path: All background information on Bill Lancaster in this chapter is from Barker 1969.

20 "My dear, I couldn't care": Spicer 2017, 19.

21 "Oh, well it is a very good": Quote and preceding paragraphs from Keith-Miller, Jessie. 1928. "Only One Frock for Half a World's Journey." *Morning Bulletin*, April 21.

21 The plane featured fresh: "The Red Rose: London to Australia in Light Plane." 1927. *The Manchester Guardian*, October 10.

21 In the end, her gear: Keith-Miller 1928. "Only One Frock for Half a World's Journey."

22 "I thought it was marvelous": Spicer 2017, 23.

23 "Women lack qualities": Lebow 2002, 4.

23 "It would be well": Ibid., 6.

23 "Most of us spread": Jessen 2002.

24 "I'm going in for everything": Lebow 2002, 152.

24 In those early years of aviation: Ibid., 7.

24 The most famous female: Lovell 2009.

25 "I am an Australian": "Woman Flying to Australia." 1927. *The Manchester Guardian*, October 15.

3 SINGLE-MINDED ABANDON

28 "My mind," she wrote: Keith-Miller, Jessie. 1928. "Only One Frock for Half a World's Journey." *The Morning Bulletin*, April 21.

28 "all the fogs in the world": Ibid.

29 This was a pattern: Spicer 2017, 29.

30 "seemed like so many clips": Keith-Miller 1928. "Only One Frock for Half a World's Journey."

30 "as if from an evil pot": Ibid.

31 "the shock of their lives": Keith-Miller, Jessie. 1928. "Red Rose in Africa." *Morning Bulletin*, May 19.

31 "If you have to make": Ibid.

32 Raising her head: Spicer 2017, 31.

32 "The sand was terrible": Keith-Miller 1928. "Red Rose in Africa."

33 When the *Red Rose*: Keith-Miller, Jessie. 1928. "Tracing North Africa." *The Mercury*, April 19.

34 The aviation world, too: Barker 1969, 30.

34 "The sails of the strange": Keith-Miller, Jessie. 1928. "Over Desert Wastes." *The Morning Bulletin*, May 20.

35 "There is no glitter": Ibid.

35 "The sun became a scorcher": Ibid.

35 "What are you doing": Ibid.

36 Later that night: Ibid.

36 "squirmed over the countryside": Ibid.

37 After such desolate landscape: Keith-Miller, Jessie. 1928. "Two Weeks at Basra." *The Morning Bulletin*, May 21.

37 The ritual, by this point: Keith-Miller, Jessie. 1928. "Kaleidoscope of Mesopotamia." *The Mercury*, April 24.

38 "They were totally confident": Spicer 2017, 33.

38 "The water is shark-infested": Barker 1969, 31.

38 "The whole expanse resembled": Keith-Miller, Jessie. 1928. "Down the Persian Gulf." *The Morning Bulletin*, May 23.

39 "a huge chunk of coral": Ibid.

39 Lancaster and Jessie were confronted: Barker 1969, 32.

4 ARRIVAL

40 the morality of the time: Barker 1969, 33.

41 After nine and a half: Ibid., 34.

41 Lancaster and Jessie had now flown: Keith-Miller, Jessie. 1928. "Another Lap of Flight: Thrills on the Journey." *The Morning Bulletin*, May 25.

41 The air force was preparing: Keith-Miller, Jessie. 1928. "Flirting with Death: Risks on the Red Rose." *The Register*, April 24.

42 "The combination of corpse and crocodile": Keith-Miller 1928. "Another Lap of Flight."

42 Lancaster and Jessie's arrival: Spicer 2017, 47.

42 Lancaster had absentmindedly left: Keith-Miller, Jessie. 1928. "Damaged Engine and Not a Rupee." *The Register*, April 27.

42 "The sea was a magnificent": Keith-Miller, Jessie. 1928. "A Forced Landing." *The Morning Bulletin*, May 26.

43 "Hold your legs up!": Ibid.

43 "Close everything up": Spicer 2017, 52.

44 About thirty minutes into: Keith-Miller, Jessie. 1928. "An Unofficial Passenger." *The Morning Bulletin*, May 29.

44 "What's the matter?": Keith-Miller, Jessie. 1928. "Snake as Passenger in Cockpit: New Use for Joystick." *The Mercury*, April 30.

44 "a heavenly blue sky": Keith-Miller 1928. "An Unofficial Passenger."

44 "I patched up my one": Keith-Miller, Jessie. 1928. "Crash at Muntok." *The Morning Bulletin*, May 30.

45 The Singapore Aero Club: Ibid.

45 "Their effort thoroughly deserves": Barker 1969, 37.

45 "Somewhere around here we'll": Keith-Miller 1928. "Crash at Muntok."

46 "The landscape seemed to have": Ibid.

46 "had fixed up a reception": Ibid.

47 a "screw being taken": Ibid.

48 "had put up a splendid": "Captain W. N. Lancaster's Fine Flight." 1928. *Flight*, January 19.

48 The *Aeroplane* noted: Barker 1969, 39.

48 When they climbed on board: Keith-Miller, Jessie. 1928. "Crossing the Timor Sea." *The Morning Bulletin*, June 2.

48 a wealthy local British: Spicer 2017, 61.

48 The lead officer had followed: Keith-Miller 1928. "Crash at Muntok."

49 For the next two months: Barker 1969, 40.

49 on February 7, Hinkler departed: Spicer 2017, 59.

50 Finally, on March 12: Keith-Miller 1928. "Crossing the Timor Sea."

50 At some unidentified spot: Spicer 2017, 63.

50 Five days later, the aviators: Keith-Miller 1928. "Crossing the Timor Sea."

50 The news of the *Red Rose*'s: Barker 1969, 41.

50 Hardly had Lancaster and Jessie: Keith-Miller, Jessie. 1928. "Darwin at Last. Red Rose in the Rain." *The Register,* April 30.

51 "I'm afraid she won't": Ibid.

51 Despite her terror, she: Barker 1969, 42.

52 "My God, what an awful": Keith-Miller 1928. "Crossing the Timor Sea."

5 GRAND WELCOMES

55 The Darwin Town Hall: Barker 1969, 44.

55 "fired the imagination": Spicer 2017, 72.

55 "The arrival of the Avian": Barker 1969, 44.

56 "[Jessie's] success in being": Spicer 2017, 67.

56 The "women of Australia": Ibid., 71.

56 "may follow where she": Ibid.

56 "simply by flying the Atlantic": Barker 1969, 45.

57 "Three cheers for your success": Spicer 2017, 80.

57 "I would be happy": "Captain Lancaster Lecture Tour of Australia." 1928. *Advocate* (Tasmania), 5.

57 "Sometimes I wish I had": Spicer 2017, 74.

58 Lyon was the son: McDonald, Ann. "Henry Lyon Jr.: An Old Sea Dog Takes to the Air." *Maine Memory Network.* https://www.mainememory.net/sitebuilder/site/272/page/531/display?use_mmn=1.

58 Now Lyon told Lancaster: Barker 1969, 46.

59 "I thought you had prohibition": Ibid., 47.

59 The women in the room: Spicer 2017, 89.

60 In August 1928: McDonald. "Henry Lyon Jr."

61 "Quite an experience to eat": Barker 1969, 48.

62 "a dead loss": Spicer 2017, 90.

62 Twenty-five hundred miles away: Barker 1969, 50.

63 When she arrived in Manhattan: "Alcohol in Airman's Compass." 1929. *The Manchester Guardian*, January 2.

64 Lancaster and Elinor Smith's return: "Missing Flyers Safe." 1929. *The Manchester Guardian*, January 11.

64 Lancaster, however: Barker 1969, 52.

6 FLYING SOLO

67 With Kiki back in England: Barker 1969, 52.

67 "I have been thoroughly": Spicer 2017, 93.

68 By March 1929, American Cirrus: Barker 1969, 52.

68 But disaster struck as Lancaster: Spicer 2017, 95.

69 For Jessie, opportunity: Jessen 2002.

69 pilot Marvel Crosson: "Woman Flyer Killed." 1929. *The Manchester Guardian*, August 21.

69 Jessie roomed in Phoenix: Spicer 2017, 107.

70 Accidents continued to plague: Jessen 2002.

70 Following her Derby performance: Barker 1969, 55.

7 A CHANGE IN FORTUNE

72 The effects of the crash: Barker 1969, 57.

73 Their situation was further: Spicer 2017, 132.

73 Finally, at a cocktail party: Barker 1969, 57.

73 "We'll get everything organized": Ibid., 58.

74 "What's the matter with you?": Ibid.

74 "You fly as well as": Ibid.

75 "Frankly," she admitted later: Spicer 2017, 139.

75 The celebrated Brooklyn-born aviatrix: Barker 1969, 60.

77 "un-airworthy crate": "Woman Flyer's Fate Is Still Held in Doubt." 1930. *The Baltimore Sun*, November 30.

77 "Everybody gives me credit": Knoblaugh, Homer. 1930. "Missing Woman Flyer Had Premonition of Tragedy." *The Free Lance-Star* (Fredericksburg), November 29.

77 "I don't know why it is": "Woman Flyer's Fate Is Still Held in Doubt."

78 "I am very anxious": "Mother Hopeful Missing Flyer Is Safe Somewhere." 1930. *The Baltimore Sun*, November 29.

78 "It is possible she was": "Woman Flyer's Fate Is Still Held in Doubt."

79 "I thought it was all over": Keith-Miller, Jessie. 1930. "Mrs. Keith-Miller Tells Own Story of Air Adventure." *Pittsburgh Post-Gazette*, December 3.

79 She hadn't been there long: Spicer 2017, 149.

80 "I am at Nassau": "Mrs. Keith-Miller Is Safe: Lands on Island in Storm." 1930. *Pittsburgh Post-Gazette*, Decemeber 2.

80 As she took off: Barker 1969, 66.

8 TO MIAMI

81 Lancaster headed to Los Angeles: Spicer 2017, 157.

82 "America gave me an opportunity": Ibid., 154.

82 Her most memorable incident: "Big Hotel Fire." 1931. *Pittsburgh Post-Gazette*, July 31.

82 While she had been crisscrossing: Spicer 2017, 157.

83 "I spent days discussing": Ibid.

83 The ruddy-cheeked, pudgy Shelton: Davis-Monthan Aviation Field Register. "William Gentry Shelton, Jr." http://dmairfield.com/people/shelton_wg/.

83 One night, when Lancaster: Spicer 2017, 157.

84 "perfect house dog": Lancaster's personal diary was reprinted in full in the *Miami Daily News*, August 5, 1932, the source for all his quotes in this chapter. According to the newspaper, the diary was read into the record in its entirety in Lancaster's subsequent trial in an effort to establish a love triangle as a motive. However, it also worked to Lancaster's advantage in making him a very sympathetic defendant.

84 "would ride out the Depression": "Mrs. Keith-Miller Continues Her Story." 1932. *Daily Express*, Oct. 28.

84 It was, rather astonishingly: Barker 1969, 68.

85 With the romance gone: My profound gratitude to Chrystopher J. Spicer for his insights, via e-mail to me, on this and other crucial aspects of Jessie and Lancaster's relationship.

85 "The windows were framed": "Mrs. Keith-Miller Continues Her Story." 1932. *Daily Express*, October 28.

86 Only a single business contact: Spicer 2017, 158.

87 "I was able to lock myself": Ibid., 159.

88 "I was cooling off": Ibid., 160.

9 FUTURE UNKNOWN

92 "We want you to fly": Barker 1969, 73.

92 "dazed" at the conversation: Lancaster's personal diary was reprinted in full in the *Miami Daily News*, August 5, 1932, the source for all his quotes (and related information) in this chapter.

92 "Captain Lancaster and Mrs. J. M. Keith-Miller": Barker 1969, 73.

94 Afterward she had fallen into: Spicer 2017, 160–61.

96 "I was pretty acid": Spicer 2017.

10 MENTAL AGONY

99 "keep sober and write": Lancaster's letters and telegrams, like his diary, were reprinted in the *Miami Daily News* and *The Miami Herald*, August 1932, the sources for all his quotes in this chapter.

108 "The risk involved is entirely": Grateful acknowledgment is made to Andrew Lancaster and Noni Couell for transcripts of Clarke's letters.

110 "I can raise funds": Barker 1969, 93.

11 EAGER, DRUNKEN LOVE

112 He argued in his claim: "Taken as Favor." 1931. *The Mail* (Australia), June 27.

113 "I am afraid that": Spicer 2017, 156.

113 "We were such good friends": Ibid.

113 "bored to sobs": Lancaster's and Jessie's letters and telegrams were reprinted in the *Miami Daily News* and *The Miami Herald*, August 1932, the sources for all quotes in this chapter, unless otherwise noted.

115 When Jessie went to investigate: Barker 1969, 91.

116 "What are you going": Ibid.

116 "They used to call him": Spicer 2017, 163.

12 THE TORTURES OF THE DAMNED

120 "Why!!" Lancaster wrote: Lancaster's personal diary was reprinted in full in the *Miami Daily News*, August 5, 1932, the source for all quotes from it (and related information) in this chapter.

122 "On our way back east": Lancaster's letters and telegrams were reprinted in the *Miami Daily News* and *The Miami Herald*, August 1932, the sources for all quotes from them in this chapter.

13 A MAN OF MANY SECRETS

125 Jessie was genuinely stunned: Barker 1969, 99.

126 "The inconceivable has happened": Jessie's letters and telegrams were reprinted in the *Miami Daily News* and *The Miami Herald*, August 1932, the sources for all her quotes in this chapter.

126 "You doubtless have read": Grateful acknowledgment is made to Andrew Lancaster and Noni Couell for the transcript of Clarke's letter.

128 "behave like a schoolboy": Lancaster's personal diary was reprinted in full in the *Miami Daily News*, August 5, 1932, the source for all quotes from it (and related information) in this chapter.

128 "Am no dog in manger": Lancaster's telegram was reprinted in the *Miami Daily News* and *The Miami Herald*, August 1932.

14 A TERRIBLE THING

130 "Hello, darling, I've missed you": Unless otherwise noted, all quotes in this chapter are from the *Miami Daily News* and *The Miami Herald*, August 2–18, 1932.

131 "I'm only going to ask one thing": Barker 1969, 103–4.

15 FORGERIES

136 "That's ridiculous," Jessie said: Unless otherwise noted, all quotes in this chapter are from the *Miami Daily News* and *The Miami Herald*, August 1932.

140 "We'd like to question you": Barker 1969, 111.

140 gripped by "desperate thoughts": Keith-Miller, Jessie. 1932. "I Appeal to You!" *Daily Express*, October 27.

144 "Say nothing whatever about it": Barker 1969, 114.

147 In a metaphorical sense: My thanks to Chrystopher Spicer for sharing his thoughts with me regarding Jessie's behavior.

16 THE SCARLET WOMAN

148 "I know I can convince": Unless otherwise noted, all quotes in this chapter are from the *Miami Daily News* and *The Miami Herald*, April 23–May 10 and August 2–18, 1932.

149 *"Reasons why Haden Clarke":* Barker 1969, 118.

150 "I wouldn't touch it": Ibid., 119.

150 "because of those damn notes": Ibid.

151 "Will everything have to": Ibid., 120.

152 "I used to ask": Andrew Lancaster 2014. *The Lost Aviator.*

153 "My Dearest Pat": Ibid.; see also Barker 1969.

155 "Your letter of July 4th": Barker 1969, 126–7.

156 "My love for Captain Lancaster": "Australian Airwoman Speaks Out Before Murder Trial." 1932. *Miami Daily News*, August 1.

17 THOSE DIM DAYS OF THE PAST . . .

162 "moral laxity": Unless otherwise noted, all quotes in this chapter are from the *Miami Daily News* and *The Miami Herald*, August 2–18, 1932.

168 "Everybody was excessively friendly": Spicer 2017, 183.

18 A TISSUE OF LIES

182 "Captain Lancaster," he asked: All quotes in this chapter are from the *Miami Daily News* and *The Miami Herald*, August 2–18, 1932.

19 AMERICAN JUSTICE IS ALL WET

191 "Captain Lancaster," Hawthorne began: All quotes in this chapter are from the *Miami Daily News* and *The Miami Herald*, August 1932.

20 THE MAN FROM AUBURN

202 "drastic action": Unless otherwise noted, all quotes in this chapter are from the *Miami Daily News* and *The Miami Herald*, August 2–18, 1932.

205 "the public's growing awe": Evans 2002.

206 "When Dr. A. Conan Doyle": Fisher, Jim. "Firearms Identification in the Sacco-Vanzetti Case." http://jimfisher.edinboro.edu/forensics/sacco1_1.html.

206 "chemistry, microscopy, handwriting": Ibid.

206 The fraudulence of Hamilton's: Ibid.

206 In 1921 Hamilton received: Ibid.

21 THE VERDICT

211 "You men are reasonable men": Unless otherwise noted, all quotes in this chapter are from the *Miami Daily News* and *The Miami Herald*, August 1932.

218 "I am delighted": "Lancaster is Freed; Spectators Cheer." 1932. *The New York Times*, August 18.

22 A TRAGIC FIGURE

220 "I have been hiding out": "Mrs. Keith-Miller Sails for England." 1932. *The Baltimore Sun*, October 15.

220 "I have not yet decided": "Captain Lancaster Plans Long-Distance Flight." 1932. *The Baltimore Sun*, October 25.

220 "I didn't have the same": Spicer 2017, 213.

221 Lancaster looked "absolutely haggard": Ibid., 215.

222 "I am going 'all out' ": "Three Long-Distance Flights." 1933. *The Manchester Guardian*, April 11.

223 "had done no flying": Barker 1969, 210.

223 "I have every confidence": "Captain Lancaster in Cape Flight Bid." 1933. *Daily Mirror*, April 12.

225 "We'll give you twenty-four": Barker 1969, 213.

226 Lancaster had planned to follow: Details of Lancaster's crash are taken from his diary, which was reprinted in full in the *Daily Express*: "The Diary of Bill Lancaster: An Incredible Story of Courage." 1962, October 22.

227 "I had a dreadful dream": Spicer 2017, 217.

227 "It is not our wish": "Airwoman to Hunt for Lost Friend." 1933. *Daily Express*, April 17.

227 "Captain Lancaster's father is now": "Lancaster Missing 12 Days in Sahara." 1933. *The New York Times*, April 25.

227 "I did not want him": Barker 1969, 216.

23 THIS PERIOD OF AGONY

230 an "indeterminate carcass": Brochard, Alain, and Michel Fernez. "A Butterfly in the Desert; Or the Tragic History of William Newton Lancaster." 3rd Transport Group, April 2009. Translated from French: http://www.3emegroupedetransport.com/Unpapillondansledesert.htm.

230 "the cabin of a small": Ibid.

230 "Now my water will give": All details of Lancaster's crash and subsequent time in the desert are taken from his diary, which was reprinted in full in the *Daily Express*: "The Diary of Bill Lancaster: An Incredible Story of Courage," October 22, 1962.

EPILOGUE: THE PAST REACHES OUT

235 "no more flying stunts": Spicer 2017, 229.

236 "most appalling shock": Ibid., 233.

236 "Anyone who has the guts": "The Diary of Bill Lancaster: An Incredible Story of Courage." 1962. *Daily Express*, October 22.

236 "I had never forgotten": Ibid.

INDEX